Operation
Totalize

Battleground Normandy

Operation Totalize

Tim Saunders

Pen & Sword
MILITARY

First published in Great Britain in 2019 by
PEN & SWORD MILITARY
An imprint of
Pen & Sword Books Ltd
47 Church Street
Barnsley
South Yorkshire
S70 2AS

ISBN 978-1-52674-126-4

A CIP catalogue record for this book is available from the British Library.

Typeset by Concept, Huddersfield, West Yorkshire HD4 5JL
Printed and bound in the UK by CPI Group (UK) Ltd, Croydon, CR0 4YY

Pen & Sword Books Ltd incorporates the imprints of Pen & Sword
Archaeology, Atlas, Aviation, Battleground, Discovery, Family History,
History, Maritime, Military, Naval, Politics, Railways, Select, Social History,
Transport, True Crime, and Claymore Press, Frontline Books, Leo Cooper,
Praetorian Press, Remember When, Seaforth Publishing and Wharncliffe.

For a complete list of Pen & Sword titles please contact
PEN & SWORD BOOKS LIMITED
47 Church Street, Barnsley, South Yorkshire, S70 2AS, England
E-mail: enquiries@pen-and-sword.co.uk
Website: www.pen-and-sword.co.uk

Contents

Introduction   7

1. Campaign Background   9

2. Operation SPRING – the 3rd Canadian Division at Tilly   21

3. II Canadian Corps' TOTALIZE Plan   48

4. The 51st Highland Division – Armoured Advance   74

5. The 2nd Canadian Division – Armoured Advance   97

6. The Bypassed Villages 117

7. The Morning of 8 August 1944 137

8. The Armoured Advance 171

9. The Second Day of TOTALIZE 203

10. The End of TOTALIZE 233

Appendix I: Order of Battle 249

Appendix II: Battlefield Tour of Operation TOTALIZE 252

Appendix III: SS Ranks and their Allied Equivalent 269

Index 270

Introduction

As is the case with most Anglo-Canadian operations in Normandy, there is enduring debate over the degree of success, or failure, of Operations SPRING and TOTALIZE. The nub of the issue is whether the commentator or historian is looking at the tactical or operational level, because in Normandy the results of operations in the eastern sector of the lodgement were rarely in accordance with each other. This book will look at both.

Those elements of the Allied armies in Normandy that had been brought back from the Mediterranean had arguably seen too much action. On the other hand, those who had been training in the United Kingdom, many since 1939, had a theoretical knowledge of war but their ranks had very little practical experience of the stresses, strain and conduct of battle against the highly-experienced commanders of the *Wehrmacht* formations they would encounter in Normandy. In many respects Lieutenant General Guy Simonds' troops who fought under his command during Operation TOTALIZE were a microcosm of General Montgomery's problem. The Canadian divisions were still learning, while the veterans of the 51st Highland Division, which had fought in the deserts of North Africa and the plains of Sicily, was under its new commander General Rennie, only beginning to get to grips with a new campaign in a very different environment.

In writing this book and having read many critiques of the Canadian army and its commanders in Normandy, I have come to the conclusion that much of the enduring criticism is almost subconsciously based on expectations founded on the performance of the peerless Canadian Expeditionary Corps of 1917–18, who were of course the pride of Canada. Therefore, blaming a tiny cadre of Permanent Force and undertrained militia officers, who had been rapidly promoted, is misplaced but laying the blame for this state of affairs at the feet of politicians is not entirely fair either when one recalls how badly Canada was affected by the Great Depression.

Two months of 'hard pounding' in the fields of Normandy had been expensive, particularly in infantry, and repeated attempts to break through the German divisions that had roped off the Allies into a bridgehead only some 10 miles deep had yielded little ground. While the American Operation COBRA had finally brought results and against flagging opposition was finally gaining momentum, the Second British and First Canadian armies, with much of the surviving German armour heading west to launch Operation LÜTTICH, the Mortain Counter-Attack, were under pressure to break out to the south.

General Simonds had seen reports of British offensives early in the campaign before his headquarters was activated in the field and two difficult operations of his own to reflect on came up with significant technological and tactical solutions that delivered a stunning success that arguably he and his formations, schooled in a deliberate and methodical tactical doctrine, were unable to exploit. The *Wehrmacht* infantry were broken but I SS Panzer Corps was given the opportunity to deploy the *Hitlerjugend* along with Michael Wittmann's Tiger tanks to first counter-attack and then block progress south.

With the pendulum of battle swinging from success through exasperation to tragedy, II Canadian Corps' Operation TOTALIZE is one of the best Allied multifaceted operations to study both at home and/or on the ground in Normandy.

Tim Saunders
Warminster, February 2018

Chapter One

Campaign Background

General Montgomery returned from the Mediterranean and took up the command of 21st Army Group in January 1944, having already rejected the detail of the COSSAC[1] plan prepared by Lieutenant General Sir Frederick Morgan. He and his staff worked to expand the landings further west to facilitate the capture of Cherbourg and to dissipate the German response to the invasion along a much wider front. This latter point is key to Montgomery's campaign plan, which he laid out to the assembled senior British, US and Canadian commanders at his headquarters in St Paul's School, London on 7 April 1944. He made it quite clear that his concept of operations was to attract the bulk of the German armour onto the Anglo-Canadian sector, giving scope for the US army to capture what was considered to be the vital port of Cherbourg and then to break out in the west. General Eisenhower, who chaired the conference, asked his multinational audience if there were any disagreements; there were none. Eisenhower wrote:

> From the beginning it was the conception of Field-Marshal Montgomery, Bradley, and myself that eventually the great movement out of the beachhead would be by an enormous left wheel, bringing our front on to the line of the Seine, with the whole area lying between that river and the Loire and as far eastward as Paris in our firm possession. This did not imply the adoption of a rigid scheme of grand tactics. It was merely an estimate of what we believed would happen when once we could concentrate the full power of our air-ground-naval team against the enemy we expected to meet in north-west France.[2]

Two of the great military truisms are that 'no plan survives contact with the enemy' and that 'the enemy always has a say'. Both of these apply to the Normandy campaign. The Germans were expected to follow military logic and fall back to a sensible defensive line. Hitler, however, ordered his troops to throw the invader back into the sea and when that had failed he demanded that no ground be given up and the Normandy beachhead be contained. Thus the original plan, briefed to commanders on 15 May, of the armies pivoting to the east on Falaise on or about D+20 did not come to fruition. Montgomery's subsequent insistence that everything went to plan did him no favours in the eyes of his critics and detractors at the time or indeed since.

The detail of where the battles were fought was inevitably changed by the enemy's 'say' in matters but 21st Army Group's overall concept of the outer western flank making its broad wheel did work. Consequently, it was

Eisenhower, Montgomery and senior Allied commanders at the Presentation of Plans.

General Harry Crerar's multinational First Canadian Army[3] who found themselves acting as Montgomery's pivot south of Caen in July and August 1944.

Repeated operations, including PERCH (12–14 June), EPSOM (26–30 June), WINDSOR (4–5 July), JUPITER (10 July) and GOODWOOD (18–19 July), to capture Caen and then advance onto the more open country to the south of the city had served to suck in the majority of the German panzer and infantry divisions on to the Anglo-Canadian front as they arrived in Normandy. A generally-accepted set of statistics is that on 5 July, two days before II Canadian Corps took over active command, some 590 panzers and 64 infantry battalions confronted Second Army, while facing the First US Army were only 215 panzers but a similar 63 infantry battalions. The balance had, however, by the end of 10 July[4] become 610 panzers and 92 infantry battalions against the British, with 190 panzers and 85 infantry battalions facing the Americans. III Flak Corps and the majority of the *Nebelwerfers* also faced Second Army.

Up against the concentration of highly-experienced German armour, Panzergrenadiers and infantry, the Canadians and those who fought alongside them were destined to have a tough fight in their drive to Falaise.

First Canadian Army

In 1918 it is said that the BEF, an army almost incomparably efficient in British military history, 'melted away like spring snow' as it was demobilized. The same was true of the Canadian Expeditionary Force but to a far greater extent. It shrank down to a permanent force of just 5,000 men and a grossly underfunded militia. Canada had emerged out of the First World War as a nation in her own right and, reflecting American Isolationism, was reluctant to spend money on her armed forces that would inevitably be called to support 'the old country' in a still dysfunctional Europe. This prospect did not sit well with the reality of the 1930s: the rise of Nazi Germany. General McNaughton, in a hopelessly optimistic moment with more than a whiff of the politician, said:

> The art of military command could be developed just as easily in civilian life as in a professional army, and that given a quick and basic

General McNaughton, Canadian Chief of the General Staff in the 1930s.

11

military education after mobilization, successful businessmen would prove very adaptable to military life in war and probably become good senior officers.

On the outbreak of war, to Canada's eternal credit there was no hesitation in joining the struggle, even though she only had a small army and a very low level of practical military knowledge. In addition, in that small army, all-arms training and exercises, other than at the lowest level, were virtually unknown. The consequence, when the necessity of rapid wartime expansion came to pass in 1939, was that Canada's military knowledge and experience was extremely thinly spread as the nation embarked on a 120-fold increase in the size of the army. In contrast Britain, which had maintained a sizeable army to police the empire and also a Territorial Army, only saw a twenty-fold increase in her 1938 strength. If Britain was forced to seriously dilute her trained manpower with conscripts, Canada was forced to virtually start from scratch. The old adage that 'a country gets the army in war that it invested in during peace' (at least in the early stages) was never more truly applied than to Canada in 1939.

The volunteers of the 1st Canadian Division, along with the support elements, numbering in excess of 20,000 began deploying across the Atlantic in December 1939 but after the fall of France, unlike their First World War predecessors, they found themselves a part of the defence of the United Kingdom.[5] Consequently, they gained no practical experience of battle for themselves or to share with the other divisions that were forming in Canada.

Brigadier Forster (wearing helmet) talks to Generals Montgomery and Dempsey during Exercise TROUSERS on Slapton Sands.

Also unlike the First World War, when the Canadian army was initially commanded by British professionals, from 1939 onwards Canada had to grow and nurture her own commanders in a rapidly expanding army. This meant short tenures of command before promotion and no weeding out of those who did not perform well in battle or could not stand up to the stress of combat. For example, it was not uncommon for a captain in 1939 to be promoted through the ranks of major and lieutenant colonel to brigadier in just over a year, having held all too briefly five appointments in the UK. No lesser person than Lieutenant General Guy Simonds rose from the rank of major at the outbreak of war to the command of II Canadian Corps in Normandy in July 1944, but this included several operational commands.

It was not until July 1943, other than the disastrous Dieppe Raid, that the Canadians were committed to battle in Sicily during Operation HUSKY. There was, however, only so much experience in gaining rotation of officers that the 1st Canadian Division, 1 Canadian Armoured Brigade and subsequently the 5th Canadian Armoured Division[6] and a Canadian corps headquarters could stand for their own efficiency. The result was that the Canadian divisions that would fight in North-West Europe, along with British war-raised divisions such as the 15th Scottish and the Territorial 43rd Wessex, would start the campaign with a well-exercised but largely theoretical knowledge of the battles that they were expected to fight. One young Canadian officer commanding a tank troop, Lieutenant Adams of

Canadian gunners in action in Sicily during July 1943.

A posed photo of training in a 'blitzed' town before D-Day.

the South Alberta Regiment, commented with some exaggeration '... we were as green as grass and if you survived, you knew how to do things ... We learned as we went along.'

This critical analysis of the Canadian army extends to its organization and training at the beginning of the Normandy campaign but not to the nearly quarter of a million individual Canadian soldiers who had to volunteered twice to get into battle in Normandy: first to join the army and then again to serve overseas. In common with much of the British army, the painful lessons of the big set-piece operations such as TOTALIZE were a part of the inevitable process of turning a theoretical knowledge into a war-winning capability.

The Campaign So Far

As a part of I Corps, the 3rd Canadian Division, followed by leading elements of the 51st Highland Division, had landed on Juno Beach during D-Day, supported by the Shermans of the 2nd Canadian Armoured Brigade. The Canadians would have reached their objective, Line OAK, 8 miles inland on the N13 highway and the Caen Bayeux railway but for the counter-attack of the 21st Panzer Division on the evening of D-Day.

The intervention of the 12th *Hitlerjugend* SS Panzer Division on D+1 prevented them from closing in on Caen from the west, but the majority of the division was later that day in place on Line OAK from Bretteville-l'Orgueilleuse, via Norrey-en-Bessin and west to its junction with the 50th (Northumbrian) Division.

While the 3rd Canadian Division was fighting the similarly inexperienced *Hitlerjugend*,[7] the 51st Highland Division had been moved east of the Orne to join the 6th Airborne Division in its long sojourn holding the left flank of the lodgement. It was, however, soon apparent that the 51st Highland Division, even though they were one of the veteran formations brought back from the Mediterranean to provide the Second Army with a backbone of experience, was not performing to expectation. They, like many who returned from campaigns in North Africa and Sicily after years of hard fighting, bemedalled, feted and believing that they had done their bit, found it difficult to get back into the swing of a new and very different campaign. Amid the hedgerows of Normandy, rapidly increasing levels of sickness, desertion and shellshock were symptomatic of the malaise. Lieutenant Alistair Borthwick of the 5th Seaforth Highlanders summed up the results of weeks of holding the line with very little offensive action:

> We had been in the line for a long time, continuously under fire and doing (as it must have seemed to many) absolutely nothing. And yet here we were, still in the same old doover, getting nowhere. The enemy mortars had our range and casualties were mounting. We were all bone-tired. When a man sees his friend killed in an attack he can understand the need for it and accepts it: but bridgeheads and buildings and army plans are abstractions too vague to be comprehended when he is sitting in a trench and seeing, day after day, four or five or six of his mates being carried off or buried. It is to the credit of the men that none of them ever did ask why, that they did accept the situation even if they did not understand it and held on uncomplainingly until the end.

A metaphorical end came on 29 July when the 51st's divisional commander from Mediterranean days, Major General Bullen-Smith, was summoned to Montgomery's headquarters where he was told by Monty 'You must go, the men won't fight for you ... you will go home now.' Major General Rennie, who had the advantage of being a Scot and having fought with the division in Egypt, was, however, available to take over command of this most mercurial of divisions, having sufficiently recovered from wounds while

Major General Thomas Gordon Rennie.

commanding the 3rd Division shortly after D-Day. The Highland Division's recovery dates from the appointment of Rennie and the prospect of a more active phase of the campaign, but at the time of TOTALIZE this was still a work in progress.

Meanwhile, the 3rd Canadian Division in their protracted and often bitter personal struggle with the *Hitlerjugend* had quickly become veterans and their time with I Corps was crowned with the difficult and costly fighting for Carpiquet Airfield and the capture of Caen. Shortly afterwards, they were joined by the 2nd Canadian Division who started to disembark on 7 July and the two Canadian formations were alongside each other in the southern suburbs of Caen under II Canadian Corps when Lieutenant General Simonds' headquarters was activated at 1500 hours on 11 July 1944.

Their first battle together on 18 July, Operation ATLANTIC, was, like its better-known partner GOODWOOD, a qualified success. The tactical aim of both operations was to gain the Verrières/Bourguébus Ridge and the largely open high ground that stretched south to Falaise. Its underlying operational purpose was to continue the process of drawing and fixing German armoured formations to the east while the Americans made slow progress through the hedgerow country to a position from which they could launch their break-out in the west.

While the three British armoured divisions committed to GOODWOOD advanced some 6 miles at a cost of 197 tank casualties,[8] the 3rd Canadian

Sherman tanks with British infantry aboard during GOODWOOD. This was the traditional way of providing battlefield mobility to infantry divisions.

Division was now, after six weeks in continual action, showing understandable signs of exhaustion. Nonetheless, their attack across the River Orne into the Colombelles steelworks and the rubble of the southern suburbs of Caen was successful but costly. Major General Foulkes' 2nd Canadian Division was launched into its first battle since Dieppe during the early evening of the 18th and 'after a sticky start' did well, crossing the Orne and starting to clear their part of the suburbs and the villages at the foot of the ridge. See map on p. 18 The following morning 5 Brigade of the 2nd Division, after a procedural and map-reading error that saw *Le Régiment de Maisonneuve* ('Maisies') forming up on their own artillery's opening barrage line, successfully attacked the village of Fleury-sur-Orne. The Calgary Highlanders then advanced and gained a tactically important knoll, Point 67, on the northern extremity of the Verrières Ridge.

On 20 July the hitherto uncommitted 6th Canadian Brigade was brought forward to develop Operation ATLANTIC's action on the high ground to the south in conjunction with the British 7th Armoured Division. Their initial objective was the kidney-shaped crest of the Verrières Ridge. The attack was initially repulsed with the tanks of the 4th County of London Yeomanry withdrawing to give fire support to Canadian infantry who would renew the attack. The Cameron Highlanders of Canada advanced from Point 67 and captured most of Saint-André-sur-Orne while the South Saskatchewan and Fusiliers Mont-Royal headed for the crest of the high ground and hamlet of Verrières respectively. Without close armoured support the Fusiliers were halted well short of their objective, while the Saskatchewans had by late afternoon advanced 1.5 miles to reach Point 88 on the crest of the ridge. At this stage rain and cloud halted help from Allied fighter-bombers who had up to then prevented German panzers from leaving cover. SS *Brigadeführer* Teddy Wisch, commander of the *Leibstandarte*, took the opportunity to launch counter-attacks against 6 Brigade. The inexperienced Canadians were caught over-extended and unbalanced by the elite and veteran SS panzer troops and forced back 'in some disorder'. They were lucky to retain a toehold on the high ground of Point 67, while in St André the Cameron Highlanders beat off heavy counter-attacks.

The Canadian official history describes the fate of the South Saskatchewans, who lost 215 men, as 'a sad affair' and states that 'the inexperienced 2nd Division had had a very nasty baptism of fire', suffering a total of 1,149 casualties. This resulted in a further churn in the Canadian chain of command at unit level as officers and NCOs found themselves stepping up to fill spaces.

During GOODWOOD the 51st Highland Division had breached both their own and enemy minefields to permit the advance of the armour and followed in their wake, taking over captured villages and suffering further casualties. With the depots empty of Scottish infantry replacements and the British already suffering a manpower crisis, numbers were made up with largely English soldiers from units that were being disbanded or

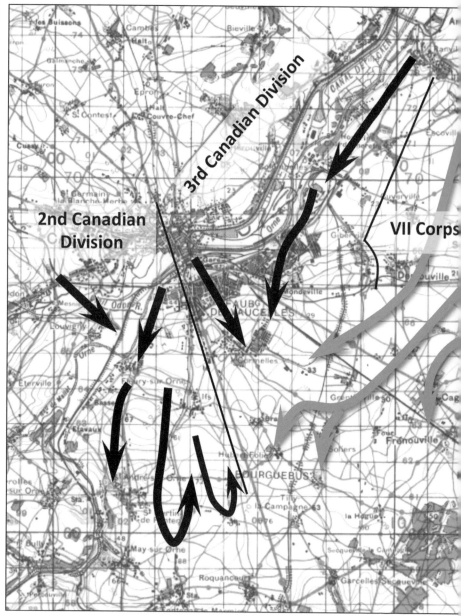

Operation ATLANTIC, 18–20 July.

soldiers fresh from English regiment's depots. This influx that the coarse filter of the replacement organization had sent the 51st further impacted on the morale of the Highlanders and resulted in General Rennie trawling the Second Army for Scots in English divisions to exchange.

In his directive M512 issued on 21 July, after a meeting in which Eisenhower was highly critical of GOODWOOD's results, Montgomery summed up the situation and gave orders:

The General Situation.

1. Since the attack of Second Army on 18 July, our general position on the eastern flank has become greatly improved. We now hold a good and firm bridgehead beyond the ORNE in the CAEN sector; and we thus have the ability to operate strongly in that sector, when desired, in an easterly, south-easterly, or southerly direction.

   In last three days we have not only improved our positions on the eastern flank, but in doing so we have 'written off' a large amount of enemy personnel and equipment.

2. Operations will be continued intensively on the eastern flank.

On this optimistic note, clearly unaware of just how concerned the Germans had been about the likelihood of a break-out south of Caen, Montgomery reorganized 21st Army Group for the next phase of the campaign.

As a result of GOODWOOD and with the Americans preparing to launch Operation COBRA and break out from Normandy, there was both the need and sufficient room on the eastern flank of the lodgement for Lieutenant General Harry Crerar's headquarters to open. Eventually:

First Canadian Army.

6. This army will take over from Second British Army the sector at present held by 1 British Corps. Command to pass at 1200 hrs 23 July.

Initially troops under command were just General Crocker's I Corps and it would be some time before II Canadian Corps came under command and Crerar was responsible for the front from the sea, south along the Amfreville Ridge towards Troarn and west to the Verrières/Bourguébus Ridge and the River Orne. In the meantime, his orders were as follows:

The immediate task of First Canadian Army will be to advance its left flank eastwards so that OUISTREHAM will cease to be under close enemy observation and fire, and that use can then be made of the port of CAEN. To achieve this, it will be necessary to push the enemy back to the east side of the R. DIVES, and to occupy such positions as will ensure that all territory to the west of the river is dominated by our troops.

Meanwhile, with the First US Army finally established on its lines of departure for Operation COBRA, II Canadian Corps would mount a fixing attack east of the Orne: Operation SPRING.

NOTES

1. Chief of Staff Supreme Allied Commander.
2. Eisenhower, *Crusade in Europe* (Heinemann, 1948).

3. Canadian, British, Polish, Dutch and Belgians.

4. The 43rd Wessex Division in Operation JUPITER had forced the Germans to redeploy the 9th *Hohenstaufen* SS Panzer Division from central reserve and fix II SS Panzer Corps to holding the ground astride Hill 112. See *Battleground* title of that name.

5. 1 Canadian Brigade did reach France in June 1940 but only by the time the French army was collapsing and they were promptly withdrawn without being in action.

6. Commanded between October 1943 and January 1944 by the then Major General G.G. Simonds.

7. While the majority of the soldiers were teenagers fresh from the *Hitlerjugend* movement, the division was built around a hard core of 1,500 highly-experienced *Leibstandarte* officers and senior NCOs.

8. British tank losses during GOODWOOD are a subject of debate, the figures being confused by authorities variously quoting the total being knocked out or otherwise disabled and those that were beyond repair. Approximately 314 tanks became casualties during the three days of GOODWOOD, of which more than half were recovered, repaired and reissued, with the remaining 130 being cannibalized for spares.

Chapter Two

Operation SPRING –
the 3rd Canadian Division at Tilly

'*Each officer, non-commissioned officer, and man must be aware that this is the struggle for the fate of Germany. Each must be willing to fight at the most decisive sector of the front. We will prove ourselves worthy of our comrades who have fallen for the greatness of our volk.*'
General der SS Sepp Dietrich, I SS Panzer Corps[1]

A full account of Operation SPRING would be a subject in itself but it does exemplify the problems faced by Lieutenant General Simonds and II Canadian Corps fighting south of Caen. Consequently, a brief account of this battle is an essential prerequisite to an account of TOTALIZE.

In late July II Canadian Corps was still under command of the British Second Army, which in Montgomery's Directive M512 was to

> operate intensively so as to secure the general line defined in para 2 [St Sylvain to Caumont], within the army boundaries, and to hold it firmly. Having gained this line, that part of the army front to the east of the R. ORNE will be kept as active as is possible with the resources available; the enemy must be led to believe that we contemplate a major advance towards FALAISE and ARGENTAN, and he must be induced to build up his main strength to the east of the R. ORNE so that our affairs on the western flank can proceed with greater speed.

Being the corps 'east of the R. Orne', this task fell to the Canadians and was coordinated to follow immediately after the US break-out, Operation COBRA.

II Canadian Corps was to advance on a frontage of 3 miles, across open fields, through the forward German positions on the Verrières Ridge. The troops available to Simonds were his own two Canadian infantry divisions, the British tanks of the 27th Armoured Brigade and the 7th Armoured Division, with the Guards Armoured Division in reserve.

The German Defenders

SS *Brigadeführer* and *General der SS* Sepp Dietrich whose I SS Panzer Corps had done so much to thwart GOODWOOD and ATLANTIC remained in position astride the Falaise road, but it was now a much-reduced corps and needed reinforcement. The combined effect of Hitler's insistence that there would be no steady withdrawal, Montgomery's concept of fixing the panzer divisions in the east and the Allied deception plan,

The *Nebelwerfer*, a six-tube rocket mortar, came in a variety of sizes ranging from 100mm to 300mm and was known as the 'howling cow' to the Germans and 'moaning Minnie' to the British and Canadians.

Although originally designed as an artillery assault gun, the *Sturmgeschütz* (or StuG) proved to be a highly-effective anti-tank weapon mounting the 75mm 40 L/48 gun.

Operation FORTITUDE, had kept the panzer divisions holding ground rather than being replaced by infantry.

Dietrich's corps consisted of three divisions: his own *Leibstandarte* and *Hitlerjugend* and the 272nd Infantry Division, the vast majority of which were either committed to holding ground or were in close reserve. The Germans could, however, plainly see the Allied build-up east of the Orne and powerful reinforcements from no less than three other panzer divisions were positioned astride the road to Falaise. Consequently, it can be said that Operation SPRING was achieving Montgomery's desired effect before it even began.

Although the panzer divisions were badly reduced in strength, the ground on the Bourguébus/Verrières Ridge played to the strengths of German weapons and equipment. The open country dotted with villages meant that they could deploy their infantry in cover and dominate the gaps with effective long-range fire. In this respect the *Sturmgeschütz*[2] III and the company of *Jagdpanzers* IV attached to the *Leibstandarte* would be highly effective. The presence of the corps' Tigers and King Tigers of 503 *Schwere Panzer Battalion* strengthened the 272nd Division. In addition, there were up to 500 artillery pieces plus mortars and *Nebelwerfers* in range. The number of panzers astride the Falaise Road was something like 180 AFVs. II Canadian Corps was facing the majority of the German armour in Normandy and more than on the entire First US Army front, just as COBRA was beginning! With these panzers Sepp Dietrich intended to fight a mobile battle, blocking and counter-attacking Canadian penetrations of the defensive positions astride the Falaise road.

I SS Panzer Corps was well-prepared, reinforced and represented serious opposition barring the route south from Caen towards Falaise; not least because their tanks out-gunned their Allied counterparts and they were fighting on favourable ground. Operation SPRING represented a formidable challenge to the Canadians.

(*Left*) SS *Brigadeführer* SS Sepp Dietrich. (*Right*) Lieutenant General Guy Simonds, Commander II Canadian Corps.

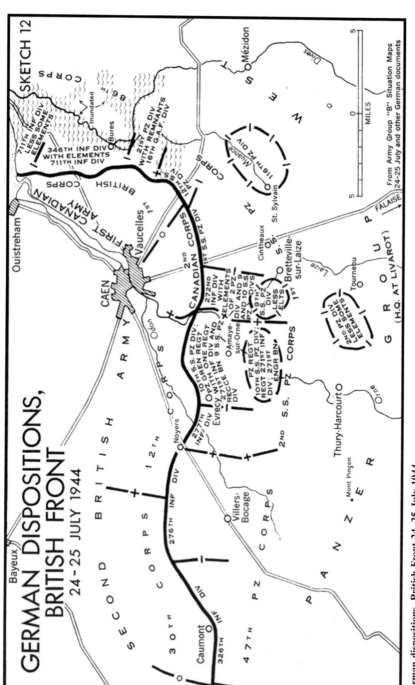

German dispositions, British Front 24–25 July 1944.

II Canadian Corps' Plans and Preparations

General Simonds' principal objective for Operation SPRING was Point 122, a piece of high ground that the Falaise road crossed on its way south. The plan was conventional and tightly-scripted, with the 6th Canadian Brigade (6 Cdn Bde) split up securing various parts of the start line during the evening of 24 July and the British 27th Armoured Brigade providing flank protection on the left. Having witnessed the carve-up of the British armoured divisions during GOODWOOD, General Simonds decided that this time the operation would start under cover of darkness. Consequently, H-Hour would be 0330 hours in order to avoid the worst of the enemy's long-range anti-tank fire. In the remaining two and a half hours of darkness, the two infantry divisions would advance with the assistance of movement light[3] to take the enemy forward positions See map on the Verrières Ridge dominated by the villages of May-sur-Orne and the on p. 26 hamlets of Verrières and Tilly-la-Campagne (Phase One). Next, fresh infantry battalions, each supported by a squadron of tanks from the 2nd Canadian Armoured Brigade (2 Cdn Armd Bde), would capture the subsequent row of villages: Rocquancourt and Fontenay-le-Marmion. All of this, it was intended, would be completed by dawn. At 'first tank light' the 7th Armoured Division would punch through to seize Point 122 (otherwise known as the Cramesnil Spur). In Phase Three, the Guards Armoured Division was to seize the high ground around Cintheaux and the river crossings at Bretteville-sur-Laize. There was even talk of Corps Recce (the Manitoba Dragoons) reaching Falaise that night but this, however, was optimistic talk![4]

General Simonds requested heavy bomber support but only sixty mediums were available to drop a mix of weapons including delayed-action bombs at dusk on 24 July. In the event, however, the volume of unsuppressed flak meant that only fifteen aircraft were able to drop their loads. The aircraft were to return in daylight the following morning and strike again at the woods east of La Hogue between 0612 and 0830 hours, as Phase Three was scheduled to be getting under way. Bomber targets were to be marked by red smoke.

Operation SPRING did not begin well. The preliminary operation on 24 July to secure the start lines in the villages of Saint-André-sur-Orne and Saint-Martin-de-Fontenay began after dark with an attack by the Cameron Highlanders of Canada (Camerons), supported by tanks of the Sherbrooke Fusiliers which only partly cleared the grenadiers of the 272nd Infantry Division who had been able to shelter in the tunnels of old iron workings. As the assault battalions came forward they found that enemy infantry was still active in the villages. H-Hour was delayed at the last moment by thirty minutes to 0400 hours.

The securing of the start line at Troteval Farm complex was slightly more successful, being complete by midnight. However, by the time the

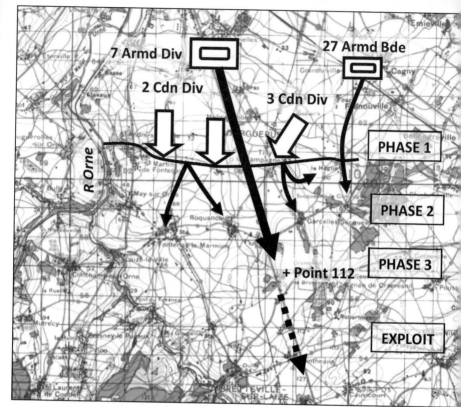

The plan: Operation SPRING.

Royal Hamilton Light Infantry (RHLI or 'The Rileys') moved forward, the enemy was again present. Either way, the start line was not secure.

Tilly-la-Campagne

The 3rd Canadian Division had a limited but what proved to be a very tough role in the first phase of SPRING. The North Nova Scotia Highlanders of 9 Cdn Bde were to attack Tilly-la-Campagne, using the road from Bourguébus as their axis of advance. In subsequent phases the Regina Rifles would attack the equally diminutive but well-defended La Hogue 1 mile to the east and the North Shore Regiment, with the support of a squadron of Fort Garry Horse Sherman tanks, would attack Garcelles-Secqueville, which was just under 1 mile beyond Tilly. In between the defended villages and hamlets lay very open and only slightly rolling countryside, but to the east or Canadian left flank lay woods that the planners correctly estimated would contain hides for German troops and would therefore receive the full attention of both bombers and artillery.

Tilly was held by the 3rd Battalion, 2nd SS Panzergrenadier Regiment and the Mk IV tanks of the 7th *Leibstandarte*'s Panzer Company. Neither

26

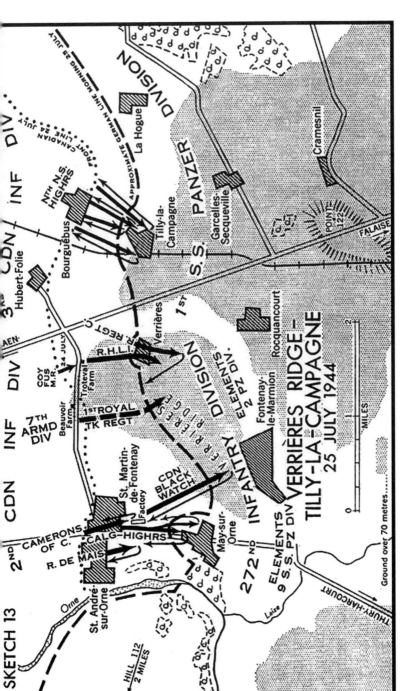

SKETCH 13

VERRIÈRES RIDGE –
TILLY-LA-CAMPAGNE
25 JULY 1944

Operation SPRING.

FRONT LINE MORNING 25 JULY
CANADIAN LINE 24 JULY
APPROXIMATE GERMAN FRONT LINE 24 JULY

S.S. PANZER DIVISION

1ST S.S. PANZER DIVISION

2ND CDN INF DIV
3RD CDN INF DIV
7TH CDN INF DIV

La Hogue
Tilly-la-Campagne
Garcelles-Secqueville
Cramesnil
POINT 122
FALAISE
Rocquancourt
Fontenay-le-Marmion
Verrières
ELEMENTS 2 PZ DIV
Hubert-Folie
Bourguébus
NTH N.S. HIGHRS
R.H.L.I.
COY FUS M.R.
Troteval Farm
Beauvoir Farm
1ST ROYAL TK REGT
St. Martin-de-Fontenay
Factory
CDN BLACK WATCH
CAMERONS OF C.
CALG-HIGHRS
R. DE MAIS.
May-sur-Orne
St. André-sur-Orne
272ND ELEMENTS 9 S.S. PZ DIV
THURY-HARCOURT
Orne
Laize
HILL 112 2 MILES
CAEN

MILES
0   1   2

Ground over 70 metres . . . .

A *Hitlerjugend* Panzer IV in Normandy.

the infantry nor the panzers were at their full establishment; 300 infantry and 8 panzers are reasonable working estimates. The hamlet's stout stone cellars had been rendered virtually shellproof by the layers of rubble and the panzers were well dug in.

Following the usual heavy artillery bombardment, the North Novas' attack did not start well. On the way to the forming-up point they were bombed by the *Luftwaffe* and D Company suffered twenty casualties before the operation had even begun. Crossing the start line as the fire plan finished, they were without the promised movement light, but eventually when the searchlights came on they silhouetted two of the three assault companies out in the open.

The German machine-gunners pinned the Novas down, the Officer Commanding C Company was wounded but the company pressed on and reached a position just north of Tilly. Meanwhile, B Company was ordered to cross the road to the left where a pair of panzers was reported. One of them was knocked out with a PIAT[5] but the surviving panzer raked B Company who were out in the open. Both the company commander and his second-in-command were killed while leading the company forward through the enemy outposts in the hedges and fields that surrounded Tilly. Few if any of B Company reached Tilly and a handful of D Company reached the forward edge of the German position and were overwhelmed by local counter-attacks.

A Company was sent forward from reserve to join C Company in an attack from the north-west and were soon fighting a confused battle with the SS Panzergrenadiers amid the ruins of the houses. Their war diary stated that 'the enemy opened the door, let them in and trapped them.' Too few Novas from A and C companies had broken into the hamlet and those that had fought amid the buildings without overall cohesion.

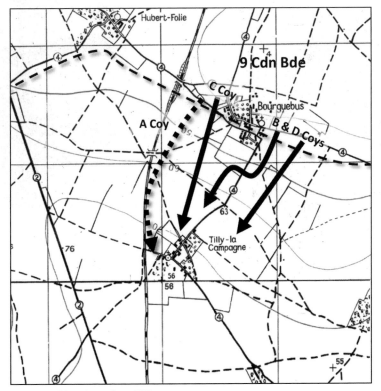

The North Novas' attack on Tilly.

A Canadian infantryman armed with a PIAT.

Reports that the Novas were in Tilly were circulating at 0430 hours, the result of seeing the red flare indicating success, but the sound of firing and calls for artillery fire, however, told a different story. At 0525 hours three of the battalion's carriers were sent forward with ammunition but entering Tilly, they ran straight into the still-active enemy panzers and were destroyed.

As a result of appeals for armoured support, the Fort Garry Horse's B Squadron was dispatched and the fifteen Shermans manoeuvred into a position from which they could shoot the remnants of B and D companies into the village. However, Mk IV panzers were waiting with their high-velocity 75mm guns, along with the 88mm guns loaded and ready. Some of the panzers fired from cover, while others manoeuvred around to the flanks and no longer cloaked by darkness, under which it was intended to have captured the forward villages, the Fort Garry's tanks were extremely vulnerable. They lost eleven Shermans knocked out and thus the second attack had failed but fighting in Tilly, with SS troops attacking individual buildings, went on all day and into the night. Over the one failing radio link, the remnants of A and C companies were ordered to 'dig in and hold on where they are' but this was eventually amended to 'make your way back to the battalion'.

Consequently, as night fell the North Novas attempted to regain their own lines. In this manner about 100 of them made it back to Bourguébus, but the losses of 196 men saw the battalion effectively out of action.

Verrières

The 2nd Canadian Division was to attack the Verrières Ridge and villages with two brigades: the 4th on the left from the supposedly captured Troteval Farm and the 5th, on the right, from within the twin villages of St André and St Martin. In Phase Two, two further infantry battalions were to advance another mile and capture the villages of Rocquancourt and Fontenay-le-Marmion, each supported by a squadron of tanks. In this phase the 7th Armoured Division would advance through the centre of the division heading to Point 122, with Canadian infantry battalions continuing their advance onto the high ground and securing the flanks.

The 4th Canadian Brigade in attacking Verrières was faced by the layered defence of the 1st Battalion, 1st SS Panzergrenadier Regiment, supported by *Sturmgeschütz* (assault guns) and Mark IV panzers. The Panzergrenadiers were mutually supported to their right by the 2nd Battalion, 1st SS Panzergrenadier Regiment centred on a group of houses on the Falaise Road.

Some 600 yards back towards Rocquancourt, dug in on the reverse slope of the Verrières Ridge was an ad hoc *Kampfgruppe* made up from all three battalions of the 1st SS Panzergrenadier Regiment. Behind them in Rocquancourt and Fontenay-le-Marmion and on the low ridge between

(*Left*) North Nova Scotia Highlanders' cap badge. (*Right*) Royal Hamilton Light Infantry cap badge.

31

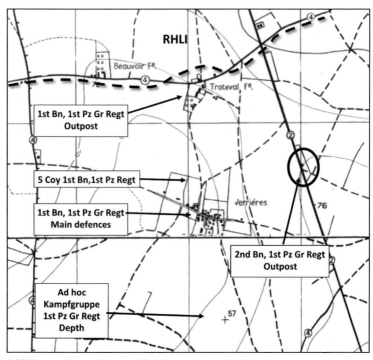

RHLI

Beauvoir Fe.

Troteval Fe.

1st Bn, 1st Pz Gr Regt Outpost

5 Coy 1st Bn,1st Pz Regt

1st Bn, 1st Pz Gr Regt Main defences

Verrières

76

2nd Bn, 1st Pz Gr Regt Outpost

Ad hoc Kampfgruppe 1st Pz Gr Regt Depth

57

I SS Panzer Corps' defence of Verrières.

the villages lay the *Leibstandarte*'s main tank strength, positioned where they could dominate the open fields to the north.

The 4th Canadian Brigade's plan was for their only full-strength battalion, the Royal Hamilton Light Infantry (RHLI),[6] to secure the village of Verrières in Phase One. This would be followed by C Squadron 1st Hussars, reinforced by troops from the 1st Royal Tank Regiment (1 RTR) advancing in support of the Royal Regiment of Canada (the Royals) south across the open fields onto the crest of the Verrières Ridge and on to attack Rocquancourt. The remainder of 1 RTR spearheading the 7th Armoured Division would advance west of Verrières from Beauvoir Farm.

As with Tilly, the attack on Verrières got off to a poor start with enemy infantry and at least one panzer being reported in the Troteval Farm area. Consequently, a delay in H-Hour was requested while two platoons of the reserve company dealt with the enemy, secured and marked the start line. This took time and when the battalion began its attack at 0410 hours, some forty minutes late, they had 'missed the timed barrage which was under Corps control'.

The *Leibstandarte*'s account describes the initial phases of the attack, the first objective of which was the hedgerow north of the village: 'At first,

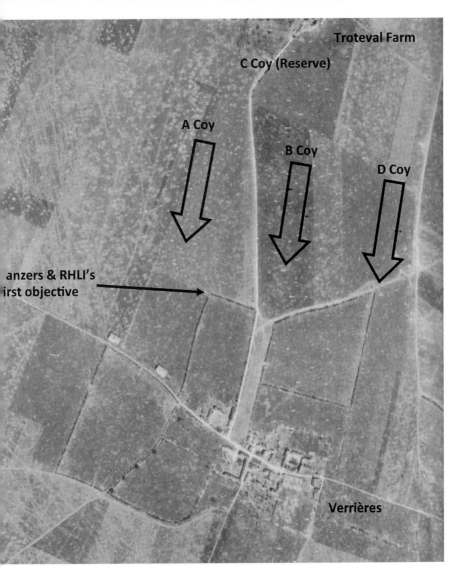

The attack of the RHLI on Verrières.

the defensive fire from the dug-in panzers of 5./*Panzerregiment* 1 pinned the attack down. Heavy anti-tank fire from Troteval drove our Panzers back, however, and we suffered losses.'

Advancing on the left flank, D Company was pinned down, suffering badly from machine-gun fire from the enemy who had all had time to recover from the bombardment. The fire of the Anti-Tank Regiment's 17-pounders enabled the company to move forward again, but by the time they approached Verrières D Company was commanded by a corporal.

A *Leibstandarte* sergeant in Normandy.

The *Leibstandarte*'s historian explains that 'The Canadians then moved forward behind a powerful rolling barrage. By 0600 hours, they had penetrated the town. We began a fighting retreat, which lasted until 0800 hours. We then abandoned Verrières.'

In this second attack a combination of the artillery keeping German heads down, a smokescreen and the RHLI following close behind the

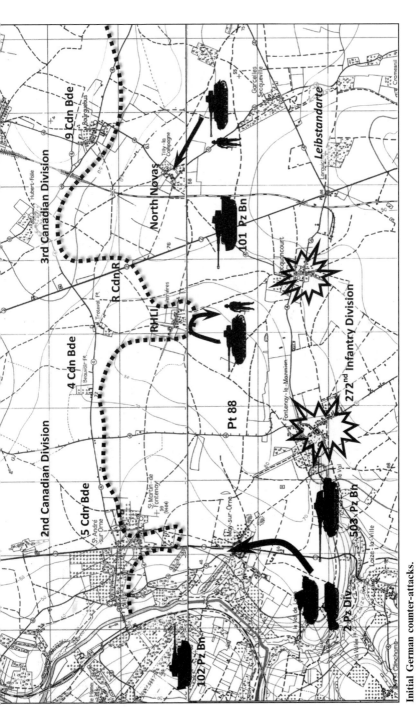

Initial German counter-attacks.

creeping barrage worked and enabled them to close on the hamlet, which was as strongly held as Tilly.

The commanding officer recorded that

> counter-attacks began immediately, causing further casualties to troops and equipment. Four of our six 6-pounder anti-tank guns were destroyed by direct fire from enemy tanks. At one period, three enemy tanks were in a forward company area before one was knocked out with a PIAT[7] and the others withdrew.

At 0700 hours General Simonds held a conference with his commanders. They agreed that with Verrières in Canadian hands, even if loosely so at this stage, Phase Two of 4 Brigade's plan could begin. C Squadron 1st Hussars and two troops of C Squadron 1 RTR equipped with Cromwells and Fireflies supported the Royal Regiment of Canada in their advance onto the Verrières Ridge. At the same time General Erskine ordered the 7th Armoured Division to begin its advance. Their first move was with 1 RTR up onto the Verrières Ridge between Troteval and Beauvoir Farms, while further right the 4th County of London Yeomanry (4 CLY) advanced towards Point 88. The Panzergrenadiers and German armour on the reverse slope were waiting for them.

The Allied armoured advance was cautious but with the situation at Tilly under control the *Leibstandarte* were able to concentrate their panzers on their left flank, i.e. around Verrières. Tigers and Panthers were able to motor up and enfilade the Royals' attack, inflicting a terrible toll on C Squadron 1st Hussars as well as the infantry. C Squadron lost fifteen of its eighteen Shermans on the ridge, being hopelessly outnumbered.

It was little better in the centre, where crossing the crest of the ridge the 7th Armoured Division's tanks came under heavy and sustained anti-tank fire and were brought to an abrupt halt. In the same area when the RHLI's

Cromwell tank of the type issued to the 7th Armoured Division.

C Company, with heavy artillery support, advanced over the crest, they found themselves amid dug-in German infantry concealed in the corn and were shot down from all sides. C Company 'was almost annihilated'.

Any vehicle going onto the ridge became sky-lined to German panzers and anti-tank guns waiting on the reverse slope. There was no way over the crest of the Verrières Ridge and the Germans renewed their counter-attacks against the RHLI in Verrières. Despite heavy casualties the Rileys held on.

At around 1730 hours General Simonds, who believed that both Tilly and May-sur-Orne were held, issued orders for a renewed advance on the Verrières Ridge. The result was as before: palls of black smoke pouring from the burning hulls of 1 RTR's tanks. In this attack the regiment lost so many tanks, around thirty, on the open slopes of the Verrières Ridge that its B and C squadrons had to be amalgamated to make a viable sub-unit.

German Counter-Attacks on Verrières

Alarmed by early reports that the Canadians had broken through and were on the Verrières Ridge in strength, *Generalfeldmarschall* von Kluge travelled to Headquarters I SS Panzer Corps to personally review the situation. He quickly authorized the release of the operational reserve to launch a corps counter-attack. *Oberführer* Fritz Krämer[8] clearly had the plans to hand because within a minute of von Kluge making his decision,

(Left) Generalfeldmarschall **von Kluge.** *(Right) Obersturmbannführer* Otto Meyer, **commander of the armoured** *Kampfgruppe* **of 9th** *Hohenstaufen* **SS Panzer Division.**

orders were on their way to *Obersturmbannführer* Harzer to 'attack north and re-establish the original HKL'.[9]

Harzer's 9th *Hohenstaufen* SS Panzer Division had two *Kampfgruppen* in reserve, named after their commanders *Obersturmbannführer* Otto Meyer[10] and *Obersturmbannführer* Zollhöfer. Meyer's armour-heavy *Kampfgruppe* consisted of the Panthers and Mk IV panzers and the armoured panzer-grenadier battalion. Zollhöfer's infantry-heavy *Kampfgruppe* was formed from the remaining infantry amalgamated into Panzergrenadier Regiment *Hohenstaufen* or simply 'H', a *Sturmgeschütz* company, and was supported by the majority of the divisional artillery.

Beginning at 1730 hours, Meyer was ordered to advance 'east of Fontenay towards Point 88' at the centre of Verrières Ridge, where the attack was to be joined from the east by elements of the *Leibstandarte*. Just as the Allied tanks had found in crossing the crest of the ridge, the Germans were exposed to the full weight of the Canadians' fire as they were in turn sky-lined and both Meyer and the *Leibstandarte* were driven back. Meyer reported at 1750 hours that 'Whoever crosses the ridge is a dead man' and moved west to support Zollhöfer.

May-sur-Orne

A mile further west, the 2nd Canadian Division's 5 Cdn Bde were in action and here conditions were if anything even more unfavourable as the attack began. The elements of 6 Cdn Bde that had been responsible for securing the start lines in St André and St Martin had by midnight only partly achieved this. H-Hour was delayed at the last minute until 0400 hours, throwing both bombardment and movement light out of sync.

The principal German formations holding the area from Beauvoir Farm to the River Orne were the seven infantry battalions of the 272nd Division. Five battalions were deployed on a frontage of just over 2 miles, with two battalions in reserve along with a panzer heavy *Kampfgruppe* from the 2nd (*Wien*) Panzer Division, which provided a mobile element with punch to the divisional reserve.

In addition, I SS Panzer Corps provided the Tigers and King Tigers of 101 *Schwere* Panzer Battalion, *Sturmgeschütz* and additional anti-tank and artillery assets, plus an infantry battalion from the 9th *Hohenstaufen* SS Panzer Division, along with the 10th *Frundsberg* Division's reconnaissance battalion. What the 272nd lacked in infantry was more than made up for by panzers and artillery firepower.

Down by the villages and River Orne the ground was not as open as the Verrières Ridge but it was eminently defensible, especially by a power-fully reinforced division. Here the German infantry also benefited from the extensive iron-ore working tunnels in the area for shelter, escape and mobility and the narrow front enabled the 11,000 men, plus the sundry attachments, to be deployed in depth. In short, while not as fanatical as the

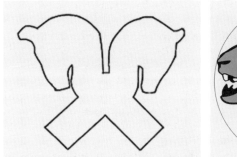

(Left) **The sign of the 272nd Infantry Division.** *(Right)* **The Tiger badge of the 101st** *Schwere* **Panzer Battalion.**

SS Panzergrenadiers, this *Wehrmacht* division still proved to be a serious enemy to contend with.

Phase One

While 5 Cdn Bde's start line was still being cleared by the Camerons, at 0300 hours the Calgary Highlanders started to move from Point 67 into St André to form up. It was immediately apparent that the area was far from clear of enemy infantry and a change of plan was also necessary when the commanding officer was told that the trees, buildings and scrub along the riverbank had not yet been cleared. Therefore, C Company was sent to protect the right flank. A combination of the fighting in the village, mortar fire, a thirty-minute delay in H-Hour and the late adjustment to the plan meant that the Highlanders 'had trouble from the beginning'. Consequently, rather than advancing quickly behind the barrage to secure the village of May-sur-Orne, the leading companies were distracted by fire from behind and the flanks.

The delay in H-Hour and the slackening of the bombardment while the fire plan 'dwelled' for thirty minutes gave the German infantry an opportunity to prepare for the Canadian assault. Advancing across 1,000 yards of flat country towards May, the Highlanders' right flank was under fire, as C Company had been unable to clear the riverbanks. The result was that B Company was badly shot up, became fragmented and went to ground. Only one platoon pressed on towards the outskirts of May just as it was getting light. The platoon commander went into the village on a reconnaissance but while he was away the 272nd Division's reserve attacked with Tigers and infantry mounted in half-tracks. The platoon promptly withdrew to the pit head known as 'the Factory'.

On the left A Company's advance was promptly forced off course by fire on their flank from their left rear – the uncleared village of St Martin – nonetheless, they pushed on to May, hoping to regain the barrage. This

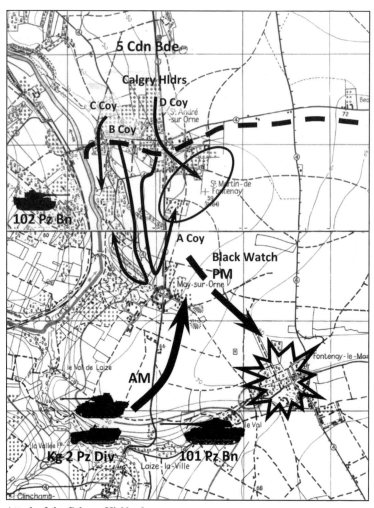

Attack of the Calgary Highlanders.

they did and reached the fields adjacent to the village but still under fire; without tank support they were unable to advance and also withdrew to the Factory. In doing so, they lost communication with battalion headquarters and the chain of command consequently continued to believe that A Company was in May.

Meanwhile, D Company, the battalion's reserve, had become hopelessly disorientated and advanced into St Martin rather than May. Here they helped to clear the village, which was to be the Black Watch of Canada's assembly area for Phase Two.

'The Factory' from German positions on the outskirts of May sur Orne.

During the attack radio communications broke down and remained almost non-existent throughout the day. As a result, little accurate information on the situation came in to the Camerons' tactical headquarters. Consequently, it only became apparent much later that the assault companies that had gained footholds in the outskirts of May during the morning had been ejected by counter-attacks.

The CMHQ[11] report summarized the difficulties faced by the Calgary Highlanders:

Errors in map reading and confusion in the darkness, as well as the presence of enemy troops behind our front, helped to prevent The Calgary Highlanders from fully reaching their objectives and making them good. Wireless communication was very bad throughout; the Commanding Officer was never able to get a clear picture of the positions of his companies and could exercise no effective control.

The failure to secure May-sur-Orne set in motion events that led to one of the enduring controversies of Operation SPRING. Even though the objective of the Calgary Highlanders had not been secured, the Black Watch was under pressure to commence Phase Two: the attack over the western extension of the Verrières Ridge to the village of Fontenay-le-Marmion. The commanding officer of the Black Watch had been killed and his senior company commander wounded in fighting to completely secure St Martin while they waited for their turn to attack. Consequently command of the

Black Watch of Canada cap badge and shoulder title.

battalion, which was at the time strung out beyond St Martin, devolved on the 24-year-old Major Phillip Griffin at about 0530 hours. As it got light it was, however, obvious to the newly-elevated commanding officer that the brigade plan had miscarried:

With a view to discovering the situation in May-sur-Orne, Major Griffin sent an officer's patrol to reconnoitre that village. This patrol entered the place and walked through the greater part of it, seeing only one German and drawing fire from one machine-gun ... It had made no contact with The Calgary Highlanders in the May area.[12]

Major Griffin came under pressure to mount the Phase Two attack and this is where the controversy lies: was Major Griffin ordered to attack? It is improbable that a young, junior officer who had been elevated to command of a battalion in the midst of action would have the presence of mind or moral authority to disobey his senior officers. He was not to know, in the absence of any concrete information, that the tanks would not be able to take up positions in May to shoot the Black Watch's assault companies into Fontenay.

As a result of the pressure a new plan was made and while this was going on the battalion intelligence officer also walked down the road and towards May and found neither Calgary Highlanders nor the enemy. As he reached the eastern outskirts of May, however, he was finally fired upon. Reporting the presence of the enemy, he was duly sent back with a patrol to clear 'the small group of enemy' flanking the start line. The conviction was clearly that May was largely held by the Camerons!

After the battle the artillery was also criticized for not giving fire support to the Black Watch's advance on Fontenay. The fire plan had been hastily adapted, again because the Calgary Highlanders were believed to be somewhere in or beyond May. This adjustment, problems with radios and the Black

Major Phillip Griffin.

Watch's own slow advance meant that the fire plan ran its course and the battalion didn't see it fall beyond the ridge, as they made their way up its forward face.

Meanwhile, Lieutenant Rawson, B Squadron 1st Hussars entered May and found only the enemy: 'My troop was belting away with machine guns at anything that looked like a Jerry position but I'm afraid it was mostly blind shooting as Jerry had turned out his usual efficient job at camouflaging.'

Most of the Hussars' Shermans that entered May were knocked out; there would be little or no direct fire support from the tanks as they were fighting for their lives. Out in the fields, advancing south from St Martin the Black Watch were already suffering casualties from both enemy infantry and artillery, with one of the rifle companies soon being commanded by a sergeant, but they pressed on up the ridge. However, as elsewhere during Operation SPRING, crossing the crestline of the Verrières Ridge was almost 'suicidal' and the battalion's problems redoubled when they encountered enemy infantry and Tiger tanks on the reverse slope. The sixty men who survived going over the crest were driven to ground. Sound working numbers are that about 350 Black Watch advanced, of whom 323 were killed, wounded and/or became prisoners of war, with only 15 returning to St Martin. Major Griffin lay among the dead on the ridge.

Zollhöfer's Counter-Attack

General Schack's 272nd divisional reserve provided by the 2nd (*Wien*) Panzer Division appears to have been committed to containing the attack on May and Fontenay along with two of his own infantry battalions. His

Shermans of the 1st Hussars with added protection of track links and sandbags to help defeat the *Panzerfäust*.

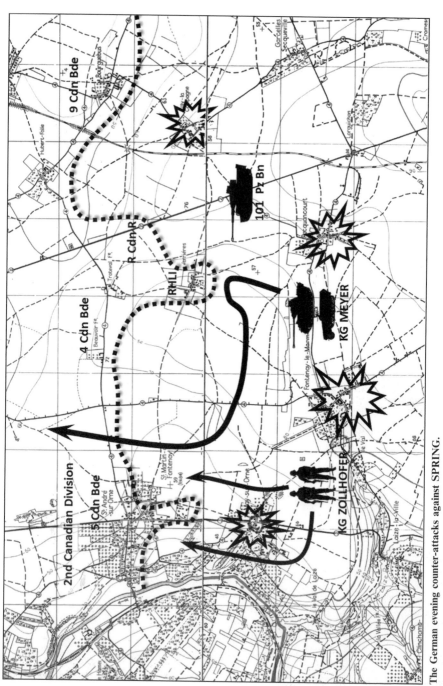

The German evening counter-attacks against SPRING.

other powerful manoeuvre unit under command was *Sturmbannführer* Brinkman's Reconnaissance Battalion[13] detached from the *Frundsberg*, which he deployed to thicken up the defensive line on the reverse slope of the Verrières Ridge, where it had contributed to the destruction of the Black Watch. To completely restore the situation on the lower ground Schack needed help from I SS Panzer Corps, *Obersturmbannführer* Zollhöfer's composite regiment from the *Hohenstaufen*.

Kampfgruppe Zollhöfer's move from their assembly area in the woods west of Bretteville-sur-Laize was significantly slower than Meyer's as the *Kampfgruppe* lacked mobility and was subject to fighter-bomber attacks. They formed up in the low ground west of Fontenay and in sweeping aside the remnants of the Black Watch and advancing up the Verrières Ridge they also had problems in crossing the open crest but they eventually managed it with considerable losses thanks to smoke and high-explosive fire. While this support was being organized, Headquarters 272nd Division was demanding to know 'Where is Zollhöfer?'

With May now obviously held by the enemy, *Le Régiment de Maisonneuve* was ordered by Brigadier Megill to resume the offensive by capturing the village, but another misbelief crept in and that was that the Black Watch, having disappeared across the ridge, had been successful. The Maisonneuves' attack began well but they were soon subjected to flanking

General Dempsey, Commander British Second Army.

fire from the 272nd's remaining positions in St Martin. At 1840 hours their situation became critical when a battalion of *Kampfgruppe* H joined in the battle around May and the Maisonneuves were forced back to St André, pursued by Zollhöfer. In doing so the *Kampfgruppe* linked up with grenadiers near the Factory and cleared the remaining Black Watch and Calgary Highlanders from St Martin and they even claim to have advanced to Point 67 before withdrawing to the villages.

The reality of the situation across the corps' front only became fully apparent as the evening wore on but, in the meantime, Canadian commanders continued to make plans to resume the attack based on a belief that May-sur-Orne was held. However, with the Germans counter-attacking vigorously, General Simonds went to see General Dempsey at Second Army headquarters with the view that Operation SPRING should be called off.

Tactically the Canadians suffered a reverse with little to show for their heavy casualties other than the village of Verrières but they had inflicted irreplaceable losses on I SS Panzer Corps. In judging the operational effect of SPRING, however, one must refer back to the task given to General Dempsey in Montgomery's directive M512, which stated

the enemy must be led to believe that we contemplate a major advance towards FALAISE and ARGENTAN, and he must be induced to build up his main strength to the east of the R. ORNE so that our affairs on the western flank can proceed with greater speed.

The degree of operational level success delivered by II Canadian Corps can be gauged by Montgomery's summary of the situation on 27 July in M515:

By our operations on the eastern flank we have pulled the main enemy strength on that side in to the area east of the ORNE and astride the FALAISE road. The enemy has tried hard to relieve his armoured divisions with infantry divisions, and to hold his armour in reserve for counter-attack. But he has failed in this; on the front of the Second British Army we now find that he has six Pz. And S.S. divisions holding the line and all these are to the east of NOYERS.

In other words, Monty had the bulk of the German armour exactly where he wanted them, for the time being!

Undoubtedly the offensive phases of Operation SPRING served their operational purpose admirably, but tactically they gave Guy Simonds plenty of pause for thought, as sooner or later he would be tasked to attack again, south through that network of German defences.

NOTES

1. *Tagesbefehl* 24 July 1944: Order of the day.
2. Assault guns. Originally conceived as a self-propelled assault artillery piece designed to support the infantry, it proved to be a highly effective anti-tank system.
3. Sometimes referred to as 'Monty's Moonlight', these were searchlights with diffused beams reflecting off clouds. They were deployed as far as possible to silhouette the enemy rather than the attackers!
4. There is the ever-present dichotomy between what a commander expects from an operation and what he and his troops hope for, sometimes desperately. It was plainly impossible to explain to soldiers that SPRING was a 'holding attack' on grounds of both security and results; soldiers simply wouldn't fight to deliver the desired outcomes.
5. The spring-propelled Projector Infantry Anti-Tank fired a shaped-charge warhead, similar to that of the *Panzerfäust* ['armour fist'] and the American bazooka.
6. The RHLI had not been committed during ATLANTIC.
7. The spring-propelled Projector Infantry Anti-Tank fired a shaped-charge warhead.

8. The highly able chief of staff of I SS Panzer Corps.
9. *Hauptkampfline*: Main Battle Line.
10. Not to be confused with either Kurt Panzer Meyer or Hubert Meyer, both of the 12th SS Panzer Division.
11. Canadian Military Headquarters, London.
12. CMHQ Report 150.
13. German panzer recce battalions were not the light armoured units typical in Allied armies but capable units that could fight for information.

Chapter Three

II Canadian Corps' TOTALIZE Plan

During the last week of July 1944, the whole complexion of the Normandy campaign changed. After six weeks of bitter fighting in the tight beachhead the under-resourced German armies had been worn down by 21st Army Group's repeated offensives and had reached breaking-point. Operation SPRING and its predecessors had played their part in weakening the Germans and fixing the vast majority of the panzers in the east away from the American Operation COBRA, which was finally launched on 25 July. Over the following three days the US offensive developed momentum south, against weak German resistance. The Allies now had their long-hoped-for break-out.

With American armour streaming south towards Avranches and out of Normandy and with the hastily-launched British Operation BLUECOAT making headway, Hitler now intervened. Following the 20 July Bomb Plot, he no longer made any pretence of listening to the professional advice of his generals who, in the prevailing climate of fear, had little stomach to do anything other than obey orders from Berlin; in this case, to mount a counterstroke against the First US Army.[1]

Hitler reasoned that with the situation in the west of Normandy rapidly deteriorating this was the main threat, and one that he had to deal with. He ordered the commander of Army Group B, *Generalfeldmarschall* von Kluge, to launch 'an immediate counter-attack between Mortain and Avranches'. To ensure his orders to attack the Americans were complied with, General Warlimont was dispatched to France where von Kluge told Warlimont that there was no prospect of success. He said that the only viable plan was to abandon Normandy and fall back to the Seine, pivoting on the strongly-held ground south of Caen. On 4 August, however, Hitler emphatically ordered that Operation LÜTTICH was to be launched.

Hitler specified using seven of the eight heavily-weakened panzer divisions in Normandy and the *Luftwaffe* would commit its remaining strength in order to at least establish air parity in an attempt to keep the Allied fighter-bombers at bay. To create the force of some 300 panzers necessary to stand any chance of success, the armour that had been massed under I SS Panzer Corps and had defeated Operation SPRING was stripped away and the remains of the *Leibstandarte, Hohenstaufen, Frundsberg* and 2nd (*Wien*) Panzer divisions joined others in night moves across Normandy between 1 and 6 August 1944. Not only had Hitler drawn his panzers deeper into the potential envelopment that was beginning to develop as First US Army turned east, but he had also left the open country south of Caen with a greatly-reduced number of panzers and had redeployed most

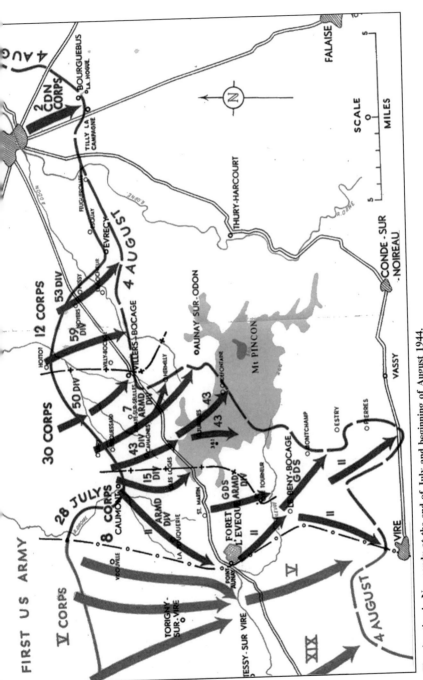

The situation in Normandy at the end of July and beginning of August 1944.

of the SS divisions that had hitherto done so much to contain the British and Canadians.

Meanwhile, with the British Operation BLUECOAT getting under way, General Montgomery had formally ordered General Crerar's newly-operational headquarters of First Canadian Army to mount an attack in approximately a week's time. He wrote:

> The general situation was now very good. We had broken out of the bridgehead and had destroyed the first hinge on which the enemy had tried to pivot. We are pressing very hard on the next key rivet of his line on the slopes of the PINCON [Mont Pinçon] massif ...
>
> The time has now come to deliver the major attack towards FALAISE, which has so long been the fundamental aim of our policy on the eastern flank. I planned that the Canadians should drive South East from CAEN to gain as much ground as possible in the direction of FALAISE, in order to get behind the enemy forces facing the Second [British] Army, and to continue the process of wearing down the enemy formations in the sector. I envisaged this operation as a prelude to subsequent exploitation of success.[2]

I SS Panzer Corps South of Caen

After its mauling in Operation SPRING, the 272nd Division was relieved in place and moved to a quiet sector in LXXXVI Corps further east, where the infantrymen took over defences from the 21st Panzer Division who were among the first to head west to face the American break-out. The *Hohenstaufen* temporarily took over the May-sur-Orne sector before also moving west for LÜTTICH. The *Leibstandarte* followed on the night of 4/5 August, with both SS divisions having handed over positions to the 89th Infantry Division. Further east the 12th *Hitlerjugend* SS Panzer Division was also being relieved and was moving back into corps reserve prior to heading west to join LÜTTICH. Sepp Dietrich's I SS Panzer Corps, however, remained in command of the Caen South Sector.

General Heinrichs' 89th Infantry Division was a newly-raised Type 44 division, coming into existence in Celle during January 1944. It was largely made up of Easterners and Germans who would previously have been exempt from service, many below 18 years of age or over 40. It had conducted its training in Norway where the demands of security operations were a continual distraction. Ordered to Normandy on 26 June, it had a long and torturous journey by troop train and then on foot from Le Havre to Normandy. The 89th started to take over the defences astride the road to Falaise on 3 August. Their presence on ground previously held by the *Leibstandarte* was only reported on the 6th after one of their ambulances took a wrong turn and drove into the Canadian positions. This was an identification that was shortly confirmed by an East European deserter. With the usual delay inherent in decoding ULTRA material, General

(*Left*) Lieutenant General Harry Crerar. (*Right*) General Heinrichs, commander of the 89th Division.

Simonds received word 'from various sources' of the redeployment of the *Leibstandarte* to the Mortain Counter-Attack. This enabled him to revise Phases Two and Three of his plan to be more ambitious.

At the tactical level prisoners were only able to furnish their questioners with the most basic information and very little detail on deployment or their commander's intent. One Canadian intelligence officer complained: 'Any attempts to clarify the situation have been frustrated by the elusiveness of live Germans and the abysmal ignorance of deserters and prisoners, who travel at night and are apparently told nothing by their superiors.'

Despite the departure of the *Leibstandarte* during the TOTALIZE planning process, effective patrolling provided information to intelligence staff that enabled them to plot the location of the 89th Division's six infantry battalions. General Simonds was able to adapt his plan as the German deployment changed. However, it took a leap of faith by some field commanders to accept that the multiplicity of slit trenches to be seen on air photos and tactical overprint maps were not all occupied by the reduced infantry strength of the 89th Division, who now held the front from the River Orne to the village of La Hougue.

The 89th Division had thirteen *Sturmpanzer* IVs attached from 217 *Sturmpanzerabteilung*. Known as the *Brummbär* or to the German soldiers as the *Stupa*, they mounted 150mm sIG 33 heavy infantry guns, which gave the division some mobile punch.

With the 89th Division holding I SS Panzer Corps' front, the 12th *Hitlerjugend* SS was the only panzer division left east of the Orne to support them

51

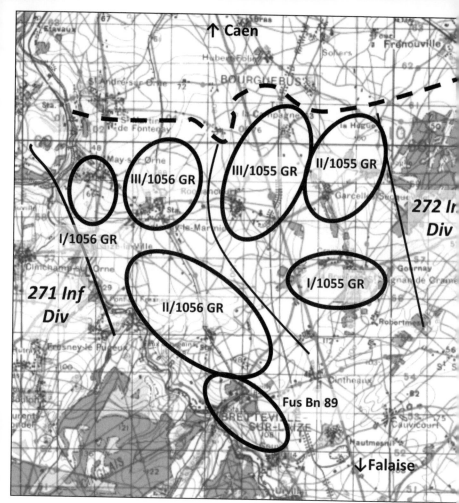

Deployment of the 89th Division astride the Falaise Road.

and they were at Hitler's insistence due to start following the other panzers west during the night of 7/8 August. The division's young and fanatical soldiers had but a single day or so out of the line, having been in action since 7 June, and were much reduced in strength. Its infantry was assessed as being only 1,500 strong, with twenty Panthers, twenty Panzer IVs and a similar number of *Panzerjäger* IVs.

Having come out of the line the *Hitlerjugend* half of the division was moved into corps' reserve, while *Kampfgruppe* Krause, supported by some of the panzers, was promptly deployed 12 miles to the west and at the time TOTALIZE was launched they were attacking a bridgehead that had been seized by the 59th Staffordshire Division at Thury-Harcourt. For the panzer crews of the remaining two *Kampfgruppen* this short time in reserve

Sturmpanzer **IV, also known as a** *Brummbär* **or** *Stupa*.

represented an opportunity to carry out maintenance of their tanks, but for the infantry they were largely employed digging a line in depth across the next piece of high ground where it was crossed by the Falaise Road north of Potigny and another on the River Laison. Their commanders, meanwhile, prepared their counter-attack options to again restore the Corps HKL.

Thin though the ranks of the 89th and the *Hitlerjugend* were, they were backed up by an extensive array of corps' assets and other attachments, some of which were in the corps' normal order of battle. The most significant of these was the remnants of 101 *Schwere* Panzer Battalion. Its ten remaining Tigers were under the command of *Hauptsturmführer* Wittmann, who had returned from Germany where he had been decorated for his part

An early version *Panzerjäger* **IV with the same 75mm gun as the Panzer IV. This one was knocked out, having already been 'half-tracked' following a final-drive failure. This would enable the vehicle to limp into battle.**

Hauptsturmführer Michael Wittmann receiving the Knight's Cross with Oak Leaves and Swords from Adolf Hitler.

(*Left*) The shield badge of the 12th *Hitlerjugend* Panzer Division. (*Right*) The Knight's Cross of the Iron Cross with Oak Leaves and Swords.

in the halting of the 7th Armoured Division's advance at Villers-Bocage (Operation PERCH) on 14 June.

I SS Panzer Corps had also retained most of their other corps troops including their artillery, the important elements of which were the heavy guns of the Corps Artillery battalion (two batteries of 170mm and one of 210mm). Consequently, when adding the divisional artillery of both the 89th and *Hitlerjugend* divisions, the corps had a significant weight of artillery firepower. In addition, there were the mortars of the 89th Division and the *Werfer* Brigade, which remained under Dietrich's command. This formation consisted of two battalions each of eighteen launchers.

Crucially, I SS Panzer Corps had also retained an ample anti-tank capability in the form of an army anti-tank battalion, plus that of the *Leibstandarte*. Together they maintained the deadly web of overlapping and interlocking arcs of fire that had proved so deadly during Operation SPRING. In addition to these guns, the corps was allocated guns from General Wolfgang Pickert's III Flak Corps. These included a significant number of 88mm dual-purpose guns, but the SS staff found it difficult to persuade their brigade headquarters to take part in the ground battle:

A Flak Brigade of three Flak Sturm Regiments equipped with between sixty and seventy 88mm AA/A Tk guns and approximately the same number 2cm anti-aircraft guns was deployed on this front. This brigade was a *Luftwaffe* formation, and did not come under the Army. It was a constant source of annoyance to the commander directing the immediate battle, who wished to employ the guns forward as effective anti-tank weapons; whereas their commander, General PICKARD [*sic*], often as not, countermanded the Army commander and moved the guns back to protect administrative sites. As a result, these 88mms were mainly deployed on the BRETTEVILLE–ST SYLVAIN line and further south.[3]

Loading a six-tube *Nebelwerfer* rocket-launcher.

The dual-purpose 88mm Flak 36 gun.

This is where the *Hitlerjugend* were preparing positions and the presence of these 88mm guns made it a second serious line that II Canadian Corps would have to breach before continuing their advance south to Falaise.

In summary, despite the inherent weakness of the 89th Infantry Division and the depleted ranks of the *Hitlerjugend*, the Germans' defence on the Verrières and Bourguébus ridges still represented a significant challenge, especially to an armoured force attempting to advance south across the open armour killing areas.

As the panzer divisions slipped away from the Orne Front, Sepp Dietrich took command of the Fifth Panzer Army during this period when General Eberbach was dispatched to command Operation LÜTTICH.

General Simonds' Estimate

Having been given a warning order on 29 July, II Canadian Corps' Commander settled down to conduct a formal estimate and he must have had the salutary experience of Operation SPRING in the forefront of his mind. Having stated his objective 'To break through the German positions astride the CAEN–FALAISE Road', he described the by now well-known strength of the German position and the fact that the Allied objectives were also all too well understood by the Germans. He concluded that:

The ground is ideally suited to full exploitation by the enemy with the characteristics of his weapons. It is open, giving little cover for

56

either infantry or tanks and the long range of his anti-tank guns and mortars firing from carefully concealed positions provides a very strong defence in depth. This defence will be most handicapped by bad visibility – smoke, fog or darkness, when the advantage of long range is minimized. The attack should therefore be made under these conditions.

In order to break through the German positions Simonds knew he had not just to cross the Verrières Ridge and Point 122 but fight his way for another 5 miles. He wrote:

> If all available air support is used for the 'first break in' [on to the Verrières Ridge] there will be nothing for the second except diminished gun support [due to range and movement], unless a long pause is made with resultant loss of speed. If on the other hand the first 'break in' is based upon limited air support (heavy night bombers), none will be available for the second 'break in' at a time when gun support begins to decrease.

This meant that the heavy bombers would be available for a second daylight strike on German in-depth positions as the operation progressed. This strike could not be on call but had to be delivered at a fixed time, thus removing an element of flexibility.

As a result of his estimate,[4] Simonds ruled out simply attempting to blast his way through with the maximum heavy bomber effort at the outset; instead he chose a more limited initial strike and to infiltrate 'through the screen in bad visibility to a sufficient depth to disrupt the anti-tank and mortar defence'. He also requested an additional infantry division and insisted that the infantry should accompany the armour and go straight through the enemy defences in the 'first break in' alongside the tanks and clear and hold objectives. This would require the assault element of the two infantry divisions, 2nd Canadian and 51st Highland, to have mobility and protection during the advance; the need for an armoured personnel carrier (APC) was reborn.[5] General Simonds later explained how the opportunity to convert Priest self-propelled guns came about:

> I was one day watching some of these vehicles and it occurred to me that, if the equipment was stripped, they would be sufficiently roomy and have adequate protection to provide the sort of vehicle I had in mind. I therefore asked General Crerar if he would intervene with the Americans to allow us to strip the equipments and lend them for this particular operation.[6]

The Kangaroo

The field regiments of Royal Artillery that landed with the leading formations on D-Day had all been equipped with self-propelled Sextons or the M7 Priests. The Priests were on loan from the US army and with a 105mm

A Canadian Bren-gunner in North-West Europe.

howitzer rather than the British 25-pounder they presented unnecessary logistic friction and were to be returned. It so happened that the 3rd Canadian Division was now out of the line for an overdue rest and its three artillery regiments were being re-equipped with towed 25-pounders. Consequently, their Priests were available for conversion to APCs.[7]

An Anglo/Canadian detachment of Royal Electrical and Mechanical Engineers, supported by Ordnance and Service Corps soldiers, known as the Kangaroo[8] Workshop, was set up and on 2 August began to 'defrock' the Priests. This involved removing the gun and its ancillary equipment plus taking out the ammunition racking, etc. The resulting large gap in the front was covered initially with armour plate but that was in short supply, so ordinary steel sheet from the Colombelles Steel Works was used but this

A Canadian 105mm Priest and crew earlier in the campaign.

steel proved unable to stop a .50 calibre bullet. Consequently, two sheets, with the gap in between being filled with sand, were used as a form of composite armour. When the Colombelles steel ran out, the Kangaroo Workshop resorted to cutting steel from landing craft that still littered the beaches, much to the annoyance of the Royal Navy!

The first vehicle off the Kangaroo Workshop's conversion line was driven to Headquarters II Canadian Corps for General Guy Simonds to inspect and pass his verdict. In the three days that followed, the workshop performed a tremendous feat of labour that saved many lives. They completed seventy-six conversions and handed them over to drivers and commanders of D and E squadrons of the Elgin Regiment[9] who became responsible for their operation and maintenance. Additional drivers were found from across the corps, including the gunners who had driven the Priests ashore on D-Day.

General Simonds had plenty of time to sell the armoured infiltration concept to his 2nd Canadian Division who, fresh from their experiences on

A 'defrocked Priest' or Kangaroo on a 51st Highland Division route south of Caen.

the Verrières Ridge, needed little persuasion but he was concerned about the 51st Highland Division's reaction:

> I was a bit worried as to how the Scots would like it, because they had the reputation of being rather canny and having their own ideas about things. General Rennie ... came over to see me as soon as they had been nominated and I had a talk with him. He was very taken with the idea and I knew from that first talk that I had his support 100 per cent and subsequently 51 (H) Div took to it with great enthusiasm.[10]

When he had originally conceived the idea of Kangaroos, General Simonds had thought he would have up to a week for training on a new and untried concept. In the event, however, 'many units only received two days' training and the last Kangaroos were only delivered to units twenty-four hours before the attack.' Lieutenant Colonel Jolly, 144 Regiment Royal Armoured Corps (RAC), recalled:

> We carried out daylight rehearsals with the 7th Argyll and Sutherland Highlanders (7 A&SH) that afternoon (5 August) and night rehearsals the following night – Lébisey Wood representing our objective. There was no time for more and the next day we crossed the Orne.

The drill in these exercises was as follows: 'The infantry companies practised embussing and debussing and runs were made to imaginary dispersal areas where the assault force debussed and attacked an objective, leaving the fortress force to secure the dispersal area.'

In some cases, during these exercises trucks were used in the columns in lieu of Kangaroos that had yet to be delivered from the workshop.

There were, however, not enough Kangaroos for all the attacking battalions. Consequently, the remainder were made up of more conventional M5A1 half-tracks and carriers of various descriptions, all of which offered some protection from small-arms fire and shell fragments.

The concept of mass armour, including the Kangaroos at night, was an innovation and was one in which not all of those who took part in the single night exercise had much confidence. Thanks to the warning orders, they already had an inkling of a novel approach but when Simonds began his Orders Group with 'Gentlemen, we will do this attack at night with armour' apparently the divisional commanders' 'jaws dropped visibly!'

Canadian Preparations

A warning order on 30 July and full orders on 4 August set the Canadians and Scots in motion, but many of Crerar's First Canadian Army combat support and logistic troops were only just arriving and had but a couple of days' grace to get everything ready to sustain a major offensive. It was, however, not just the logistic units that were still arriving in theatre but armoured formations as well. The 21st Army Group's planned schedule of arrival of armoured divisions and brigades had been disrupted by Hitler's insistence on roping off the beachhead and not falling back to a more defensible line. Consequently, it was only in the last days of July and early August that the First Canadian Army received its additional armoured formations: the 4th Canadian and the Polish armoured divisions.

With the need to waterproof their vehicles and be ready to be called over to Normandy at short notice in the event of a collapse of the German Seventh Army, both divisions had been denied the use of their armour for almost two months. For the infantry this was not too serious as dismounted exercising continued, but for armoured regiments this represented a serious loss of condition and focus while waiting. Consequently, the tactical and operational lessons coming back from Normandy could only be discussed by 4th Canadian Armoured and the Poles but crucially they could not be tested or practised during pre-deployment exercises.[11]

Historians have persistently been critical of Major General George Kitching's inexperienced 4th Canadian Armoured Division during the Normandy campaign. The preparation of the division had a lower priority than the three British armoured divisions along with the armoured brigades that were to deploy early in the campaign. This manifested itself in just a handful of divisional exercises in late 1943 (a full seven months before deployment) and little all-arms training at a level that would test the division's staff and their procedures. Even though his division could be described as undertrained, General Kitching himself had a sound military

Generals Simonds and Kitching watching training in the UK in early 1944.

background dating back to 1929 in the British army. In 1939, however, he joined the Canadian army and like so many of the senior Canadian commanders his rise through the ranks and appointments was speedy. His operational experience was as a staff officer with the 1st Canadian Division during the invasions of Sicily and Italy and a few months in late 1943 commanding the 11th Canadian Infantry Brigade in Italy. Kitching demonstrably had as much practical experience as most senior Canadian officers before returning to the UK on promotion to command the 4th Canadian Armoured Division. As highlighted above, in the months leading up to their deployment Kitching had not had the opportunity to properly exercise his staff or that of his brigades in the field.

The 1st Polish Armoured Division was formed in Scotland from the remnants of the 10th Motorized Cavalry Brigade under General Stanisław

Major General Stanisław Maczek.

Maczek during 1942. Some 30,000 Polish soldiers and civilians had escaped from their own country via Rumania and on to France in 1939 and early 1940 and eventually reached Britain. In May 1943 the Polish Armoured Division moved to Newmarket in Suffolk to undergo five months of training on tanks and armoured warfare in general. As other divisions found, training on the heathlands of Suffolk and Norfolk bore little resemblance to the ground in Normandy and proved to be poor preparation.

Even though many Poles had far more practical combat experience from earlier in the war, the Polish Armoured Division suffered from many of the same problems as their Canadian Allies. When the two formations assembled in Normandy during the last week of July and the first few days of August, they discovered that they were going to be thrown into battle without that gentle introduction to the conditions found in real battle that Montgomery strove to provide to his newly-arrived divisions.

The state of preparedness of the 2nd Canadian Division has been covered in the previous chapter but the 51st (Highland) Division was having difficulties of its own. As renowned, suntanned and bemedalled veterans of the Eighth Army they had returned to a cold, drab wartime UK winter. They had been much admired, indeed feted, but their training and, in common

A Sherman of the Polish Armoured Division coming ashore at the Mulberry Harbour's Tank Landing Ship berth only days before TOTALIZE.

with some other Mediterranean formations, preparation for the campaign was characterized by a reluctance to engage in new ideas and they were far from their top form. Captain Aitkinhead wrote '... we had six months in the UK, saw our loved ones and were stationed mainly in the Home Counties. We became perhaps too soft and relaxed ....' On top of this, their experience in the beachhead, sitting in defence for long periods taking casualties, was guaranteed to make matters worse. For instance, 7 Black Watch had just received its fifth commanding officer in six weeks, the result of sackings and casualties, and all-ranks casualties exceeded 300.

Lieutenant Colonel Carr, the Highlanders' Commander Royal Engineers, wrote to his wife describing the cause of and the resulting malaise that had beset the division:

At the end of six weeks we were very tired, even the gunners and sappers. There was no let up. Pinned up in our little corner under steady shellfire by day, and air attack by night, every 24 hours brought its trickle of casualties. Sleep was difficult, chiefly because we have lived in our own gun line for so long. After the Caen battle we found ourselves relegated to holding the shattered ruins of villages, splintered leafless woods smashed in our previous six weeks fighting, reminded at every turn by the sights and smells of our hastily buried dead caused by our fruitless endeavours, you can imagine a certain depression setting in.

The return of Major General Rennie was the beginning of a process that would later in the campaign see the restoration of the Highland Division's

Major General Rennie and aide-de-camp aboard a Jeep.

fortunes but in the short term being released from holding ground on the eastern flank brought a boost to morale. Lieutenant Robinson of 1 Black Watch said 'It was basically a return to offensive action after weeks spent in the woods ... that put us back on our feet again.'

II Canadian Corps' Plan

It is widely accepted that TOTALIZE was seen by General Simonds as an opportunity to establish himself as a corps commander of repute and was above all determined for his corps to do well after the difficulties and disappointment of Operation SPRING. His plan was somewhat complex and inflexible because, even though he had ruled out using all the heavy bomber support available at the opening of the battle, he was going to use it in two bites. The problem was that assembling the might of the Allied bomber barons took time and lacked sufficient flexibility to keep pace with developments on the ground.

Simonds gave orders to his divisions on 4 August. The operation was to be carried out as follows:

(a) Phase I – Break through the FONTENAY LE MARMION–LA HOUGUE position.

(b) Phase II – Secure the high ground West of the main road–Point 180–Point 195–Point 206 and East of the road at Point 170–Point 159.

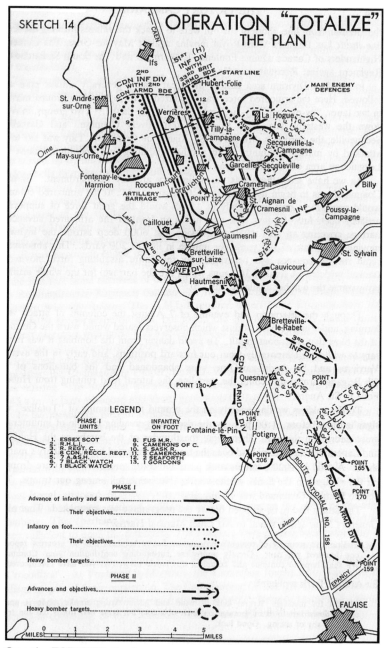

Operation TOTALIZE: the plan. (Colonel Stacey, *The Victory Campaign*)

(c) Phase III – Exploit as ordered by Commander 2 Cdn Corps.

For Phase I, 2 Cdn and 51(H) Divs, each with an armoured brigade under command and with their leading infantry brigades carried in Armoured Personnel Carriers, are to move by night on the Right and Left respectively of the road CAEN–FALAISE. The following tasks are laid down:-

(a) 2 Cdn Div
    (i)   Capture as first objective CAILLOUET–GAUMESNIL and woods Point 122.
    (ii) Mop up area MAY SUR ORNE–FONTENAY LE MARMION–CAILLOUET GAUMESNIL– ROCQUANCOURT.
    (iii) Reorganise in the above area: protect the Right flank and form a firm base for launching of Phase II.

(b) 51(H) Div
    (i)   Capture as first objective LORGUICHON Wood– CRAMESNIL–ST AIGNAN DE CRAMESNIL and woods to the South–GARCELLES SECQUEVILLE.
    (ii) Capture in succession SECQUEVILLE LA CAMPAGNE and the wooded area to the East.

Meanwhile, 4 Cdn Armd and 1 Polish Armd Div are to move up behind the assaulting divisions so as to be positioned on the Corps Start Line ... by the morning D plus 1.

Originally it was intended that in Phase Two the 4th Canadian Armoured Division would fight its way through the second German position on a narrow front with the Poles remaining in reserve. With receipt of the news that the *Leibstandarte* had slipped away, a conference was held at Corps HQ at 1000 hours on 6 August. General Simonds had decided to take full advantage of the reduced opposition expected on the corps' front and, 'having broken through the forward defences, launch the two armoured divisions directly through to the final objective.'

Phase II was planned to start at 1400 hours D plus 1. At this hour the armoured divisions were to pass through the infantry and go straight for the final objectives ...

(c) 4 Cdn Armd Div
Position itself facing West and South on the high ground Point 180–Point 195–Point 206 and keep contact with the enemy within the arc formed by the roads FONTAINE LE PINMESLAY and FALAISE–ARGENTAN.

(d) 1 Polish Armd Div
Position itself facing East and South on the high ground Point 170–Point 159 and keep contact with the enemy within the arc formed by the roads FALAISE–ARGENTAN and MONTBOINTCONDE SUR IFS.

During this phase, 2 Cdn and 51(H) Divs were to secure the Right and Left flanks at BRETTEVILLE SUR LAIZE and the woods South-East of ROBERTMESNIL respectively. 3 Cdn Div was to be ready to move forward on orders of the Corps Commander and take over the area HAUTMESNIL–BRETTEVILLE LE RABET and the high ground Point 140.

In Phase Three the corps was to exploit south on General Simonds' orders.

It is worth noting Simonds' orders contained a paragraph on 'Aids to Navigation in Phase I':

(a) Leading tanks will have positions and bearing of thrust lines fixed by survey.
(b) Bofors barrage, co-ordinated by CCRA 2 Cdn Corps, will be fired over divisional thrust lines.
(c) Wireless direction beam, two per divisional front, under direction of CSO 2 Cdn Corps.[12]
(d) Target indicator shells will be fired under divisional arrangements on thrust lines. 2 Cdn Div RED indicators, 51 (H) GREEN indicators.

The main effort was explicitly the penetration of the German positions by the armoured columns to a depth of some 5,000 yards. In doing this they would, of course, bypass the defended villages and it was the task of the dismounted infantry to capture and hold these points. In the Highland Division, 152 Brigade was in sequence to secure Tilly-la-Campagne, Lorguichon Wood and Secqueville-la-Campagne before exploiting to secure Poussy-la-Campagne, Tilly and Conteville. In Phase Three, 153 Brigade was to be responsible for expanding the penetration eastwards by clearing the flanking woods.

For Phase One, the 2nd Canadian Division allocated the assault role, alongside 2 Canadian Armoured Brigade, to 4 Canadian Infantry Brigade (4 Cdn Bde) and 8 Recce Regiment (the 14th Canadian Hussars). The latter were to form the division's fourth assault column. The 6 Cdn Bde on foot was to clear the Orne Valley villages, namely May-sur-Orne, Fontenay-le-Marmion and 5 Cdn Bde was to be held as General Foulkes' reserve.

General Crerar had repeatedly emphasized that phasing of corps and divisional plans was to be progressed smoothly and that it was all-important to maintain both the momentum of the attack and the initiative. As has been highlighted, the plan had a fundamental flaw that could potentially lose these vital elements of success if not regarded flexibly.

Assembly and Move Forward

The 51st Highland Division had finally come out of the line on 31 August and moved to a camp between Caen and Juno Beach for a rest and to take in casualty replacements. First to move back to the front in trucks through the ruins of Caen was 154 Brigade, who were to begin training on the Kangaroos. Recce and orders groups followed as battle procedure swung into action. The other brigades and divisional troops followed across the Orne over subsequent nights up to that of 5/6 August and regrouped for the coming operation with their allocated battle groups in their hide/assembly areas.

Between 3 and 6 August the forces that were to make up the Phase One assault columns started their training. In the case of 154 (Highland) Bde and 33 Armd Bde, this was in the area north of Caen and 4 Cdn Bde and 2 Cdn Armd Bde assembled at Lébisey and as already mentioned conducted rehearsals, allocating and adding the Kangaroos to the assault columns as they arrived from the workshop.

The 4 Cdn Bde assembled into four columns, each with their own objective, and 154 Bde into three columns. Each column's composition was

Soldier of the 51st Highland Division in Normandy.

A Canadian column carrying out daylight rehearsals.

different depending on obstacles and tasks, but a generalization of grouping would be as follows:

Navigating tanks (and/or recce troop of the armoured regiment)

Gapping Force	Troop of tanks
	1 or 2 Troops of Sherman Flail tanks[13]
	1 or 2 Troop of AVREs (Armoured Vehicle Royal Engineers)
Assault Force	Infantry Battalion mounters in Kangaroos or other armoured vehicles
	Remainder of squadron or regiment of tanks
	Armoured and infantry HQs
	Attachments (anti-tank guns, machine guns, etc.)
Fortress Force	1 Squadron of tanks.

Two squadrons of flame-throwing Crocodile Tanks were to remain at the rear on call.

During 5 August the Germans withdrew from the much-disputed villages of St André and St Martin as they were being subjected to enfilade fire from XIII British Corps who had advanced south on the west bank of the Orne. 5 Cdn Bde was ordered to follow up and ordered the Black Watch of Canada to secure May-sur-Orne, but as they advanced their attack was broken up by heavy mortar and machine-gun fire:

Further East, 4 Cdn Armd Div tested the defences of TILLY LA CAMPAGNE and LA HOUGUE. The former village had always been stubbornly defended by SS troops and 1055 GR, which was taking over at this time, proved no exception to this rule. Both attacks were repulsed with losses in infantry and tanks and proved beyond doubt there had been no withdrawal in this sector.

Elsewhere, patrols were also met with heavy fire. Across the front the Germans were very much still in place and there had been no general withdrawal.

On 6 August the 51st Highland Division's assault group moved to their assembly area at Cormelles without incident. During the night the

A Churchill Crocodile conversion 'flaming'.

Another conversion, the M4 Sherman Crab Flail Tank.

remainder of the division returned to the line taking over the front east of the Falaise road, with 152 Bde at Hubert-Folie and Bras, and 153 Bde occupying the line Bourguébus–Soliers–Grentheville. For the Canadians:

> The following afternoon and evening [7 August], 2 Cdn Div was assembling between FLEURY SUR ORNE and IFS. The weather was fine, and although the area was secure from direct observation, the vehicles raised clouds of dust which must have been visible from the enemy Ops. However, no air action or shelling by artillery resulted.

The Highlanders' columns formed up at 2200 hours and started to move forward at 2215 hours and it is reported that 'The columns were formed up exactly as they intended to cross the start line.'

Hopes ran high that TOTALIZE would 'prove to be decisive'. During 7 August corps and divisional commanders issued their obligatory message to the troops, all including emotive phrases, but General Simonds went further, reminding his soldiers that 8 August was the anniversary of the 'Black Day of the German Army' in 1918 and the beginning of their Canadian forebears part in the Hundred Days that brought the Great War to an end. Hope and expectations were high.

NOTES

1. *Generalfeldmarschall* von Kluge, commander Army Group B, had warned Hitler on 22 July that German forces in Normandy were verging on collapse but he was ignored and instructed to stand firm.
2. Montgomery, *Normandy to the Baltic* (British Army of the Rhine Stationery Services, April 1946).

3. British Army of the Rhine Battlefield Tour – Operation TOTALIZE. G (Trg) BAOR June 1947.
4. Presented verbally on 31 July to General Crerar and formally signed on 1 August 1944.
5. The need for an infantry-carrying tank had been auctioned in 1917 and II Australian Corps used Mk V* tanks to move machine-gun sections forward during the first day of the 1918 Battle of Amiens in August 1918.
6. Ibid. (Directing Staff Edition).
7. Permission had to be obtained from the Americans for the conversion with suitable assurances that the process could be reversed.
8. 'Kangaroo' became the generic name for all conversions of tracked armoured vehicles to armoured personnel carriers.
9. Their correct title was 25th (Armoured Delivery) Regiment.
10. The 51st Highland Division was in reserve and was transferred to the Canadians from I Corps for TOTALIZE.
11. The British army traditionally lacked a strong unifying doctrine due to the multitude of different factors across the Empire. In the case of armoured doctrine in 1944, it was heavily influenced by the Eighth Army's experience in North Africa.
12. Chief Signals Officer.
13. Attached from the 79th Armoured Division, 'Hobart's Funnies'.

Chapter Four

The 51st Highland Division –
Armoured Advance

There was to be no signature preliminary bombardment that would warn the Germans of an impending attack. As darkness fell, however, the distant throb of 1,120 Lancaster and Halifax aircraft grew into a roar and then at 2300 hours the bombs fell on five target areas for forty minutes. The targets for the RAF's 1,000lb and 500lb bombs were the villages and woods to the flank of the night's advance. A 21st Army Group note records:

> This bombing was intended to destroy the enemy defences and tank harbours by blast and fragmentation in forty-five minutes [*sic*]. Although the forward troops would be moving ahead while the latter part of this bombing was actually going on, their advance to the initial objectives on either side of the FALAISE highway would not bring them within the danger zone of 2,000 yards from the bombers' targets.

The accuracy of the bomber strike was aided by Canadian 25-pounders firing coloured marker flare shells, and searchlights at a low angle pointing due south were a further aid, but such was the stillness of the summer night that Air Chief Marshal Harris signalled General Crerar 'Regret lack of wind and accumulating smoke made it unsafe to put down last third on each objective but hope two thirds did the trick.' Some 641 aircraft had dropped 3,458 tons of high explosive but in this mission the RAF lost ten aircraft to flak over the battlefield during their bombing runs. These losses to the guns of III Flak Corps were comparatively light in comparison with a similar-sized raid over Germany.

Back at divisional command post east of Potigny, the *Hitlerjugend*'s commander *Standartenführer* Kurt 'Panzer' Meyer heard 'A continuous booming and rumbling north of Bretteville announced the anticipated Allied offensive shortly before midnight. Air attacks hammered the positions of the 89. Infanterie-Division and created a fiery glow in the sky. The front was on fire!'[1]

With the aid of SS liaison officers with forward divisions, as usual the German reaction was swift, in fact so swift that the leading elements of the *Hitlerjugend* were on the move before the Allies had crossed their start lines. Kurt Meyer continued:

> The first bombs automatically tripped the alarm for the units. Reconnaissance units moved north and tried to contact the engaged regiments of the 89. Infanterie-Division. Hour after hour passed in gloomy expectation of the coming day. The giant hammer blows of the enemy bombers told us more than any mortal could. The drumming of the

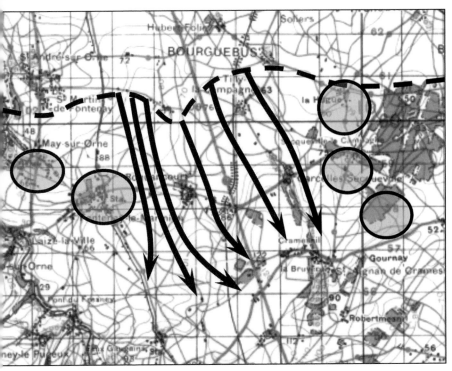

Bomber targets at 2300 hours on 7 August 1944.

bombs and shells drew our attention. There was no point in wanting
to escape this hellfire; its throat had already opened to receive us.

Having received authority to deploy from I SS Panzer Corps, Meyer issued
orders as soon as the attack was confirmed. *Kampfgruppe* Waldmüller was
to move to occupy positions to block any advance south along the axis of
the Caen–Falaise road and Krause was ordered to return with his *Kampfgruppe* and be prepared to launch a counter-attack with Waldmüller.

As the bombing reached its crescendo, the Allied columns started to
move forward from their forming-up places following a route lit with
lamps on 5ft piquets; right green and red left. They crossed their start line,
the Grentheville–Hubert-Folie–St André road, at 2330 hours; a full ten
minutes before the bombers departed. They advanced, slowly to start with,
speeding up to 5 miles per hour. Leaving just minutes for the bombers to
get clear, the massed artillery opened its fire plan at 2343 hours. The
Canadian Official Historian recorded:

> Its first task was to lay in front of the armoured advance a barrage
> covering an area 4,050 yards wide and 6,000 deep astride the high-
> way, moving at the rate of 100 yards per minute in lifts of 200 yards.
> This abnormally rapid rate of advance was occasioned by the entire
> assaulting force moving in tracked vehicles. A total of 360 guns would

Standartenführer **Kurt Meyer, before promotion but wearing his Knight's Cross and Oak Leaves.**

fire the barrage: for the whole artillery programme the number available was 720.

The rate of advance of the barrage, however, proved to be difficult for the tightly-packed columns to keep up with in the darkness and more importantly the dust thrown up by the bombing, barrage and tracks.

Even though the 89th Division's report states that 'the psychological effect of the extraordinary bombardment on personnel was comparatively quickly overcome', it describes the paralysing effect of the 'detonations, the near misses, air pressure blasts as well as grit and dust, as well as direct hits affecting sight and movement, which caused military disruption as troops were unable to respond in a truly fit condition.'

The 51st Highland Division's part in the initial stage of the operation was to be carried out by 154 Bde and 33 Armd Bde formed into two columns. That on the left consisted of a single armoured regiment and a battalion of infantry, while the right was a double column of infantry and tanks. The armoured regiment's commanding officers were responsible for the navigation of their column and for getting the infantry on to or within assault distance of their objectives. The two routes they were to take ran 'roughly parallel with the main road CAEN–FALAISE and the columns were to by-pass the village of TILLY LA CAMPAGNE on either flank.'

In the case of the Highland Division the columns of about 200 vehicles each were deployed 4 vehicles abreast and nose to tail, just 2 yards apart. The column was almost 300 yards long. The brigades deployed with

144 RAC [Royal Armoured Corps] and 7 A&SH [Argyll & Sutherland Highlanders] leading on the right axis were directed on CRAMESNIL. See map on p. 82 Behind them were 148 RAC and 7 BW [Black Watch], which were to capture GARCELLES SECQUEVILLE. ST AIGNAN DE CRAMESNIL was the objective of 1 N YEO [Northamptonshire Yeomanry] and 1 BW on the left.[2]

Tanks of 33 Armoured Brigade moving forward on 7 August 1944.

The Right Column

The column on the right route was commanded by Lieutenant Colonel Jolly of 144 Regiment RAC:

> On the night 7/8 August, my regiment's task was to escort 7 A&SH, to cross the road which was our start line at 2330 hours, by-pass TILLY to the West, deal with any opposition on the centre line, and put the infantry down 3 miles from here outside the village of CRAMESNIL, which was their objective. The infantry was then to dismount and capture the village by night attack. At first light the tanks were to occupy battle positions previously selected from air photographs as the enemy was expected to react with an armoured counter-attack, which he did.

Colonel Jolly would command and decide when and where the infantry would debus, all depending on ground and enemy encountered. To make this work Lieutenant Colonel Meiklejohn in 7 A&SHs' command vehicle had an extra No. 19 Set on 144's regimental radio net in order to monitor and keep up with the developments at the head of the column. In addition, the regiment provided its second-in-command to the infantry battalion headquarters and at company level squadron liaison officers mounted in their tanks to help coordinate the activities of infantry and armour.

This unusual (at the time) communication and liaison was necessary due to the unique level of integration of infantry and armour in pursuit of a specific tactical solution. Neither 144 nor the Argylls, nor indeed any other armoured regiment or infantry battalion taking part in TOTALIZE had trained or taken part in such an endeavour before.

The two navigators Captains Osborne and Pickering, the leading element of 144 RAC, mounted in light tanks of the Recce Troop set off with the assistance of the overhead Bofors tracer and 'They each had a P 8 compass and were also trying to use a wireless beam method whereby they heard a series of dots if they went too far to the Right and dashes if they went too far to the Left.' Colonel Jolly recounted:

> The Regimental Navigator, leading the column, had so far not heard a sound from his beam wireless, either dots or dashes, but his compass had been working fairly well. But when the barrage started, the needle immediately swung wildly to all points of the compass and became useless. He could see nothing in the dense dust cloud and his light tank almost immediately fell into a bomb crater about ten feet deep.

This early problem about 1 mile from the start line was compounded when Captain Pickering, attempting not to wander off his bearing, ran into another crater and suffered the same fate. Without their navigators the column had to rely mostly on sense of direction as the green marker shells being fired on the objectives by the Canadian 25-pounders were not yet

One of the numerous tanks that ditched in shell or bomb craters on the night of 8 August.

visible through the dust and odd belt of trees. Every five minutes, however, the bursts of Bofors fire directly down the axis of the column's advance more or less kept them on track, but there was a significant obstacle ahead: a railway line. Colonel Jolly explained:

> From the air photographs it looked as though the cutting through which the railway runs was likely to be an obstacle except for a stretch of about 500 yards South of TILLY ... As TILLY itself was strongly held I wanted to give it as wide a berth as possible and this therefore reduced the area for crossing the railway to the immediate neighbour-hood of a certain railway hut.

Even though the head of the column was more or less on course, Colonel Jolly described the 'utter disintegration of the column which occurred' behind him:

> The confusion was indescribable. Everyone had been told to keep closed up and follow the tank in front but it was soon obvious that it

The point where the battle group crossed the railway line (now a new road).

was the blind leading the blind. Great shapes of tanks loomed up out of the fog and asked you who you were: Flails seemed to be everywhere, and their great jibs barging about in the dust seemed to add to the confusion.

It was clearly not just the British who were confused: a tank became separated and drove unmolested through a village 'that shouldn't have been there', only to find that it was Tilly, the most heavily-contested and defended spot on the Normandy Front! A Sherman flail of B Squadron 22 Dragoons was not so lucky and was knocked out as it approached Tilly trying to get its bearings. Another tank of the Northamptonshire Yeomanry, from the left column, had lost the shaded convoy light of the Sherman in front of him and 'after driving around spotted another dim glow to which I headed'. Only at daylight did he realize that he had joined 144 RAC's column.

A Sherman 'flail' or Crab.

In this confusion officers dismounted from their tanks and were leading others on foot with the benefit of less heavily-shaded torches. In this manner Major Reid commanding A Squadron now leading the regiment found the railway line, located the hut, the nearby level crossing and fired a Verey light. Colonel Jolly continued:

... when I arrived at this point he was just beginning to lead the way across, followed by a Firefly of his leading troop. Suddenly there were two flashes in quick succession accompanied by showers of molten sparks as the enemy Bazookas [*Panzerfäusts*], fired from behind the hut, hit the tanks. The leading one did not brew up and everyone bailed out without serious injuries including the Squadron Leader and the regimental navigator who had climbed on board the Squadron Leader's tank when his own went into the bomb crater ...

The second tank brewed immediately. The wireless operator was wounded but the other three members of the crew were killed. The tank commander could be seen trying to free himself, but then collapsed and was engulfed in flames. A good deal of rather indiscriminate shooting followed, of more or less equal danger to both sides, and a dismounted tank party threw a number of hand grenades into the hut area.

Three Germans were killed and the remainder withdrew as the column crossed and attempted to reform, but this was easier said than done. Colonel Jolly ordered B Squadron 'to make for the burning tank and take over the lead' while A Squadron regrouped, but B was equally disorganized and was 'trying to disentangle some of the tanks from a Canadian column which had come over our side of the road'. It was a slow business gathering the column at the rail crossing. Colonel Jolly explains the exasperating situation:

I have never realised before how dependent one is, when controlling tanks by wireless, on sub-units and individual tanks knowing where they are in relation to each other. In this situation different squadrons and troops were all mixed up. An order might be given to Baker 3: 'Move straight to your front and halt when you get to the other side of the railway.' But Baker 3 was probably over on the FALAISE road and the order did not make sense to him. Able 3, who was the chap who was really being spoken to, only heard a call for Baker 3, so did not take any notice – so nothing happened, or only very slowly.

Meanwhile, the second-in-command of 144 RAC, Major Lovibond, had left the infantry to find out what was happening ahead of them and in doing so had collected half a dozen tanks. He located the railway 200 yards left of the crossing and found it to be not as much of an obstacle as expected. Amid the dust, despite their proximity he was unmolested by the

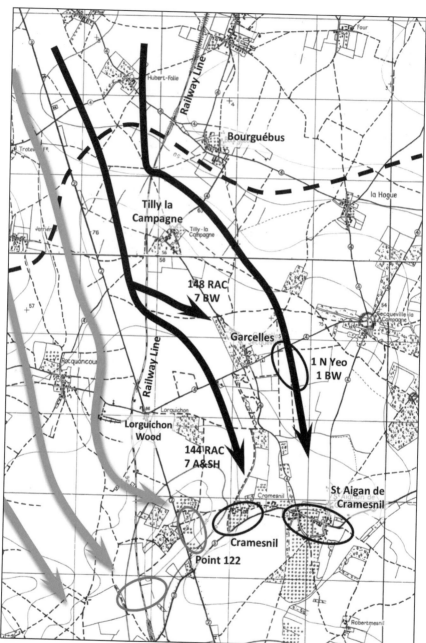

The planned routes of 153 Brigade's columns.

defenders of Tilly. Consequently, he and his small group crossed and were ahead of the main body. Colonel Jolly recalled that Major Lovibond

> announced on the wireless that he was just entering the last field before the objective. In fact, he had gone one field too far and almost immediately one of the tanks with him came up on the air and reported 'Able 16 has just been blown to bits'. His tank had been hit by a Bazooka at close range and brewed up immediately.

Major Lovibond and the regimental signal officer, who was sharing the tank, were both killed and two other crewmen wounded, with only the driver escaping unhurt. It would appear that they had indeed gone one field beyond the debussing point and, consequently, closed to within range of the enemy infantry and their *Panzerfäusts*. The remaining tanks pulled back.

While the action just short of Cramesnil was going on the head of the column had crossed the railway and was now heading deep into enemy territory, but further back 7 A&SH were only very slowly trundling forward past Tilly. Lieutenant Colonel Meiklejohn recalled:

> It was here that the first enemy was encountered and B Coy came under Spandau fire and several hand grenades were thrown at the company HQ troop carrier; one which landed inside was promptly picked up and thrown back by one of the signallers. The post was soon dealt with, two Germans being killed and three wounded, but in leading the men to it, the company Second-in-Command was shot through the stomach and had to be left behind in charge of a stretcher bearer, an elderly man called Cameron. When the column had moved on and left them, three Germans appeared out of the darkness and made for them. But Cameron ran at them with his Sten, killing one, wounding another and putting the third to flight.

Meanwhile, up ahead, having crossed the railway the majority of 144 RAC was fairly well-formed and all was quiet around Lorguichon Wood at this juncture, which they passed to the east; nonetheless Colonel Jolly commented that 'we passed it with some trepidation'. A little further on

> We realised that we were nearing our objective when we were asked by 1 N YEO-1 BW to desist from 'brassing up' any more hedges as they were getting most of the benefit of it. Their Centre Line took them the other side of that line of woods [between Garcelles and Cramesnil], and they were now fairly close to us on our left. I had been counting the hedges from my gridded air photographs and reckoned that we were now in the field where the infantry were due to debus.

Colonel Jolly duly issued the code-word LILY at around 0400 hours. This told Lieutenant Colonel Meiklejohn that they had reached the dismounting area.

As the infantry moved on towards the village it was soon all too apparent that the enemy was still present behind them in Garcelles and Lorguichon Wood. As 144 RAC's tanks were leaguering up in the darkness prior to deploying forward at first tank light, which was still an hour hence,

> there was another of those now all-too-familiar showers of sparks from one of the tanks in the leaguer. The shot had come from behind us and we concluded that it was from an anti-tank gun by-passed in the LORGUICHON Wood area. The tank 'brewed up' at once and all except one member of the crew were killed. We were in a very vulnerable position and it was an unpleasant situation waiting in the dark for the next tank to go up. However, the rest of the night was uneventful and we never solved the problem of who fired that last shot as no anti-tank gun was found the next day.

Despite the earlier confusion Colonel Jolly and the rest of his regiment had delivered the Argylls to their debussing point 3 miles into enemy territory with minimal casualties. Some of the junior officers, no doubt thinking only of the difficulties of the last few hours, were later 'surprised to be told that this was a success' but a significant success it was. Guy Simonds' vision and risk had worked.

The Argylls' Attack on Cramesnil

With the dismounting area reached, primary command was transferred to Lieutenant Colonel Meiklejohn, whose immediate task was to capture the village of Cramesnil. The Argylls were also to prevent interference from Lorguichon Wood, which the column had bypassed and was to be screened by 4 Platoon until 5 Camerons (152 Brigade) cleared it at a later hour, having advanced on foot.

Colonel Meiklejohn recalled how he ordered all four rifle companies to debus short of Cramesnil:

> It was very difficult to see just where we were. In addition to the dust of the barrage and the tanks, there was a very heavy ground mist which was aggravated by the smoke from burning haystacks. I reckoned we were pretty close to the village for I had seen the loom of LORGUICHON Wood to the Right and I thought I had recognised from the air photographs the line of tall elm trees at the beginning of the debussing field. The column seemed to be pointing in the right direction. Odd Germans were appearing out of the corn and giving themselves up ...
>
> OC B Coy asked me for a direction but all I could tell him was to go on the axis of the tanks. This he did and he had only passed the head of the column by a few yards when he hit the debussing point – a tribute to the accuracy of the tank's navigator.

A pre-operation photograph of a well-laden Kangaroo.

Major McKinnon recalled that from the railway

> to the debussing pt. things were pretty confused with a few tanks burning here and there and Spandau fire on all sides. The debussing pt. was reached at about 0400 hrs and 'B' Coy collected itself by degrees and moved off to its objective which was the rear of the village of Cramesnil.
>
> 'A' Coy whose objective was rt. and forward of 'B' Coy arrived at the debussing pt. In driblets as did 'D' Coy who were to go left and forward of 'B' Coy. However, both Companies soon collected themselves.

As B Company was well-concentrated they were ordered to attack at once, so as not to lose the morale effect of the arrival of the tanks that had arrived immediately in front of the enemy. At the same time Colonel Meiklejohn's attached battery commander called for fifteen minutes of fire on a pre-arranged artillery target at the eastern end of the village. This was in order to prevent interference with B Company's attack and to soften up A and D companies' objectives. See map on p. 86

The 1st Battalion 1055 Grenadier Regiment held the villages of Saint-Aignan-de-Cramesnil and Cramesnil, plus the woods and orchard to their south. Conventionally, they would have been expected to deliver counter-attacks to restore the positions of the forward battalions. The German opposition that the Argylls faced in Cramesnil was probably an infantry company:

> The Company advanced two platoons up and one back and had to pass through the Bosche DF, which hadn't so far slackened off. They

85

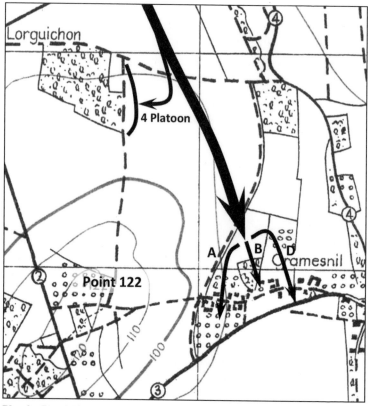

Plan for 7a A&SHs' attack on Cramesnil.

were ordered not to use their rifles and Brens as the tanks had been told to fire at any rifle and LMG [Light Machine Gun] fire. In spite of these various handicaps however, the company pushed on and the thick visibility enabled it to surprise the Germans out of their holes ... the leading troops came upon twelve Germans including a CSM [Company Sergeant Major], in the open. They killed five and took the rest prisoner. In a short time, the Company had got on and mopped up all its objective.

The commanding officer and the battalion tactical headquarters (Tac HQ) had also dismounted and had followed B Company as far as the outskirts of the village, from where Colonel Meiklejohn could best control the developing battle.

A and D companies were, however, both so scattered and mixed up that it took them the whole of the fifteen-minute bombardment to gather their men. The headquarters of A Company, for instance, had arrived at the debussing point accompanied by only one section, but it was able to launch its attack at nearly full strength only a few minutes after the last shells fell on Cramesnil. A Company advanced with

> two platoons up, 7 on the Right and 9 on the Left. 7 Platoon went down the line of the hedge ... and immediately ran into strong opposition from an enemy position of about platoon strength dug in in front of the line of houses. The slits were in the field but bolt holes had been dug through to the houses so that it was easy for the Germans to escape at the last minute. They used their PIAT and mortar against the walls of the house and the blast was very effective. They then assaulted through the orchard and suffered a number of casualties from small grenades slung between trees. In the close fighting they killed a few Germans and took 15 prisoners but their platoon commander, who had led them very gallantly, was mortally wounded and died later in the RAP.

No. 7 Platoon, having broken into their part of the village, paved the way for the left platoon which manoeuvred to the end of a row of buildings and methodically cleared their way through them. With the leading two platoons giving covering fire from their flanks, the third platoon was able to advance through the centre and clear the orchard as far as the hedgerow and road.

Both A and D company were assisted by B Troop 33 Anti-Tank Battery, equipped with M10 Tank Destroyers, who had come up while the infantry were reorganizing to help the hold against the inevitable counter-attack. Contrary to their usual insistence (quite correctly) that they were not tanks, the troop commander was, according to the Jocks' commanding officer, willing to help at close quarters: 'I had thought he would want an infantry escort to get his guns up to their positions, but so far from wanting an

The view north out of Cramesnil towards the Argylls' debussing area.

A knocked-out M10 Achilles Tank Destroyer.

escort, his idea was to lead my companies on to their objectives with his vehicles.'

With assistance from the M10s and the enemy reeling from the bombardment, D Company on the left had 'a very easy passage and captured its whole objective with negligible opposition'. In the hedgerows bounding the orchard at this extremity of the village they also captured about six *Nebelwerfers*, which were all loaded and ready to fire.

Once 5 Camerons arrived at Lorguichon Wood at 0445 hours and took it over from 4 Platoon. On their way to join the rest of the battalion in the village 4 Platoon beat the hedges and ditches around the field where Support Company were setting up their mortar line and mustering their vehicles. In doing so they flushed 'quite a few Bosches out of them' who were part of the forty unwounded prisoners gathered under the control of the regimental sergeant major and the battalion's provo staff, prior to being marched back to brigade headquarters for questioning. Colonel Meiklejohn, however, took the opportunity to speak to them:

> They were all from 89 Div and seemed quite glad to be captured. They said they had only moved up the night before and had not had time to settle in. Their officers had left them about a quarter of an hour before the attack went in, telling them to stay put. They were very bitter about this.

By 0500 hours, the village was firmly in the hands of the Argylls and as dawn rose the tanks deployed forward into cover on the southern side of the village and its orchards. At first light all that remained was to task patrols to clear west towards the inter-divisional boundary and link up with the Canadians at Point 122. Major McKinnon concluded that 'the situation looked pretty heartening'.

Casualties at this stage had been low, especially when compared to normal dismounted attacks, being one officer and two other ranks killed and one officer and eighteen other ranks wounded. Eight tanks had been knocked out.

Right Column: Garcelles

Meanwhile, 148 RAC with 7 Black Watch (7 BW) had been following behind 144 RAC and 7 A&SH on the right route until they had crossed the railway, where they would turn left, dismount the infantry and clear the woods and the adjacent village of Garcelles. The village was held as a part of the 2nd Battalion 1055 Grenadier Regiment's defensive positions, probably in company strength.

While ahead of them 144 RAC and the Argylls were clearing Cramesnil, at 0400 hours the navigators of 148 RAC had located the road that would be their axis of attack and could see the outline of the northern tip of the wood that extended 400 yards south to Garcelles. 7 BW debussed in the open, 500 yards from the wood and at 0430 hours began their attack. Major Russell felt that the battalion was back to its old self as it cleared through the woods taking on machine-gun positions one after the other in a thoroughly businesslike manner.

Within an hour Garcelles was in the hands of 7 BW and was being cleared in detail by its companies. Casualties had been remarkably light,

Cap badges of (*left*) Argyll and Sutherland Highlanders and (*right*) Royal Armoured Corps.

but the Jocks' trenches were still shallow when the enemy artillery started to seriously play on the village and woods at 0700 hours and casualties mounted.

The effect of armour driving right on past them into the rear of their divisional area had clearly and understandably undermined German morale in Garcelles. The commanding officer recalled being told about '... an intercepted message, which I believe, proved the consternation that was felt by the enemy commanders at armoured columns motoring through their lines in the dark.'

The Left Column

In a very similar operation Lieutenant Colonel Forster's 1st Northampton-shire Yeomanry (1 N Yeo) and 1 Black Watch, commanded by Lieutenant Colonel Hopwood, were to advance, bypassing Tilly to the east. During planning getting across various sunken roads around Bourguébus and the railway line emerged as the immediate problems for the Left Column. Captain Tom Boardman, second-in-command of A Squadron recalled:

> In front of our start line there were two nasty ditches where roads went through cuttings and we weren't sure if tanks could get across them. I was sent out on a reconnaissance and there I was with a sapper and an infantry officer crawling on our bellies, which as a tank officer I hadn't done since the officer training corps and we could hear German voices the other side of the cutting – not at all what I was used to! The banks had to be blown before we could cross and so it was arranged. In the event this was done and they were marked with coloured lights.

Captain Boardman, having seen the location of German outposts on the railway line and the problem it represented, was nominated by Colonel Forster as navigating officer. He recounted that

> When we were all lined up, it was a lovely evening. All the navigation aids were supposedly marvellous but they were useless and even the

The official Northamptonshire Yeomanry Cap badge (*left*) was not available and the regiment used their collar dog instead; the horse on a blue patch (*right*).

tracer overhead was lost in the mass of other tracer. It was prayer and luck; I relied on the compass.

1 N Yeo actually had more success with the radio direction equipment than 144 RAC and in the early stages easily heard the dots, dashes and the null point (on course) in between, but once they were in the heavily-shelled area and having to avoid craters, they regularly lost the signal and eventually gave up veering to right and left in an attempt to pick it up. Captain Boardman's verdict was that it was a distraction when attempting to command a tank and use the compass at the same time.

As navigating officer, Captain Boardman bore a lot of responsibility:

By the time we reached the road crossing we were getting a bit disjointed and I called up Colonel Forster and asked if I could fire Verey lights. The disadvantage was that they lit me up and attracted a lot of enemy small arms fire. I eventually ran out of cartridges and dismounted to get some more from the other navigating tank 20 yards away and I nearly fell into a slit trench full of Germans. We just looked at each other and I went on my way. I was happy to ignore them as there was little I could do and they were happy to stay put in the bottom of their trench!

The problems the column faced in reaching Saint-Aignan-de-Cramesnil are summed up in this account:

Hundreds of vehicles added dust from their tracks to the clouds already raised by the barrage. Drivers were blinded and struggled with the contrasting glare of the searchlights which gave the dust clouds a strange glow. They could only just discern the nearest dim convoy lights in front of them. They crawled along in first gear at about 100 yards per minute towards their objectives 5,000 yards deep in enemy territory. Collisions happened, when vehicles lost the convoy lights and wandered from the column and in the confusion some of the lost vehicles were fired on by their comrades as they returned from an unexpected direction and some were knocked out by enemy's action.

Lieutenant Ian Hammerton, leading one of the troops of flail tanks attached to the Highland Division from the 79th Armoured Division, was towards the front of the column but found no mines, having narrowly missed the corner of two minefields!

We trundled forward, all eyes straining to see in the pitch blackness. As we reached the near edge of the German positions, our visibility was reduced to zero. The bombing and shelling had created so much smoke and dust that it was impossible to see even the pin-point red rear lights of the tank in front although our jib and rotor kept bumping into that tank. We proceeded by fits and starts, the radio filled with messages of bewilderment and complaints about the impossibility of

91

A 5.5in medium gun belonging to one of the AGRAs.

seeing anything. Our own gun flashes were blinding in the darkness. Above us, on the underside of the low clouds, shone Monty's Moonlight, which cast an eerie glow over everything. We were only able to keep some sort of direction by means of the Bofors tracer shells fired overhead every few minutes indicating the main axis of the advance. Then we heard that a tank had been bazookered and we saw a glow of fire in front, then another and another.

Lieutenant Hammerton's flail tank did not fall victim to either the *Panzerjäger* or the *Panzerfäust* but fell into a crater, broke a track attempting to extricate itself and became stranded. One flail disappeared and was only found knocked out well to the west by Hammerton during a post-war visit, while others became disorientated and were lost in the dust that enveloped the battlefield. With the flails getting lost it was fortunate that at this stage of the campaign the Germans had few mines available to them.[3]

Lieutenant Ian Hammerton of the 22nd Dragoons.

The Germans claim to have inflicted armour casualties to the left column during its move past Tilly. One tank was hit by a *Panzerfäust* and there

92

were claims of up to eight tanks by the *Jagdpanzer* IVs of No. 2 Company of the *Hitlerjugend*'s *Panzerjäger* Battalion 12, who were operating on the column's left flank, having been dispatched there to replace the panzers redeployed for Operation LÜTTICH. Only four Shermans belonging to A Squadron 1 N Yeo were knocked out, but three were also knocked out during the armoured advance past Tilly. Lieutenant Colonel Hopwood recalled that shots 'came from an enemy self-propelled gun which followed the column a short distance and knocked out two Kangaroos which were carrying B Company men.'

At the front of the column Captain Boardman had his compass 'boxed' or calibrated to take into account the metal of the tank in which it was mounted. He explained:

> I mainly relied on compass not daring to traverse my turret which would screw it up and mileage travelled. Eventually I arrived at this belt of wood outside St Aignan on the north tip. I contacted the Colonel and said 'I think I have arrived'. He replied, 'Hang on' and came up in his Sherman accompanied by Colonel Hopwood in his Honey light tank.

The infantry commanding officer had little faith in the operation and believed that the chances of arriving in the right pace were slim, but peering through the wooded hedge at the silhouette of the village in front of him, illuminated by Monty's Moonlight, he expostulated 'Fuck me Tom, we've arrived in the right place!' Colonel Hopwood[4] later recorded that

> owing to the excellent navigation on the part of the Northamptonshire Yeomanry and by dint of good driving, well over 90% of the column arrived at the debussing area some 800 yards short of St Aignan at 0315 hours, some four and a half hours after passing the start line.

From the nominated debussing point to Saint-Aignan-de-Cramesnil there was flat uncut corn offering little cover for the Jocks and a good field of fire for the Germans and the village was typical of those found across Normandy. It was stoutly-built and surrounded by apple and thick hedges and banks, which in the case of St Aignan extended approximately 1,000 yards to the south of the village. Colonel Hopwood had planned to clear a strip of wood to the right of the debussing area that ran up to the village:

> On arrival at the debussing area, however, a change of plan was made owing to the 'going' being better than anticipated. It was decided to motor right up to the objective under cover of a pre-arranged artillery concentration (Code word BRIMSTONE) from 0325–0345 hours, and fire from the two leading squadrons of tanks.

The leading companies were to clear through the village, while D Company in reserve remained with battalion headquarters on the northern side

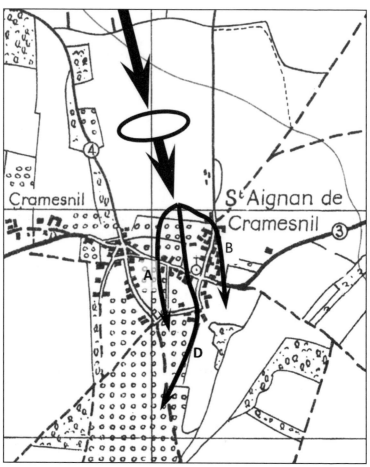

1 Black Watch's plan for the assault on St Aignan. D Company was initially in reserve and C Company had been temporarily disbanded because of casualties earlier on in the campaign.

'clearing up any pockets of resistance which might be left'. With the gunners firing a heavy BRIMSTONE artillery concentration, one fired by all guns available in the division, the assault began. Even though the hedge and its bank was less of an obstacle than had been expected from examination of air photographs, getting the tanks and Kangaroos across it was slow but Colonel Hopwood recalled

> motoring over the last 800 yards to the objective was entirely successful owing to the heavy artillery concentration and secondly to the magnificent fire support given by [A and B squadrons of] the

Northamptonshire Yeomanry from their 75s and Brownings, which plastered every place that could possibly have held an enemy post. On debussing, slight confusion was caused by a thick ground mist which was accentuated by the Cordite smoke from the artillery concentration, and by the fumes from the exhausts of the tanks and Kangaroos. In spite of this however, 'A' and 'B' Companies maintained direction and advanced to their respective objectives.

There was opposition to be 'mopped up'. For example, as B Company reached the edge of the village,

> A Spandau opened fire from a house wounding one man and holding up the final advance of the company. An anti-tank gunner who was moving with the company to recce a position for his guns immediately dashed into the house with a Sten gun, killing the two Boche who were manning the Spandau. He carried out this action without assistance, thereby allowing the remainder of the company to continue its advance unhindered.

B Company took seventy-nine prisoners from the 1st Battalion 1055 Grenadier Regiment. The remainder of the company holding the village that had not been killed or wounded withdrew hastily south.

By 0530 hours, the forward companies had reached their objectives and D Company advanced through them to complete the clearance of the orchards to the south of St Aignan. By 0600 hours battalion headquarters had also moved across the village to a point from where it could better control the coming defensive battle against the expected German counterattack. By the time it was light, 1 BW was digging in and the tanks and the supporting arms were moved up to join their designated companies.

The field across which the Black Watch assaulted St Aignan.

During this period while A Company's officers and NCOs were siting trenches there were still Germans around, especially beyond the village. Colonel Hopwood explains:

> As this company was getting into position on the far side of St Aignan, a Boche patrol consisting of seven men advanced through the orchards towards the company who were preparing to dig in. This patrol which possibly did not realise the situation, as it was far too small to take on the company, was immediately spotted by a Bren gunner who opened fire, killing five and wounding one, the remaining man being taken prisoner.

In the same manner as 144 RAC at Cramesnil, the Shermans of 1 N Yeo deployed forward of the village at dawn to take up their positions on the extremity of the orchard from where they could cover the open fields to the south.

With the objectives taken, in accordance with orders, all of the Kangaroos, carriers and loaned vehicles, less those belonging to the Derbyshire Yeomanry (the 51st Highland Division's Recce Regiment) and the divisional artillery were to be mustered under an officer of the Yeomanry and sent back to 1 Gordons for their part in the attack on Secqueville-la-Campagne and its woods.

NOTES

1. Meyer, Kurt, *Grenadiers* (J.J. Fedorowicz, 1957).
2. G (Trg) HQ BAOR Battlefield Tour 'Operation TOTALIZE'. June 1947.
3. This is in contrast to the Bocage and Operation BLUECOAT where mines abounded but the front had been stable here from the early days of the campaign.
4. This language was apparently 'quite out of character for Colonel Hopwood'.

Chapter Five

The 2nd Canadian Division – Armoured Advance

On the afternoon of 7 August 1944, Canadian elements of Lieutenant General Simonds' Corps that were to launch the initial assaults were crossing south over the River Orne, returning from their training grounds and heading to their assembly areas on the dusty plains south of the Faubourg de Vaucelles. They had been told that this was to be the long-awaited break-out from the tight confines of 21st Army Group's beachhead south of Caen.

Major General Foulkes' 2nd Canadian Division had been out of the line since Operation SPRING and was now to play a leading role in the break-in battle during Operation TOTALIZE and their task was even more complex than that of the 51st Highland Division. They were to move in four columns rather than two and seize objectives on the ridge extending westward from the key terrain of Point 122 to the River Orne.

Brigadier Wyman, Commander 2 Canadian Armoured Brigade (2 Cdn Armd Bde), had two of his own regiments, the Fort Garry Horse and the Sherbrooke Fusiliers, Brigadier Ganong's 4th Canadian Infantry Brigade (4 Cdn Bde), plus the 8th Canadian Reconnaissance Regiment (8 Cdn Recce Regt) under command. In addition, specialist assault vehicles from the 79th Armoured Division were grouped with the armoured force and, on arrival at the objective, they would be joined by the division's medium machine guns, M10 Tank Destroyers and engineers.

In their account of the operation the Essex Scottish emphasized that 'The four columns were simply to make a swift dash between the enemy's

Major General Charles Foulkes.

A Canadian divisional sign. The background for the yellow maple leaf was blue for the 2nd Canadian Division and green for the 4th Armoured Division.

foremost positions to a dispersal area in his rear, where the infantry would dismount, seize their objectives, and prepare to hold them against counter-attack.'[1]

Three of the columns, each carrying a battalion of infantry, were to advance in a compact formation, side by side, from the area of Beauvoir Farm, bypassing Rocquancourt to the west, while the fourth column (8 Cdn Recce Regt), would cross a start line at Troteval Farm and bypass Rocquancourt to the east. After that the Recce Regiment was to cross the railway line and clear the woods up to the rounded and dominating bulk of Point 122 just east of the Caen-Falaise Road. The other three columns were to head for a central dispersal area and assault on foot: namely Caillouet (Essex Scottish), the Quarry (Royal Hamilton Light Infantry (RHLI or 'Rileys')) and the high ground between the railway and the road (Royal Regiment of Canada (R Regt C or 'The Royals')).

Some have been critical of using the light armour of 8 Armd Recce Regt as an additional column rather than in its proper role out in front, albeit bolstered by a couple of troops of tanks. Based on previous experience and in the conditions likely to be encountered, it is hard to imagine what they could have achieved in the recce role during the initial stages of the attack. Few can, of course, have envisaged the desperate necessity of firing Verey flares to indicate the way whilst in the midst of the enemy.

The Canadian methodology was similar to that of the Highlanders, including navigators:

> At the head of each [column] was a heavily armoured advanced guard or 'gapping force', consisting of two troops of Sherman tanks, two troops of 'Flails', and a troop from 69 Assault Sqn RE [AVRE –

A rear view of a Kangaroo complete with its former artillery unit markings.

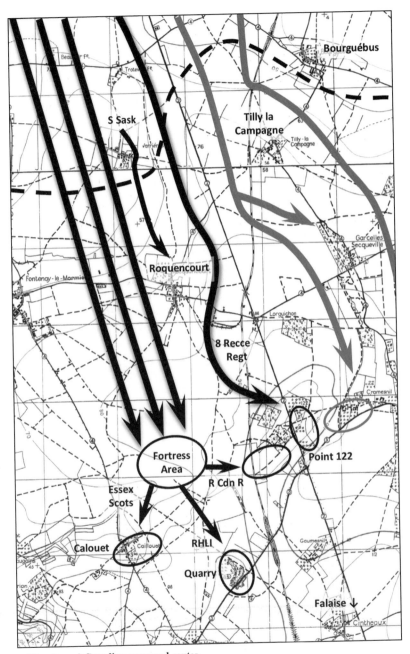

The planned Canadian armoured routes.

99

Armoured Vehicle Royal Engineer]. The Shermans were to lead with the 'Flails' following behind ready to clear any mines encountered by the sappers, working from their AVREs.

The difference was that the AVREs were to mark the routes with the tapes plus red and green lights that they usually used for marking minefield lanes. Following on behind was the main body, led by another squadron of Shermans, with the infantry battalion riding in its Kangaroos or aboard assorted carriers. Another difference was that 'Bringing up the rear in each case were more tanks known as the "fortress force", charged with making

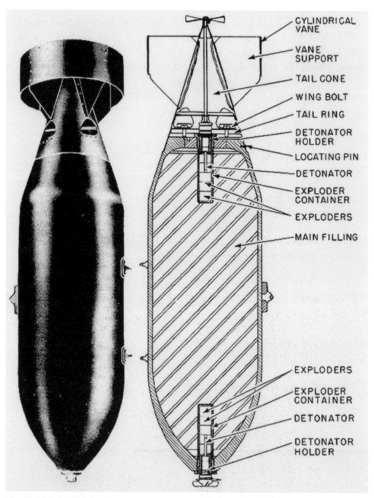

CYLINDRICAL VANE
VANE SUPPORT
TAIL CONE
WING BOLT
TAIL RING
DETONATOR HOLDER
LOCATING PIN
DETONATOR
EXPLODER CONTAINER
EXPLODERS
MAIN FILLING

EXPLODERS
EXPLODER CONTAINER
DETONATOR
DETONATOR HOLDER

The British 1,000lb MC (Medium Capacity) Bomb Mk 1.

the dispersal area secure and providing a firm base from which the infantry could assault on foot.'

Of the mass of armour assembling on the plain below the Verrières Ridge, the adjutant of the Calgary Highlanders (5 Cdn Bde) remarked in the battalion war diary that 'The concentration of troops and armour within the small area of Ifs is a sight to behold.' Another officer explained that 'I left my tank and walked back to the end of the regimental column, we were closed so tight that my feet never touched the ground, I just stepped from tank to tank.'

A glance at the map will show that the armoured advance would bypass the villages of May-sur-Orne and Fontenay-le-Marmion on the low ground to the west and, as already mentioned, Rocquancourt to the east, all of which had been a considerable source of trouble during Operation SPRING. As in the 51st Highlanders' area, the flanking villages on the low ground would be bombed at the opening of the offensive and then attacked by 6 Cdn Bde, while the Germans were still reeling from the effects of the RAF's 500lb and 1,000lb bombs. This, however, meant that due to the proximity of the bombing, St Martin and Verrières would have to be evacuated and the attack would start from behind the St André–Hubert-Folie road.

Advancing on foot at the same time as the armoured columns, 6 Cdn Bde, now armed with plans of the tunnels and mine workings in the area that had helped to thwart 5 Brigade during SPRING, would capture the villages and the surrounding areas with the support of the Sherman tanks of the 1st Hussars.

Initially 5 Cdn Bde was to be held in reserve south of Ifs but Brigadier Megill was 'to be prepared to restore the momentum of the attack, should it be lost'. His main task was, however, to be during Phase Two, when, on

Brigadier Megill.

The entrance to one of the mine workings being guarded by Canadian infantrymen.

orders from General Foulkes, his brigade was to advance on the western flank from the high ground secured in Phase One and capture Bretteville-sur-Laize with the support of the tanks of the 1st Hussars.

The war diary of 2 Cdn Armd Bde records that

For the assembled troops waiting in the darkness on the night of 7/8 Aug the heavy rumble of aircraft passing overhead was the immediate overture to battle. Promptly at 2300 hours the bombers began to unload over the enemy positions, marked by our artillery shells Operation 'TOTALIZE' had begun.

Half an hour later the solidly-packed, slow-moving armoured columns and the marching infantry crossed their start lines on the Hubert-Folie–St André road. The initial Canadian experience in the columns is remarkably similar to that of the Highlanders, the official account of their operations reading as follows:

> At first the enemy appeared to be overwhelmed with confusion, but he recovered sufficiently to react with his artillery and mortars. It is not surprising that collisions occurred, that vehicles strayed from the route, even that some of the stragglers came to be fired on by their friends.
>
> The Germans were clever enough to add to the confusion by firing smoke-shells to thicken the ground mist that was coming up on the night air.

Matters were not helped by the flail tanks of the 1st Lothian & Border Horse. A Canadian observation is that the 'confusion was made worse by the flails who had not been present at the rehearsal and who lost station very early in the proceedings.' In an operation as novel and complex as that being executed by General Foulkes' division, their absence from the rehearsals due to Second Army operations in heavily-mined areas was highly regrettable.

The noise of the battle had also to be contended with but, as Lieutenant Blackburn explains, it was loudest at the artillery's gun positions:

> The overpowering crash of guns on all sides in response to yells of fire from GPOs [Gun Position Officers] is beyond anything you've experienced before in Normandy. Not only are there 720 guns of all kinds

A Sherman 'flail' or Crab that has just crossed one of the Orne bridges in Caen.

supporting Totalize, but so concentrated are they that their thunderous roar makes voice communication impossible. Even shouting directly into another man's ear is ineffective, and the only sure way to communicate anything important, even down in the command post dugouts, is to write it out.

And so it is for the next hour as the stupendous bombardment straddling the Caen-Falaise highway ploughs a swath 4,000 yards wide and 6,000 yards deep. Every two minutes the guns lift 200 yards. And the mediums are superimposed 400 yards in depth.

In addition, of the 720 guns, 312 of them, including some heavies from the Army Groups Royal Artillery, fired a twenty-minute intense counter-battery bombardment on 'known enemy gun positions'.

In the confusion of darkness, noise, dust and smoke, parts of the columns that should have bypassed Rocquancourt to the west 'went astray'. According to 2 Cdn Armd Bde: 'Instead of all passing west of the village, the three right-hand columns took wrong routes. R. Regt C. [Royal Regiment of Canada] Went to the east, RHLI actually drove through the village, and although Essex Scot kept to the west as intended, they completely lost their bearings.'

The delay resulted in the protective effect of the bombardment being reduced, as the barrage continued to march on through the German positions in its tightly-choreographed lifts, allowing enemy infantry to recover their sensibilities before the arrival of the armour.

In contrast to the 51st Highland Division, the Canadians found that the radio direction equipment worked well to start with but, as the navigators

The 5.5in Medium Guns were the mainstay of the Army Group's Royal Artillery.

A tank silhouetted by Movement Light or Monty's Moonlight.

climbed over the Verrières Ridge heading south, the signal being propagated from the low ground behind them became weak and eventually unusable. To compensate, an increase in the strength of movement light was requested but even this could not penetrate the all-enveloping murk. An increase in the rate of overhead fire of the Bofors was called for, which the navigators reported was useful in locating the dispersal area. Red 20mm tracer was fired straight down the divisional axis, while green tracer was fired down the inter-divisional boundary, i.e. above the Caen–Falaise road.

8 Reconnaissance Regiment (14th Canadian Hussars) – La Guerre

8 Cdn Recce Regt, with attachments from the 79th Armoured Division and two troops of C Squadron Fort Garry Horse, made up the bulk of the left column. Being immediately to the west of the Caen-Falaise road, they had the easiest navigational task and the benefit of the comforting tapes laid by the AVREs, plus the associated green and red lane marker lights every 150 yards. All was going well when, according to Sergeant Wilson, commander of a carrier section:

> A tank on our right went up in a burst of flame and then another to our front. We were 'bogged down' it seemed. 'A' Squadron on our right was having a field day shooting into the German masses.
>
> Major Scott, our Squadron leader, had jumped out of his vehicle and was directing the troops to dig-in. While doing so, he was caught in a burst of machine gun fire and was killed.

Meanwhile, Brigadier Wyman realized that 8 Cdn Recce Regt was also having orientation problems but of a different nature from the other columns, when just after midnight a series of conflicting reports had climbed the chain of command. The Canadian report records that:

There was already considerable uncertainty at HQ 4 Cdn Inf Bde as to where this column actually was, and doubt increased when wireless contact was lost at 0148 hours. There was no more news of the column on the left until shortly after 0200 hours, when 8 Cdn Recce Regt reported being approximately level with the northern outskirts of Rocquancourt, and several hundred yards short of the position reported much earlier. While these confused messages were reaching brigade, the column had encountered the enemy and lost two tanks, suffered casualties and captured prisoners identified as belonging to a battalion of 89 Inf Div.

8 Cdn Recce Regt had been brought to a halt by opposition in the small group of buildings clustered around the La Guerre mine shaft between Rocquancourt and the road. It is also probable that it was their supporting tanks from the Fort Garry Horse that crossed the Caen–Falaise road and ran into 144 RAC, as mentioned in the previous chapter, during an attempt to bypass the village and mine workings further to the east. The resulting fratricide could have contributed to Lieutenant Colonel Always' decision to halt 8 Cdn Recce Regt rather than attempt to push on in growing light to Point 122. Sergeant Wilson recalled that

By morning, we had managed to get down roughly three feet into the hard chalk. When we looked about it was the weirdest sight we ever hope to see. The vehicles were in a slight depression roughly in a circle, as the caravans of the old west might form up while under attack by Indians.

(*Left*) **The 8th Reconnaissance Regiment's cap badge, as worn during the Second World War.** (*Right*) **Essex Scottish cap badge.**

106

Point 122

The original plan for the R Regt C is described in their war diary:

Our own Coy objectives were as follows:
'A' Coy – left forward – to occupy the orchard on the east side of the CAEN–FALAISE Highway immediately around POINT 122.
'B' Coy – right forward – to occupy a copse to the south-west of the crossroads.
'C' Coy – to move as left reserve Coy, and to take up a position immediately around the crossroads.
'D' Coy – right reserve Coy, to occupy another copse north-west of the crossroads.

Within a mile of their start line events were already gaining their own momentum. As they approached Rocquancourt the Royals' column ran into that of the RHLI, which created a confused traffic jam to the north of Rocquancourt, from which the Royals could only extricate themselves by going around the village to the east. Interestingly the column must have driven right past the enemy force that was blocking 8 Recce Regt! During this confusion the Royals' B Company and B Squadron became detached, with parts ending up joining the RHLI's column and others remaining around Rocquancourt.

Even though the Royals had gone off course, they eventually shook themselves free of trouble and continued the advance. To compound their

The Royal Regiment of Canada's objectives: the plan.

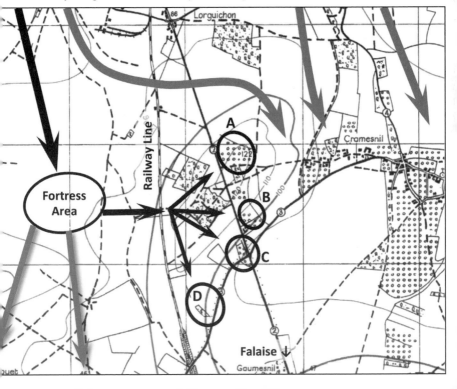

difficulties, the overhead Bofors tracer had long since stopped, as had the green flare shells that had been fired on the objectives, once the eighty available shells had been expended. Consequently, the Royals overshot the planned dispersal area, where the infantry should have dismounted and advanced between the railway line and the Caen-Falaise road towards the forward slope of the ridge. Instead they had continued on south with their infantry still aboard the Kangaroos. Lieutenant Colonel Anderson, his company commanders and their forward observation officers (FOO) dismounted to confer, minus of course B Company who were still missing. Their war diary records:

> At 0300 hrs, the remainder of our column, while somewhat scattered at times, had passed through the Bde dispersal area, and turned north-west. The original point at which we intended to cross the railroad tracks to move to our objective was not located by the leading tanks, and our column eventually crossed the tracks about a mile to the north.

Turning the column around and retracing their steps back towards Rocquancourt was a slow business but

> By 0430 hrs the Bn less 'B' Coy and some elements of 'C' Coy was concentrated in the low ground between the railway tracks and POINT 122. The absence of part of our forces, the change in the direction from which the attack was to be launched and, above all, the urgent necessity for prompt action in order to reach the objective before daylight necessitated considerable changes in our plan. It was of paramount importance that the dense concentration of vehicles be relieved before first light exposed them to enemy observation. 'D' Coy were complete, and 'A' Coy were complete insofar as personnel were concerned although they were now loaded on five Priests instead of the original eight as three had suffered mechanical breakdowns en route. The CO, therefore, ordered 'A' Coy to proceed with all possible speed to their original objective while 'D' Coy was to take the copse which had originally been the objective of 'B' Coy.

Once across the railway line, A Company took a south-easterly bearing to the top of the looming bulk of Point 122. With the danger of attacking in daylight and the already improving visibility as the dust cleared, the company commander elected to keep the infantry mounted and drive as far as possible before debussing. A Squadron of the Sherbrooke Fusiliers were the only tanks with the Royals and deployed to the flanks and rear to give covering fire. The Canadian report states that at 'About 0500 hours, when it was beginning to get light, the battalion put in its attack ... deficient some anti-tank guns, tanks and kangaroos, which had become casualties.' The war diary records

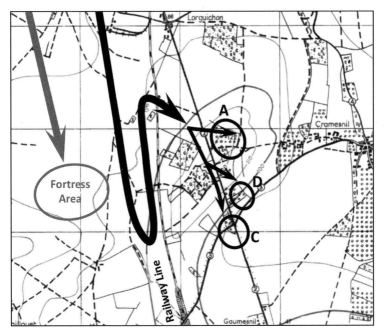

The Royals' revised plan.

Faint signs of daylight were already beginning to appear as 'A' Coy moved forward up the hill followed by 'D' Coy. They were fortunate in quickly recognizing their objective, and the Priests were driven right into the orchard without encountering any opposition. As the plns [platoons] moved towards their respective areas heavy small-arms fire came skimming over the top of the hill from the south. It is suspected, although never confirmed, that this fire came from our own tanks who were making a belated attempt to support our troops onto their objective. 'D' Coy were equally successful in reaching their objective, and the remainder of the Bn and supporting arms moved up at 0600 hrs.

The company of 1st Battalion 1055 Grenadier Regiment on the feature, according to prisoners 'had withdrawn at approx 0400 hrs in the morning'. Point 122, which had originally been an Operation GOODWOOD objective back on 18 July, was finally in Allied hands and by 0600 hours the Royals were digging in.

The Quarry

Meanwhile, it had taken the RHLI longer to get clear of and on past Rocquancourt, during which time they collected disorientated sub-units including the lost troops from the Royal and the Sherbrooke Fusiliers, including a gapping troop. Resuming the advance, the column crossed an abandoned airstrip under small-arms, mortar and anti-tank fire from the west, where the Essex Scots were in difficulty. Consequently, by the time they had re-gathered elements of the battalion in the dispersal or 'fortress area' and the infantry dismounted, it was getting light. Their objective, the Quarry, lay some 800 yards ahead on the ridge. The volume of fire coming from the ridge was such that 'they were unable to advance to their objective. The enemy had four tanks and a self-propelled gun firmly established in the nearby quarry. The force therefore dug in as far forward as possible and prepared to defend themselves against counter-attack.'[2]

These 'tanks' were almost certainly *Panzerjäger* IV from No. 2 Company of SS *Panzerjäger* Battalion 12. For the Germans it was readily apparent, despite communication difficulties and the abrupt change of Allied tactics to a night assault, that this was a major attack and that the 89th Division was in trouble. Consequently, having conferred with I SS Panzer Corps at 0400 hours (Allied time) *Obersturmbannführer* Hubert Meyer ordered *Sturmbannführer* Günter Woost to motor forward with his two remaining companies to support the 89th Division and to join No. 1 Company, which was already in action on the left flank of the 51st's assault. On their arrival at the front before first light, General Heinrichs (89th Division) deployed the self-propelled company (No. 2) to the ridge and the towed company (No. 3) astride the Caen-Falaise road.

The RHLI had been blocked by the 89th Division's timely reinforcement of *Panzerjäger* and driven to ground in a very open area. Some cover

One of the *Panzerjäger* IVs belonging to the *Hitlerjugend*.

The combat load of a Canadian infantryman.

was, however, to be had from the embanked hedgerow that marked the forward edge of the fortress area and some sunken tracks that criss-crossed the area.

The Essex Scottish

The Essex Scots, making up the right column, had as mentioned above encountered an anti-tank gun, north of the lateral road between Rocquancourt and Fontenay. This gun's crew stood and fought despite all the difficulties, which makes it entirely possible that this was one of the *Leibstandarte*'s guns that had been left behind to stiffen the 89th Division. The Essex Scots' difficulties, however, had already begun about half an hour after crossing the start line.

The leading company, A Company, became disorientated when they lost touch with the gapping force ahead of them. Mounted in an unarmed FOO version of a Sherman, Captain Grange from the 4th Canadian Field Artillery Regiment confesses all!

> [I was] . . . following our tanks guided by the white tapes the engineers were laying down up ahead but in the dust, the other tanks get away out of sight, and I am lost.
>
> Of course, I carry on but go the wrong way. And then to my horror I find all the [A Company] Kangaroos and carriers following me. We all end up in Rocquancourt. Fortunately, the village is in the process of being abandoned (or at least that is how it seems to me), with them going out the back way as we are coming in the front, probably believing they are surrounded from the great numbers of people passing by them. Anyway, where I am, there is really no fuss. In fact, I am surprised at how little opposition there is. Some shots are fired, but none from my tank I can tell you. And after it's all over, I find my tank is the only one there – all the others have gone to the right place. On top of everything, my tank is just a dummy – its gun couldn't fire anything! Then, when dawn comes, I discover huge quantities of infantry have followed me instead of the right people.

Captain Grange was thanked for his action by the Essex; little did they know. The majority of the battalion had been brought to a halt not knowing where they were and he was thanked for being the only tank that had remained with them, complete with dummy gun!

At 0100 hours A Company reported that the 'visibility is virtually nil and over the next hour there were frequent stops whilst stragglers were collected'. The advance, however, continued very slowly, 'with everyone trying to recognise landmarks'. At 0115 hours, A Company reported that it had found and joined up with the squadron of Sherbrooke Fusiliers again and 'that they were in front of the objective and about to attack it'. 'Almost immediately an 88mm opened up on the column at a range of 200 yards, setting fire to some half-tracks. This split the column into two and threw it into a state of great confusion.'[3]

One witness believed that the enemy had started firing into the clouds of dust and smoke at the sound of tracks and the roar of engines and then continued to do so by the light of burning armoured vehicles:

> Some of the leading vehicles went on, whilst others in the scramble to move out of the line of fire of the 88mm, reversed into each other. Difficulties were increased by the number of stragglers from other columns who had previously joined on and who now thought it was not such a healthy spot to be. No contact could be made with the Commanding Officer nor with A Coy.

What the Essex had run into was a substantial part of the 3rd Battalion 1056 Grenadier Regiment dug in on the reverse slope of the Verrières Ridge between Rocquancourt and Fontenay. The column's planned route across the ridge should have avoided them; nonetheless they brought the Essex to a halt with anti-tank fire. Consequently, as reported to Headquarters 4 Cdn Bde at 0357 hours, in the absence of the commanding officer, Major Burgess, the second-in-command, ordered the infantry to debus from their carriers as the dust was settling and visibility was improving. While they dug in and the column was being rounded up, Major Burgess

> collected the remaining company commanders and a troop leader from 1 LOTHIANS, the only tank commander who could be found. A short conference was held. No one knew in what direction CAILLOUET or the debussing area lay, but all agreed that they were beyond both.

Meanwhile, a platoon was dispatched to deal with the crew of an 88mm gun but it was driven back by machine-gun fire. The rest of the battalion was digging shell scrapes and the painfully slow process of collecting stragglers continued.

At 0430 hours the commanding officer, Lieutenant Colonel Jones, was back in radio contact and able to pass a message 'that all was now clear and the column was to continue the advance'. Before this could be put into effect the colonel's radio link failed again. 'Whilst the column was being re-sorted, the Second-in-Command walked to the nearest village, found it to be ROCQUANCOURT and that his Commanding Officer was there and had been wounded.' Apparently, as Colonel Jones approached the village in darkness he had run into a group of Germans and in the ensuing fire-fight he and several others had been shot and were eventually evacuated.

On returning to the battalion, Major Burgess was briefed that fourteen half-tracks had been knocked out or were missing, two M10 Tank Destroyers had been brewed up and the squadron of Sherbrooke Fusiliers' tanks were not with the battalion, having gone on when the column originally split.

An abandoned 88mm Pak 43/41 west of Rocquancourt; possibly the one that gave the Essex Scots so much trouble.

The Essex Scots, as the sky lightened to the west, were in the fields digging in a short distance south of the Rocquancourt-Fontenay road, still a good 2,000 yards short of their objective of Caillouet. It took until 0845 hours for elements of the battalion and its supporting arms, less the tanks, to be ready to resume the advance.

The Tanks

What of the tanks, most of whom had lost some or all of their following infantry? In the case of those with the Essex, most of the Sherbrookes had carried on and had arrived at the dispersal area where they had waited; tanks on their own being, of course, unsuitable for clearing the village of Caillouet. In another instance, Major Radley-Walters' A Squadron of the Sherbrooke Fusiliers was with the Royal Regiment of Canada. He recalled:

> My column, as we came through Rocquancourt was supposed to come out [on the west] of Rocquancourt. We all got pushed out to the east and once we got through, I realized that Rocquancourt was on my right. I had to get down into Gaumesnil.[4] I got next to the railroad track and had to find a place to cross over. Then I had the railroad track on my right and the road on my left and I couldn't get lost.

Major Radley-Walters led his tanks, minus a troop that had joined the RHLI, on south to the forward edge of the ridge.

114

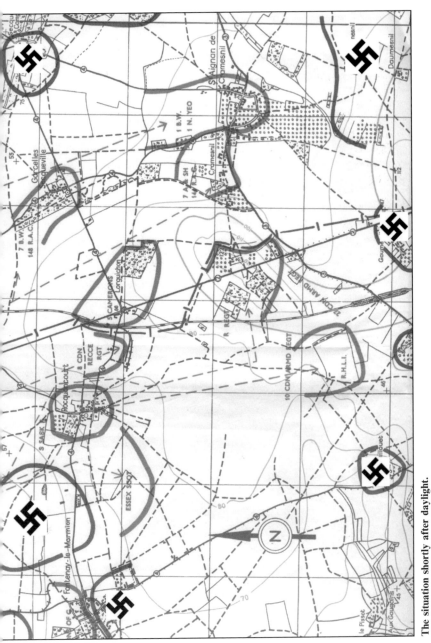

The situation shortly after daylight.

The essence of the plan had worked. Most of 4 Cdn Bde were established beyond the interlocking arcs of the enemy's anti-tank and machine guns that had stopped Operation SPRING in its tracks. The Canadians generally felt that due to the requirements of the campaign, there had been a rush to get into action. Consequently, the men were tired and that the armoured advance may have been significantly better if the whole force had had the opportunity to train together over a longer period.

The relative inexperience of the Canadian infantry of course contrasts with that of the veteran 51st Highland Division who, when opposition was encountered, nonetheless pressed on, ignoring those elements of their units that had become disorganized or irrevocably lost. As the Canadians had found out on the ridge around the Quarry that morning 'being firstest with the mostest'[5] was still important. For example, the Highlanders, with the company of *Hitlerjugend Panzerjäger* IVs operating on their open left flank, continued the advance through the murk to secure their objectives by between 0500 and 0600 hours rather than stopping to deal with them.

NOTES

1. As with the Highland Division, the general arrangement was that while mounted in the columns the armoured brigade/regimental HQs were in command, with command transferring to the infantry HQs once they had debussed.
2. The Divisional Chief of Staff, *Obersturmbannführer* Hubert Meyer (not to be confused with the divisional commander Kurt 'Panzer' Meyer), stated that there were unlikely to have been panzers that far forward so early in the battle. Interview with the author, April 2009.
3. While some sources state that the 89th had a company of 88mm Pak 43 guns in its *Panzerjäger* battalion it can seem that every anti-tank gun was 'an 88' and every tank a 'Tiger'. This far forward at this stage of the battle it was likely to be one of the 89th's own guns.
4. His Phase One objective was on the ridge between road and railway. Only later was A Squadron ordered forward to Gaumesnil.
5. A traditional military corruption of the Confederate Civil War cavalry commander Bedford Forrest's maxim: 'get there first with the most men'. He was famous for his speed of movement.

Chapter Six

The Bypassed Villages

As the British and Canadian armoured advance got under way, the dismounted infantry battalions of the 2nd Canadian and 51st Highland divisions began their assaults on the village strongpoints that the columns were to bypass in their drive into the depths of the German position. It was hoped that with the enemy 'unhinged' by the passage of the armour, the villages, such as May-sur-Orne and Tilly-la-Campagne, which had been thorns in the Canadian side for several weeks, would finally and easily fall to the Allies. The *Leibstandarte*'s infantry and many of the tanks had departed west to take part in the Mortain Counter-Attack and been replaced by the largely-untried 89th Division but even so, in well-prepared positions they would be tough nuts to crack.

In comparison with the Canadians, the part to be played by Brigadier Cassels' 152 Highland Brigade in the capture of the villages of Tilly and Lorguichon was more conventional and less glamorous but no less important. It was fully appreciated that the Germans would launch a full-blown counter-attack to restore the *Hauptkampflinie* ('front' or 'main battle line') and the villages if still held by the enemy would form important pivots around which the *Hitlerjugend* would manoeuvre.

At the same time as the armoured columns of 154 Brigade crossed their start lines, a single battalion from 152 Brigade was to advance from its position around Hubert-Folie and capture Tilly-la-Campagne. With the armoured columns to either flank moving at little more than walking pace, the 2nd Battalion Seaforth Highlanders (2 Seaforth) were to advance between them. Brigadier Cassels recalled that 'We thought that the rumble of armour from each side and behind would make the Tilly garrison look eagerly over its shoulder and "pack in" comparatively easily.'

Elsewhere, the 5th Cameron Highlanders (5 Cameron), also on foot, would follow 154 Brigade and attack the Lorguichon hamlet and wood, plus clear the railway cutting to the north of the houses. 152 Brigade was to hold a battalion (5th Battalion Seaforth Highlanders (5 Seaforth)) in reserve to help 154 Brigade, if necessary, in Phase One. In Phase Two 5 Seaforth were to capture and occupy Secqueville-la-Campagne and the woods around the village. Finally, 153 Brigade, the divisional reserve, was to hold the area of Bourguébus–Four–Grentheville as a firm base for the attack until relieved later in the battle. See map on p. 118

Of this plan, Brigadier Cassels commented:

It is clear that this was a very big commitment for one brigade, but in view of our original, but false, premise [that the Germans in Tilly would collapse], I was reasonably happy about it. The only point that

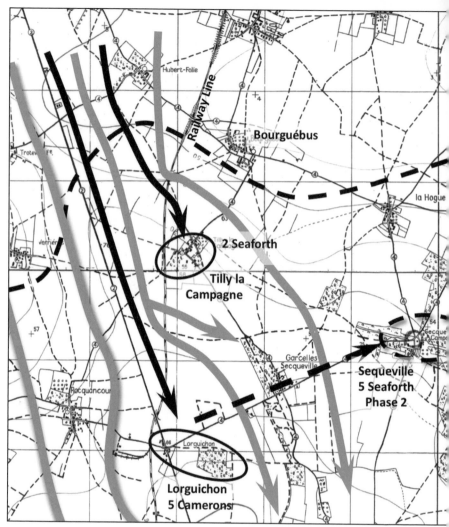

No. 152 Highland Brigade's plan and objectives.

worried me was that I could not allot any reserve for the TILLY
battle as 5 SEAFORTH had to be left untouched in case 154 (H) Bde
wanted it. After discussion with the Divisional Commander I was
allowed to allot one company of this battalion as reserve, if required,
for 2 SEAFORTH.

Tilly-la-Campagne

Taking the village that had been held so stoutly by the enemy during
Operation SPRING and subsequent days was to be the objective of Lieutenant Colonel Andrews' 2 Seaforth. His problem was that Tilly was not to

be bombed by the RAF due to its proximity to the start line and the routes of the bypassing columns. In addition, it was not going to be heavily bombarded as the artillery barrage would advance beyond it in just three minutes. According to the operational report the Seaforths did have 'Additional support from 4.2-inch mortars and one machine gun platoon was, however, allocated, with artillery concentrations on call after the completion of the barrage.' Much of this support could only be used after the passage of the flanking columns.

Tilly was now held by a reinforced company of 3rd Battalion 1055 Grenadier Regiment and, as before, the heart of the defences was the trenches that radiated from the cellars now covered with the addition of thick layers of rubble, which made them proof to all but direct hits from the heaviest shells. The outposts of the German defences were pushed as far forward as the level crossing. Major Gilmour described these as 'a network of trenches dug along the hedgerow' that extended back towards the village. Based on the expectation of an early surrender of the enemy company, the Seaforths' plan was to envelope Tilly. They would advance on the village with two companies, A and D, supported by B Company, with C in reserve. In the second phase

> B Coy was to follow behind A and D as far as the level crossing and as soon as D Coy was reported on its objective, but without waiting for it to be mopped up, B Coy was to move by the Right flank to an objective on the Southern edge of TILLY.

In the third phase C Company, commanded by Major Gilmour, was to move round whichever flank was considered to be most hopeful and take up positions astride the Tilly–Garcelles–Secqueville road. As fighting in the

The site of the level crossing. The railway has gone and the crossing is now on the edge of an industrial estate.

ruins of Tilly, in which the enemy were strongly positioned, would be next to impossible, the final clearance would be done by daylight. Major Gilmour recalled that:

> The village would therefore be closely surrounded by infantry and further cut off by the advance of the armoured columns. The centre of the village was to be cleared at first light and companies had been given definite sectors for which they were responsible.

Major Gilmour outlined the battalion's advance on the railway crossing:

> In order to cover the 1,500 yards in the eighteen minutes available, the companies were forced to advance in file down the only available track and deploy into formation for the attack at the level crossing. The manoeuvre of deploying whilst on the move without a pause had been practised beforehand. To have advanced deployed all the way from

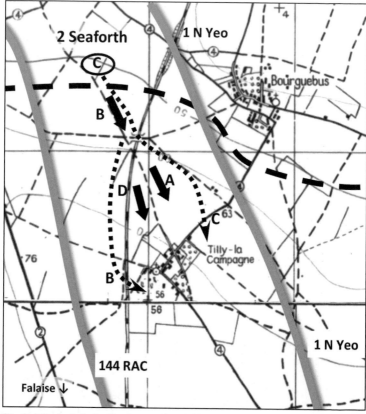

The 2nd Seaforths' plan for the attack on Tilly.

the Start Line through the high standing crops could not have been done in the time available.

A and D companies made good progress as far as the railway line but A Company in particular had now fallen well behind the barrage. As the leading companies approached the railway crossing, however, the Seaforths were quickly disabused of their optimistic notion of an early surrender by the enemy, as they were 'greeted with heavy small arms and machine gun fire'. With the barrage having passed over Tilly quickly the banks of dust that swirled around the armoured columns were notably absent at Tilly. Brigadier Cassels recounted: 'The artificial moonlight and the rising moon made visibility too good: it was possible to see men moving at about 200 yards, and as a result, heavy casualties were suffered.'

D Company had kept closer to the barrage by following the railway to the right and reached its objective on the outskirts of the village, surprising and mopping-up some enemy positions on the way. In 'confused fighting and mopping up for about an hour' they cleared the wood and scrub on this flank of the village. A Company on the left was pinned down, was under heavy fire and had sustained many casualties clearing a hedgerow about halfway to the village. Only slow progress was made and Brigadier Cassel's diary records 'Little definite news was heard until 0045 hours, when the left company was reported to be in the orchard on the outskirts of the village and engaging the enemy in close fighting.'

B Company in Phase Two without the benefit of proximity to the barrage was slower in moving and encountered enemy who had reoccupied their outpost positions, which had earlier been cleared by D Company.

The view from the area of the railway crossing towards Tilly. The few hedges have long since gone.

Consequently, B Company, who had veered off course, was pinned down by the railway behind D Company for the rest of the battle.

Meanwhile, on the left Major Gilmour had brought C Company forward:

The badge of the Seaforth Highlanders.

> On reaching the level crossing my company met with fairly heavy mortar fire (about 0015 hours). As I did not expect an immediate move, I ordered platoons to dig shallow slits in the plough and went to find the Commanding Officer and get some orders.
>
> The Commanding Officer considered that things were going alright on the Right but that the hedgerow position must be captured before dawn as it commanded the approaches to TILLY in daylight. He therefore ordered me to go and assist A Coy take the position and proceed to my original objective afterwards. I got A Coy runner to guide me to its HQ, telling my platoon commanders on the way what was happening.
>
> On reaching A Coy commander, I found that one platoon had walked right on to an enemy position which appeared to have recovered from the effects of the barrage and opened up on the platoon at point blank range and practically wiped it out. The other platoon of A Coy was also depleted.[1]

The two company commanders conferred and decided to bring up one of C Company's platoons and carry out a reconnaissance by fire to locate the enemy's left flank around which another C Company platoon would manoeuvre and attack from the rear:

> By the time orders were issued and A Coy's ammunition replenished, over an hour had elapsed before all was ready (about 0300 hours). The drawing of the enemy's fire was successful and showed the enemy's Right flank. I therefore ordered the other platoon round in a wide sweep giving it fifteen minutes before covering fire was opened. It was then to rush in from the Right behind the position.
>
> The attack was not successful. The flanking platoon took too narrow a sweep and bumped the end of the position and was repulsed. The platoon withdrew after some difficulty, taking its wounded with it. The platoon commander's body along with five others was found next day almost on top of the enemy trenches.

Brigadier Cassels commented: 'The enemy fought stubbornly, bringing down heavy automatic fire, and had at least one SP gun in action on the North-East side of the village.' By now the dawn was lightening the sky to the west and A and C companies were in what was described by Major

Gilmour as 'a hopeless position on a bare slope within a few yards of the enemy (within grenade range) and almost out of ammunition. In consultation with A Coy Commander I therefore decided to thin out and withdrew to the cover of the railway.'

Meanwhile, back on the right flank Captain Murray's D Company of 5 Seaforth was deployed from reserve and ordered to attack Tilly from the west, as it was believed from reports that the two right companies of 2 Seaforths were close to their objectives. The brigade commander stated that

> it was intended that D Coy 5 SEAFORTH should attack between them. In fact, the company which should have reached the south-west end of TILLY LA CAMPAGNE was north-west of the village. As a result, the attack by D Coy 5 SEAFORTH was made by one platoon only, the remainder of the company providing fire support on the open right flank. This platoon was held up on the Western outskirts of TILLY LA CAMPAGNE near the [second railway] crossing, having suffered heavy casualties.

Captain Murray was among those killed and it was clear to Brigadier Cassels that something drastic had to be done, and at

> about 0330 hours I asked the Divisional Commander if I could use the whole of 5 SEAFORTH. He agreed. This of course was alright in theory, but not so hot in practice, as 5 SEAFORTH had made no study whatsoever of the problem, having been given two other tasks later in the battle. I saw the Commanding Officer at about 0400 hours and told him the situation.

Lieutenant Colonel Walford 'was somewhat taken aback' by the change in task. While 2 Seaforths' two companies were to attack from the west he was to break into the village at its eastern extremity after a renewed artillery and machine-gun bombardment. This necessitated the withdrawal of A and D companies of 2 Seaforth to a safe distance behind the railway crossing. The attack was to be renewed at 0610 hours but was delayed by a combination of the change in task and mist to a new H-Hour of 1000.

The British Bren gun was the mainstay of the rifle section, but it had a much lower rate of fire than the MG42.

Meanwhile, Brigadier Cassels was pressing divisional headquarters for tank support and received a squadron from 148 RAC who motored back north from Garcelles where they had been in action with 7 Black Watch. At 0830 hours, in the mist and smoke the tanks followed the road and drove straight into the village where they were subject to sniper and machine-gun fire. Major Gilmour, now back at the level crossing, recalled that:

> At dawn we heard tanks in the direction of the enemy. They were firing with their machine guns apparently in our direction. At first, I thought that it was a counter-attack, but they appeared out of the mist and were seen to be Shermans which had come through TILLY from the south and also taken the hedgerow position from the rear.

Over the next hour the squadron manoeuvred and engaged the village from south to north with high-explosive shells from their main armament and their machine guns. Germans who appeared from the hedges and trenches with their hands up were sent back to the Seaforths as prisoners of war.

The Germans had been shocked by the unexpected arrival of armour in the midst of their position and having been softened up by tank and artillery fire. Just before the infantry were to renew the attack, word was received from

> The Squadron Commander [who] reported that he had received an offer of surrender from the garrison. 5 SEAFORTH attack was called off and the remnants of A and C Coys of 2 SEAFORTH returned to TILLY with the tanks. The remainder of the garrison then surrendered.

The battle for the ruins of Tilly-la-Campagne was finally over on the morning of 8 August 1944 and at 1050 hours, the sole surviving German officer and about thirty prisoners marched out of the village. The cost of this final attempt to capture Tilly had once again been high.

Lorguichon

Meanwhile, 5th Battalion Queen's Own Cameron Highlanders (5 Camerons), the third battalion of 152 Brigade, was already in action. They had set off on foot from La Guinguette on a night march of more See map on p. 118 than 2 miles to their objective. They were to follow behind the two armoured battle groups that made up the right column. It had been a slow and much-delayed move behind 7 Black Watch's vehicles, with the dismounted infantry constantly fearing that the armour they could hear all around them would blunder into them and mangle them with their tracks.

At 0130 hours, 5 Camerons was ordered forward by 152 Brigade. Passing the tail of the right column to the west, they advanced through the tall wheat towards Lorguichon, a hamlet and level crossing on the Falaise Road adjacent to La Guerre where 8 Cdn Recce Regt was being held up. A couple of hundred yards to the east of the hamlet was the not insubstan-

124

Searching German prisoners.

tial Lorguichon Wood, which had earlier been bypassed by 144 RAC and 7 A&SH on their way to Cramesnil. This was a company objective.

At 0335 hours the Camerons were reported to have reached Lorguichon but from the amount of firing it was obvious to brigade headquarters that they were not yet 'firm'. While two companies spent more than an hour clearing the houses and the surrounding area, another company fought its own battle in the wood, which had earlier been bypassed with little trouble and was not secure until 0600 hours.

The 5 Camerons' casualties had been light, but this was only the first action in what was to be a long day for the Highlanders.

6th Canadian Infantry Brigade

The task of Brigadier Young's 6 Cdn Bde was to secure the villages bypassed in 2 Cdn Armd Bde's columns, namely from west to east May-sur-Orne, Fontenay-le-Marmion and Rocquancourt. May and Fontenay were both bombed in the RAF's pre-H-Hour strike, but this was largely ineffective as an operational research report makes clear:

Fontenay-le-Marmion This target was bombed by 153 Lancasters dropping 825 tons ... No bombs fell on the village itself; there were a

125

few in the fields to the east, but the great concentration was straddled across the little hamlet of LE VAL, which is half a mile west of the target ... Debris and craters made the roads through LE VAL quite impassable.[2]

It was a similar story at May-sur-Orne where 'Damage inflicted on the enemy was negligible' and the report concludes that 'the bombing appears to have been no assistance to them [the Canadian infantry] in taking these points.' In fact, the bombing proved to be a hindrance: 'The flares had just faded out when the bombers arrived. Some bombs fell short amongst the men who were waiting to advance; this caused some confusion and did not improve morale!'

The brigade task had been increased in scope when General Simonds had heard of the departure of the *Leibstandarte* and 'it was decided to take advantage of the effects of the bombing and commit all three battalions of the brigade at H hour.' The amount of artillery support was, however, even less than that available to 152 Highland Brigade at Tilly. The British Army of the Rhine account explains that 'Further, the barrage did not include ... [May or Fontenay] and only very limited fire support could be provided there until the barrage was completed.' The lack of indirect fire support was, however, again compensated to some extent by the allocation of the division's 4.2in mortars (Toronto Scottish Regiment) and a squadron

A Toronto Scottish carrier and crew. These carriers provided mobility for the mortar and machine-gun platoons.

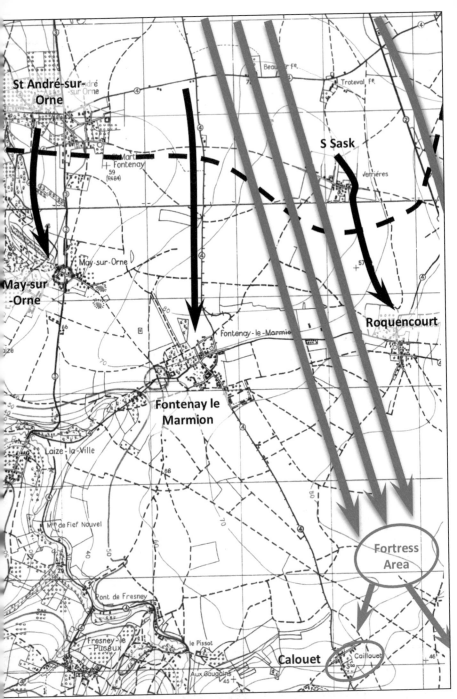

The Canadian infantry brigade's plan and objectives.

of Crocodiles, flame-throwing variants of the Churchill tank, from 141 Regiment RAC.[3]

Battalion objectives were for *Les Fusiliers Mont-Royal* (FMR) May-sur-Orne, the Queen's Own Cameron Highlanders of Canada (Camerons of C) Fontenay-le-Marmion and the South Saskatchewan Regiment (S Sask or Saskatchewans) Rocquancourt. Squadrons of Shermans from the 1st Canadian Hussars were to support the infantry battalions.

May-sur-Orne

The village was strongly held by the 1st Battalion 1056 Grenadier Regiment who had taken over the well-developed defensive positions from the SS in and around the battered village, up on the western extremity of the Verrières Ridge and in the woods on the banks of the Orne. To the west of them, on the river line was the boundary with the 271st Infantry Division.

The FMR had an unfortunate start. The Germans had again sheltered in the deep mine workings around May while the bombs fell. Consequently, when the FMR's leading companies were seen forming up in the ruins of St Martin, they were heavily shelled and mortared, and the French Canadians suffered significant casualties. This caused a delay as it was necessary to reorganize the companies, which were already badly under strength. Now with less than forty men each, they advanced south across

The battle-damaged church at May-sur-Orne.

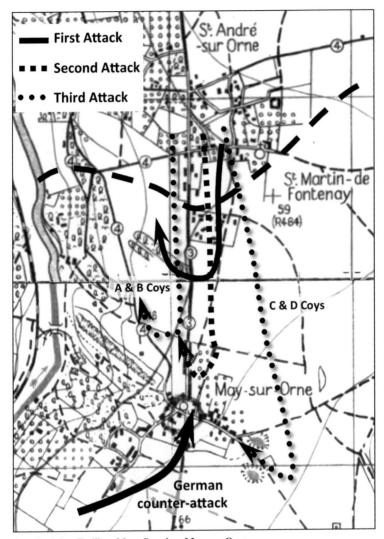

Attack of *Les Fusiliers Mont-Royal* on May-sur-Orne.

the 1,200 yards of largely open fields. With the Germans ready and waiting and the scene illuminated by flares, the Fusiliers made little headway before being forced back into cover.

The second advance, however, benefited from smoke and dust, which enabled the leading companies to approach the woods and orchards on the northern edge of the village. Supported by fire of the 4.2in mortars, one of D Company's two platoons broke into the outskirts but was immediately

129

driven out by a vigorous German counter-attack. The battalion was forced to pull back to the edge of the woods.

The battalion again regrouped and called for artillery support from the guns that had by then finished the creeping barrage and were now 'on call'. Having reorganized and with the artillery softening up the village, at 0430 hours all four companies took part in a silent attack. A and B companies

Mine workings at May-sur-Orne.

were to advance astride the axis of the road using the silhouette of the battered church spire to guide them, while C and D attempted to infiltrate via the quarries to the south-east and into the village. The FMR got to within 300 yards of the village before they were spotted. Their war diary recorded that 'The silent attack had so far been successful but at this point a German officer or NCO was observed going around putting his sleepy men on alert.'

As the French Canadians stealthily approached the houses, flares again illuminated the scene and numerous well-sited enemy machine guns, posted on the flanks of the village, with interlocking and overlapping arcs of fire brought the attack to a prompt halt with considerable casualties. At daybreak May-sur-Orne was still firmly in enemy hands.

Fontenay-le-Marmion

In the centre of the brigade area, Lieutenant Colonel Runcie's Camerons of C had to advance 3,000 yards across open fields, up over the western end of the western part of the Verrières Ridge and down to the village of Fontenay, which was in dead ground. They, however, had the advantage of the north-south running mineral railway immediately on their left to guide them to Fontenay. If this was an advantage, they had several factors working against them! The rifle companies were only sixty to seventy strong and once again there was only minimal indirect fire support available and the Germans, realizing that the bombing heralded an attack, adjusted their deployment. The operational researcher, in assessing the effect of the bombing, concluded that:

> POW reports state that, when the bombs fell on May-sur-Orne ten or fifteen minutes before the [air] attack on Fontenay-le-Marmion, the tanks and MT [mechanized transport] which were in the latter were pulled out and the troops in the trenches to the north were told to hold on as a counter-attack would be launched in the morning.

The Camerons' C and D companies led the attack with B Company in close support and A Company in reserve. Trouble, however, began just over 1,000 yards beyond their start line on the St André–Hubert-Folie road. D Company encountered isolated enemy outposts of the 3rd Battalion 1056th Grenadier Regiment and machine guns that were firing blind through the clouds of dust and smoke.

16 Platoon was pinned down by machine-gun fire and when 18 Platoon launched a left flanking attack to deal with the enemy, they too came under heavy mortar fire pinning them down as well. Both platoons eventually extricated themselves by crawling forward through the enemy's arcs of fire.

The next problem was a minefield laid across their axis of advance, which brought the Camerons to a halt and Royal Canadian Engineers were brought forward to breach it and mark a lane for the infantry, all of which

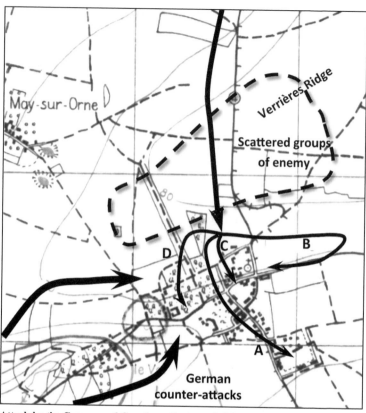

Attack by the Camerons of Canada on Fontenay-le-Marmion.

took time. Once through the minefield the shelling and machine-gunning
continued, principally because the Camerons were advancing straight
through an enemy battalion position on the reverse slope of the Verrières
Ridge! Neither Germans nor Canadians could properly see what was going
on amid the shroud of dust. Colonel Runcie reported that 'the enemy were
firing wildly in all directions'. Having passed through the Germans,
advancing on a narrow frontage, the Camerons left numerous active enemy
positions behind them. In addition, a significant portion of their men had
become separated from their sub-units in the reduced visibility and confusion. During this period the commanding officer was missing and was
later found wounded.

At around 0100 hours, the battalion reached the outskirts of Fontenay
with the rifle companies each around twenty to thirty strong, but groups
of disorientated Canadians drifted in over the next few hours. Despite
the lack of numbers, the Camerons went straight for their objectives with

Major Ganong's D Company fighting their way into the houses. At the same time, further to the left, the enemy allowed the forward platoons of C Company into the village and then engaged those following behind, C Company's HQ and 15 Platoon, preventing them from moving forward. Consequently, 13 and 14 platoons were isolated in the village. 15 Platoon and Company HQ worked their way around further to the left flank and reached their objective where they hoped to find the other two platoons but they were not there. The missing Camerons were eventually able to link up with elements of B Company to the east of the village and prepared for the expected enemy counter-attack.

B Company's initial objective was a set of small workings referred to as 'quarries' to the east of the village, where the enemy was known to be dug in. They attacked with 11 Platoon forward, 10 Platoon left rear and 12 Platoon right rear. Sergeant Mahon was awarded the Military Medal for his part in the stiff fight for the quarry. Having cleared the enemy from this area, B Company headed for the outskirts of Fontenay-le-Marmion where they were to link up with C Company in the buildings and orchards around the church.

Fighting to clear the houses in the part of the village that the Camerons held went on all night; by 0630 hours, however, the Camerons of C had culminated: they had suffered additional casualties, were running low on ammunition and to complicate matters further, elements of the German battalion on the ridge, which they had sliced through under cover of darkness and obscurity, were now behind them and active! The situation grew worse still: 'As the mist cleared … the 88mm gun, which had caused so much trouble to the armoured columns, now controlled the CAMERONS of C's axis … its axis was cut and no one could get to it nor could any wounded be evacuated.'

One of the surviving stout old stone buildings in Fontenay around which the Camerons of C fought.

In the circumstances, the company commanders initially agreed to hold on where they were but somehow Major Ferguson, their brigade major and former second-in-command of the battalion, got through to Fontenay to take command and ordered action. Clearly believing that securing the remainder of the village was within the capability of the depleted battalion, he gave instructions to the company commanders to each clear a sector. A Company, for instance, was to advance some 300 yards through the village and drive the remaining Germans out of the square block of houses at the southern extremity of Fontenay. Major Cavanagh in his debrief said:

> By 0700 hrs, 8 August, the dust had settled sufficiently so that visibility was good and we pushed off sending back word about 0800 hours that we were reasonably well established in our area. Counter-attacks soon developed on us from south and east. As I arrived on the position with only 50 men, with which I had to hold an area about half a mile, I asked for assistance. The enemy were infiltrating through the town and between us and the town so that information got through very slowly. Counter-attacks continued all that morning. We were able to hold on only with the small arms fire which we had.

The Camerons were counter-attacked by tanks and on several occasions were all but surrounded, but they maintained their tenuous hold on the rubble of Fontenay.

Rocquancourt

The South Saskatchewans (S SASK R) had the advantages of advancing between two of the armoured columns, 8 Recce Regt on the left and the Royals on the right and with the support of the barrage. Although the armoured advance didn't work out as planned, the defenders of Rocquancourt, a company of the 3rd Battalion 1055 Grenadier Regiment, had the alarming spectacle of armoured columns to both their left and right. Not only that, they must have been very surprised to have the RHLI's column drive directly through the village without seriously molesting it! Advancing from Troteval Farm with A and D companies deployed forward, C in support and B in reserve, the S SASK R followed the track south-east via the hamlet of Verrières:

> The battalion was determined to get to ROCQUANCOURT as close behind the barrage as possible. In spite of darkness, the standing crops, shell holes, slit trenches and machine gun posts, some of which were manned and had to be dealt with, the leading company, according to the personal account of its Commander, 'A' Company hit the village right on the nose close behind the barrage. In the orchard there, we captured six mortars, their detachments and ammunition complete.

By following as close behind the barrage as possible and ignoring as much enemy fire as they could, A Company had broken into the orchard while the enemy was still reeling from the effects of the artillery and Lieutenant Colonel Clift said that 'Enemy heads were still underground when we arrived.' With the orchard on the right secured by A Company, D followed and the others passed through, so that by 0100 hours the village had been taken but it took until 0445 hours to clear the last resistance and round up prisoners. To the left 8 Recce Regt was having its difficulties around

The ruins of Rocquancourt church after the battle.

Le Guerre and to the right the Essex Scottish had tangled with elements of the German battalion dug in on the reverse slope of the Verrières Ridge: 'By first light our defence and the digging-in was completed. A slight flurry occurred then, when tanks were heard approaching in the mist, but they turned out to be ours which were coming back for repositioning.'

152 Highland and 6 Cdn brigades had been largely successful and, as will be seen, their tasks completed during the course of the morning of 8 August. Success was achieved, but at a price. On foot they lacked the protection of the Kangaroos and other armoured carriers and had, except in the case of the S SASK R, not benefited from the bombardment. With their already thinned ranks, they had been up against largely unsubdued German infantry. In comparison with some of Montgomery's other offensives around the eastern hinge of the lodgement, Phase One of Operation TOTALIZE can be firmly regarded as a considerable success.

NOTES

1. Due to a lack of replacements, all four rifle companies were reorganized as two rifle platoons and a support section, with the spare Bren gun, 2in mortar and PIAT. Gilmour, BAOR Battlefield Tour 1947.
2. Report No. 8 by No. 6 Operational Research Unit, OPERATION TOTALIZE, RAF Heavy Bombing on night of 7/8 August 1944.
3. 141 Regt RAC was formed in November 1941 by the conversion of the war-raised 7th Battalion, Buffs (Royal East Kent Regiment) to the armoured role. Eventually they took over Churchill Crocodile flame-throwing tanks and joined the 79th Armoured Division during the Normandy campaign.

Chapter Seven

The Morning of 8 August 1944

'We have to risk everything. A breakthrough has occurred near Caen the like of which we have never seen in the west.'
Generalfeldmarschall von Kluge, am, 8 August 1944

While fighting was still in progress at points along the 7,000-yard frontage of II Canadian Corps' breakthrough, the immediate consideration for 154 Highland and four Canadian brigades and their armoured support was to dig in and prepare to hold their gains against the German counter-attacks. For the Germans it was to contain the Allies, and if possible regain ground through immediate response, before launching larger operations to restore the original *Hauptkampflinie*. For General Simonds, although some of the armoured objectives had yet to be secured and the villages on the flanks were still being cleared, it seemed that he had a gap into which he could launch the 4th Canadian and Polish Armoured divisions and, in doing so, maintain momentum and gain the success that he and his corps so earnestly desired.

Immediate German Counter-Attacks

As the morning mist burned off at 0830 hours, the German counter-attacks were already well under way. These were the immediate reactions to the loss of ground that their tactical doctrine called for, from the lowest level of command upwards. These attacks were designed to exploit enemy disorganization at the end of an assault or at least to be delivered before they were properly dug in and the new defences properly coordinated. Two months into the campaign, every Allied combat soldier knew exactly what to expect and to dig as fast as they could, but it was slow going once they were down into the chalk. Colonel Hopwood of 1 Black Watch in St Aignan commented that 'The battalion were allowed about two hours grace to organise themselves for defence before the enemy started to shell and mortar on a fairly heavy scale.'

At first mortar bombs and shells were fairly arbitrarily scattered, but as light and visibility grew, so did their accuracy. The battalions, who with the benefit of the Kangaroos and armoured carriers had suffered few casualties during the first phase, now faced a steadily mounting number of casualties and their evacuation.[1] Little of the newly-taken ground was immune from heavy German fire, as the Allies had in effect driven a salient into the enemy line. Consequently, not only could the 89th Division's artillery engage but also that of flanking formations, namely the 271st and 272nd divisions.

Standartenführer Kurt 'Panzer' Meyer had put the 12th *Hitlerjugend* SS Panzer Division on alert as soon as the bombing that heralded the offensive started. Consequently, leading units such as the *Panzerjäger* battalion had been in position before dawn to attempt to contain the Canadians. Meyer himself was on the road:

> I raced towards Bretteville with some dispatch riders before daylight to obtain an overview of the previous night's events ... I talked to Mohnke in Urville[2] and received the first reports on the night's events. The positions of the 89 Infanterie-Division had been overrun; the division was as good as destroyed. Only a few individual strongpoints were still intact; they were like islands in the stream of battle, giving the attacking Canadians a hot reception time and again.
>
> There were no communications whatsoever with the units at the front and the surviving pockets of resistance fought on independently. There was no cohesion to the defence; they had to rely on their own resources.

As Meyer drove on towards the front he could see how serious the situation was for himself:

> Bretteville was impassable. The bombs had blocked the streets with rubble. We moved across open fields to try to reach Cintheaux that way ... I found a platoon of *Panzerjäger* from *Kampfgruppe* Waldmüller at Cintheaux. With foresight, Waldmüller had already moved the platoon there during the night. The place was under artillery fire.

This platoon of 75mm Pak 40 anti-tank guns was a part of the towed company of SS *Panzerjäger* Battalion 12. Meyer drove out of the village and on a short distance to the main road:

> I couldn't believe my eyes. Groups of German soldiers were running south in panic down both sides of the Caen-Falaise road. I was seeing German soldiers running away for the first time during those long, gruesome years of genocide. They were unresponsive. They had been through hellfire and stumbled past us with fear-filled eyes. I looked at the leaderless groups in fascination. My uniform stuck to my body; the heavy burden of responsibility made me break out in a sweat. I suddenly realized that the fate of Falaise and the safety of both armies depended on my decision.
>
> I stood up in the Volkswagen and moved in the direction of Caen. More and more confused soldiers approached me fleeing southwards. I vainly try to stabilize the collapsing front. The appalling bombardment had unnerved the units of the 89. Infanterie-Division. Rounds landed on the road, sweeping it empty. The retreat could only continue off to the sides of the road. I jumped out of the car and was alone in the middle of the road.

A 75mm Pak 40 positioned to fire through a loop-holed Norman stone wall.

I slowly approached the front and addressed the fleeing soldiers. They were startled and stopped. They looked at me incredulously, wondering how I could stand on the road armed with just a Schmeisser. The young soldiers probably thought I had cracked. But then they recognized me, turned around, and waved to their comrades to come and organize the defence around Cintheaux. The place had to be held at all costs to gain time for the *Kampfgruppen*; speed was imperative.

'Panzer' Meyer, having seen the situation at the very front for himself, drove back to Bretteville to organize the main counterstroke:

While with Mohnke, I saw the commander-in-chief of the 5. *Panzer-Armee, General der Panzertruppen* Eberbach. The general had come to see for himself the effects of the earlier Allied attacks and make decisions based on personal observation. The commander-in-chief gave me full freedom of action and agreed with my estimate of the situation.

Meanwhile, elements of the 89th Division who reported that 'The psychological effect of the extraordinary bombardment on personnel was comparatively quickly overcome' and divisional headquarters were steadily gaining control over the confusion of the night. General Heinrichs was forward on the right flank south of Saint-Aignan-de-Cramesnil where he considered the greatest threat to be and the divisional adjutant was with

(*Left*) *Standartenführer* **Kurt 'Panzer' Meyer in combat dress.** (*Right*) *General der Panzertruppen* **Heinrich Eberbach.**

the Fusilier Battalion on the Caen-Falaise road. Both officers were shoring up the defence and urging units into action, reinforced by elements of the *Hitlerjugend* that had come forward during the night.

The first significant sized counter-attack began at 0830 hours, when the Canadians on the ridge beyond Point 122 adjacent to the Caen–Falaise road saw four panzers, two Panthers and probably a pair of Mk IVs leading dismounted infantry coming in their direction. Beyond Cramesnil more *Hitlerjugend* panzers opened fire on the Royals on the ridge:

> At approx 0830 hrs, the enemy counter-attacked with tanks. Panther tanks moved up the CAEN–FALAISE Highway, and we were also fired on by tanks from the far side of CRAMESNIL. One Panther tank penetrated our positions and approached within about 25 yds of Bn HQ. Heavy casualties, both in personnel and vehicles, were suffered by the fire of MMGs [Medium Machine Guns] attached to the Bn. Our 3″ Mortar Pln also suffered heavily, losing four carriers complete with ammunition that were burned out and two mortars. Three mortarmen were wounded. One of our SP A/Tk guns was brewed.

The Royal Regiment of Canada's mortar line and that of the supporting platoon of Toronto Scots' 4.2in mortars had been caught while they were still digging in, and the single tank in the area was knocked out with the carriers suffering the same fate one by one. Both of these mortar platoons were necessarily much further forward than the artillery because of their

140

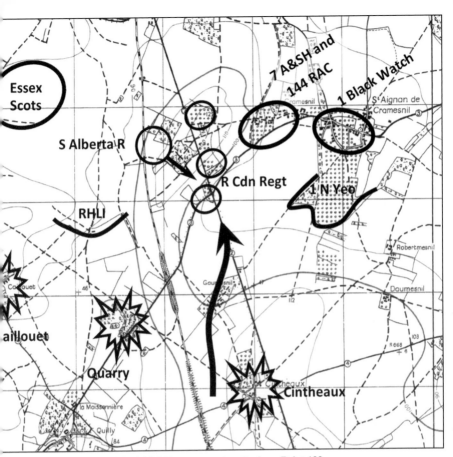

Approximate line of the initial German counter-attack on Point 122.

relatively short range.[3] The Torontos also lost medium machine guns to enemy fire before the German attack petered out.

As the counter-attack developed, Captain Bill Waddell, one of the artillery Forward Observation Officers of 4 Cdn Fd Regt who was with the Royals' forward company, went back on foot to get the Sherman tanks of Major Radley-Walters' A Squadron of Sherbrooke Fusiliers from the leaguer. He led them forward to good fire positions from where they were able to engage to good effect. The Royals' battalion second-in-command, Major Young, witnessed Waddell in action:

> This guy is standing out in the open, all by his bloody self, pointing out a German tank here,

The Military Cross.

141

another there, yelling at our tanks, 'Hit the goddam thing!' or words to that effect. Those are his fire orders. Oh yes . . . incredible! With him pointing and the tanks shooting, they knock out three, maybe four, of them – one or two self-propelled guns, and a couple of tanks.

A Squadron claimed four kills, 'the first of many that day' but lost two tanks in the process. Captain Waddell, however, was awarded a very well-deserved Military Cross.[4]

To Bomb or to Go!

'The break-in had caught the enemy unaware. It remained to be seen how effectively we could pursue our initial advantage before he should have time to recover his balance and strengthen his rear defences.'

Colonel Stacey, *The Victory Campaign*

Brigadier Wyman from his 2 Canadian Armoured Brigade (2 Cdn Armd Bde) command tank in the dispersal/fortress area, south-west of Rocquancourt, signalled the 2nd Canadian Division at 0615 hours that 'The [objective] area is securely held by our forces and the situation appears to be entirely suitable for further ops to begin.' This was clearly a premature verdict, with only Point 122 and the area where the Caen-Falaise road crossed the ridge in Canadian hands; while to the left the 52nd Highland Division was only just completing consolidation and beginning to dig in and, most importantly, to his right most of the ridge and the villages had yet to be secured.

As the mist started to burn off Lieutenant Colonel Gordon of the Sherbrooke Fusiliers went forward to join A Squadron and look out over the empty open ground to the south of Point 122. He radioed brigade headquarters and requested permission to continue the advance, but Brigadier Wyman had already been told not to go any further forward. Nonetheless the brigadier went up to the ridge to see the open road south for himself. Even though officers then and since have argued that 'there were more Germans behind us than in front of us', he reiterated that the brigade was to form a firm base for Phase Two. Wyman was soon wounded up on the ridge and his influence in subsequent decision-making as the man on the spot was sorely missed.

The abiding question at this stage in the battle is that with the success of the first phase of the operation, should the second bomber strike have been cancelled in order to exploit what would surely be a fleeting opportunity? Much criticism has been levelled at General Simonds both at the time and subsequently, not least from the commander of the 12th SS Panzer Division, *Standartenführer* Kurt 'Panzer' Meyer, who couldn't believe that the Allies didn't advance.

Simonds, however, had a relatively narrow window in which to make his decision whether to confirm or call off the second bomber strike. This had

One of the bridges built over the Orne by Canadian engineers in Caen, but these were traffic bottlenecks.

to be made and communicated by 0726 hours and at that time the situation was far from clear, but there was a further hour and a half during which the bombers could still be recalled. At the time he made the decision:

> A sizeable portion of the Phase One objective still had to be cleared and secured. Progress in bringing forward two rather than the original one armoured division for Phase Two had led to reported congestion and delay.

In addition, as a former gunner officer, Simonds appreciated that momentum during Operation GOODWOOD had been lost partly due to a failure and/or inability to bring forward adequate artillery fire support to blast the armour through the rapidly-forming German defences on the Bourguébus Ridge. In the same operation, the Royal Air Force had also been criticized for not carrying out interdiction in depth to prevent I SS Panzer Corps forming the new line. Consequently, a signal was sent to the 8th USAAF confirming that the bombing was to go ahead.

The window for Simonds' decisions closed at 0900 hours, which was the 'abort deadline' for the American bombers to be recalled. At this time Headquarters II Canadian Corps was receiving reports of the 0830 hours counter-attacks described above, and again the situation was still far from clear. As the attacks ebbed away after 0900 hours, even had Simonds wanted to call off the American air strike, the lead bomber formations were already airborne and beyond the point of recall.

A final factor was that it would have put General Crerar in a politically difficult situation to cancel a bomber strike for which he had lobbied the reluctant 'bomber barons' so earnestly only days before.[5]

In short, Simonds could not take the risk, as the extent of his success overnight was still far from clear back in Headquarters II Canadian Corps at the time he could call the bombers off. Additionally, as will be seen, the two armoured divisions were far from poised, ready to advance at a moment's notice. Culturally, British and Canadian commanders liked a 'tidy battlefield' and secure lines; consequently, the infantry commanders were busy consolidating and unable to organize an exploitation. Nonetheless, Colonel Gordon of the Sherbrooke Fusiliers wrote in 1960 'I thought a great opportunity was lost and that we could have been in Falaise in an hour or so, had we started soon after first light.'

The 2nd Canadian Division

On the 2nd Canadian Division's front, in 4 Cdn Bde's area the village of Caillouet, the objective of the Essex Scots, still had to be taken and the RHLI had dug in short of Point 46 and the Quarry. Of 6 Cdn Bde's tasks, only Rocquancourt was secure, the Camerons held Fontenay 'lightly' and *Les Fusiliers Mont-Royal* had yet to capture May-sur-Orne. General Foulkes wanted these objectives 'cleared up'.

As early as 0705 hours 8 Recce Regt, who were digging in east of Rocquancourt, out of significant contact with the enemy, were ordered to move to support the Essex but as they moved west they became entangled with Germans in the crops around Rocquancourt who had been bypassed during the night. By 0900 hours only a fraction of the recce troops had shaken themselves free and at 0910 the Essex Scots' war diary records that:

> Imperative orders came down from Divisional Headquarters for the battalion to take Caillouet with the aid of 8 Cdn Recce Regt, whose position had presumably been eased by the advance of 51 (H.) Inf Div, and who were no longer needed at Point 122. But 8 Cdn Recce Regt was unable to move forward from its position near Rocquancourt, and by 1025 hours Essex Scots came to a halt when they observed that their objective was 'picketed with Tiger tanks'.[6]

Without tanks the Essex Scots fell back to positions a mile from Caillouet and requested armoured support. Later in the morning with a heavy preliminary artillery bombardment and a squadron of Shermans from the Sherbrookes they attacked the village, which was reported as being in the hands of the Essex by 1300 hours. Meanwhile, now isolated on the ridge, the Germans in the area of the Quarry had withdrawn and the RHLI moved forward to occupy the ground.

In 6 Cdn Bde's area, Fontenay-le-Marmion was not fully cleared or indeed secure, with the Camerons having lost a second commanding officer killed and a third wounded in a matter of hours. The volume of enemy artillery fire increased noticeably, and the Germans were seen to be preparing to counter-attack again but that did not materialize. It is probable that the attack was broken up by Canadian artillery fire while still forming up.

With the situation largely under control in Rocquancourt, Brigadier Young was allocated two companies of Saskatchewans, their carrier platoon

Operations to complete the capture of Phase One objectives.

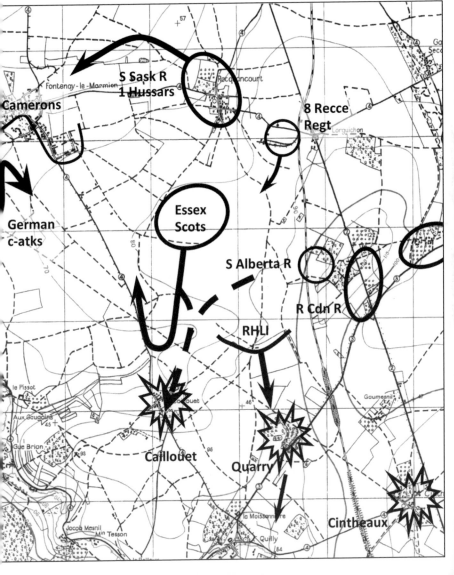

and C Squadron of the 1st Hussars to assist at Fontenay. Heavy fire from the objective, however, prevented them from advancing directly down the line of the Rocquancourt–Fontenay road. Instead they were forced to take a circuitous route north clearing as they went the remaining German pockets out of the crops, banks and hedgerows on the reverse slope of the Verrières Ridge. Having linked up with the Camerons they mounted attacks from two directions, finally capturing the village in the early afternoon. Some 250 Germans from the fields and Fontenay itself were taken prisoner by the Saskatchewans. When counted, the FMR's mortar platoon had eighty Germans, mostly from 3rd Battalion 1056 Grenadier Regiment, in their makeshift 'cage' alongside their mortar line. An area held by this number of enemy in an urban setting, let alone those who had escaped or continued to fight in the fields around the village, had been way beyond the capability of the Essex Scots, a single largely unsupported and under-strength infantry battalion.

The Germans, holding out in their solidly-built defences and the mine tunnels of May-sur-Orne, had continued to defy the FMR and deny them the capture of the village. Throughout the morning the French-Canadian infantry who had fallen back to the area of La Cité de la Mine continued to be subjected to machine-gun, artillery and mortar fire and required assistance. Having dispatched tanks and infantry to support the Camerons, Brigadier Young took the remaining squadrons of the 1st Hussars further west, along with the Crocodile flame-throwers from A Squadron 141 Regt RAC that had been brought forward from the suburbs of Caen. It was

Infantry clearing houses with the help of a PIAT.

decided that the whole squadron would engage with flame rather than a single troop as normal.

The attack was to be launched from the area of La Cité de la Mine ('The Factory') after a five-minute, short but heavy bombardment that was to be followed by a smokescreen being laid on the flanks of the attack, which would again be from the north. The key part of the attack is recorded by Captain Storrar, second-in-command of B Squadron, in the war diary:

> The plan was to attack with four Tps up on the village, with one Tp right of the main CAEN–MAY SUR ORNE rd and three Tps left of the rd. FUP behind the Mine bldgs, which were held by us. SL the line of the Mine bldgs. H hr when the Crocodiles crossed the SL. The four comd tks were to give covering fire and smoke from the area of the Mine bldgs. The length of the adv being some 600yds. Arty concs went down on the village, and subsequently on the back of the village to prevent any enemy getaway.
>
> The Crocs pressured up a mile from the FUP and 2 Tp had to be dropped because of their trlr and gun troubles. The attack then went in at 1505 hrs with 1 Tp right and 3 and 4 Tps left as per diagram.
>
> The whole front area of the village was flamed and the slit trenches on the eastern edge. From the SL to the objective all tks fired 75mm and Besa even whilst the flame was being used.

The maximum range of the flame was 110 yards, so the Crocodiles needed conventional suppressive fire from the command tank's 75mm main armament and machine guns to close within that range across 600 yards was entirely necessary. The flame was a weapon that was both loathed and feared by the Germans. The sight and sound of the lance of flame in this case prompted most of the enemy to attempt to flee, if they had not already been incinerated. The infantry was deployed one company either side of the road and followed the Crocodiles closely. A Corps HQ report described the process:

> The general plan was that behind each tank would move two sections following very closely on the [flame fuel] trailer behind the tank. As

The diagram from B Squadron's after-action report to illustrate their flame assault.

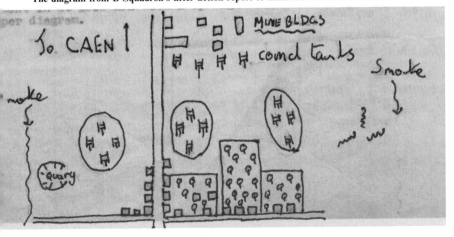

A Churchill Crocodile flame-thrower in action.

the tank approached a house it would fire, knock a hole in the house [with its 75mm], then squirt the liquid flame into the opening thus created. Immediately the section directly behind the tank would dash for the doorway and clear the house as quickly as possible.

The tank meanwhile moves forward down the line to the second house and turns its turret against it. Gun and flame thrower repeat their actions and the second section of infantry following the tank is available for clearing this house. These two sections thus alternate in entering the buildings set ablaze by the tank and the sections of the reserve platoon following further in rear occupying the buildings already searched.

Even though most of the enemy had fled, it took over an hour to work through the village and secure it, in the process rounding up more than 100 prisoners.

The Crocodiles had made all the difference and the village, or at least the rubble of May-sur-Orne was finally in Canadian hands. Captain Storrar wrote 'The dream of a whole squadron being used together materialised' and B Squadron's conclusion was that 'This attack bore out the contention that the effect of flame is increased out of all proportion when used en masse.'

Preparations for the 12th *Hitlerjugend*'s Counterstroke

As he drove forward in the early hours of 8 August, *Standartenführer* Meyer had an advantage:

> A lucky coincidence was that I knew the terrain in great detail. I had been there with my old reconnaissance battalion in the autumn of 1942, and we had conducted plenty of exercises. I knew, therefore, that the high ground at Potigny dominated the terrain and the Laison sector was a natural tank obstacle. The Canadian attack had to be halted north of Potigny or the fate of the 7. and 5. Armeen would have been sealed.

The plan he made based on this estimate was as follows:

> I decided to defend Cintheaux with those forces already employed and to launch an attack east of the road with lightning speed and all available units. By doing that, I hoped to disrupt the enemy's intent. I designated the woods south-east of Garcelles as the objective. Because a large quarry made a tank attack south of Cintheaux unlikely, I had no fears there. We had to risk the attack to gain time for the Laison sector. The attack was planned to start at 1230 hours [1330 Allied time].

It is worth noting that with the disparity of forces Meyer had at an early stage decided that he could only disrupt the next phase of the battle that would surely see the use of an Allied armoured division, rather than restoring the *Hauptkampflinie*. See map on p. 151

Back in the woods and farm buildings just to the east of Potigny *Obersturmbannführer* Hubert Meyer, the chief of staff, had the *Hitlerjugend*'s divisional staff working on assembling the division, producing orders for the counter-attack and the new defensive line on the high ground north of the River Laison.[7] He had anticipated Kurt Meyer's intention, who recorded that 'In the meantime, Hubert Meyer had directed *Kampfgruppe* Waldmüller to Bretteville-le-Rabet. From there it could be employed based on the situation.' While in Bretteville-sur-Laize the divisional commander penned a message with the broad outline of his plan, which was sent the 9 miles back to his headquarters by dispatch rider. He later wrote that his outline plan was:

1. *Kampfgruppe* Waldmüller, reinforced by the I./SS-Panzer-Regiment 12 and the remnants of *Schwere* SS-*Panzer-Abteilung* 101, counter-attacks to seize the high ground south of St Aignan.
   Note: Allied intelligence overestimated the number of Panthers available. The *Hitlerjugend*'s war diary gives a strength of nine operational tanks and a similar number in short-term repair. It is generally accepted that eight to ten Tigers mostly of 3 Company were available plus four *Brummbär Sturmpanzer* IV. The infantry was *Sturmbannführer*

149

(*Left*) *Obersturmbannführer* Hubert Meyer (before his promotion). (*Right*) *Sturmbannführer* Johann 'Hans' Waldmüller, Commander 1st Battalion, 25th SS Panzergrenadier Regiment.

Waldmüller's 1st Battalion, 25 SS Panzergrenadier Regiment, which was approximately 200 strong.

2. Divisional *Begleitkompanie* [Escort Company], reinforced by the SS-*Panzerjäger-Abteilung* 12 advances through Estrées and takes the high ground west of St Sylvain.

Note: I SS Panzer Corps' *Begleitkompanie* was also grouped with this force.[8] SS-*Panzerjäger-Abteilung* 12 was already deployed. Meyer is in error here; I Panzer Corps did not have an organic anti-tank battalion, it was either an army heavy *Panzerjäger* battalion or the *Leibstandarten* that had been left behind. Their task was to occupy blocking positions.

3. *Kampfgruppe* Krause, reinforced by the II/SS-Panzer-Regiment 12, disengages from the enemy, occupies the high ground west of Potigny and defends the area between Laison and Laize.

Note: *Sturmbannführer* Krause commanded 1st Battalion 26 SS Panzergrenadier Regiment who that morning was counter-attacking the 59th Staffordshire Division's bridgehead at Grimbosq. The figure of thirty-nine operational Mk IV panzers being available is correct but given losses and Allied observation a significant number if not all of the 2nd Battalion's Mk IVs were grouped with Waldmüller for the attack.

4. Divisional command post at Potigny; I will be with *Kampfgruppe* Waldmüller.

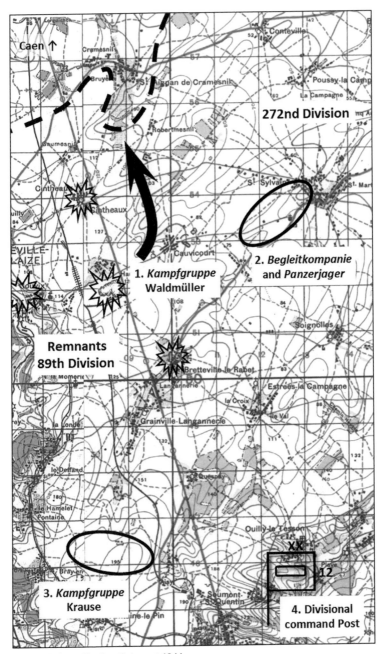

The *Hitlerjugend*'s plan, 8 August 1944.

His plan made and being put into effect by Divisional Headquarters, Kurt Meyer

> met Waldmüller north of Bretteville-le-Rabet. Together we drove to Cintheaux to determine the present situation. Wittmann's Tigers were already in position in cover of a hedge east of Cintheaux without having taken part in the fire fight so far. Cintheaux was under artillery fire while the open terrain was fairly free of fire. From the northern edge of the village we spotted massive tank columns north of the road to Bretteville-sur-Laize. The tanks were assembled in packs. The same picture offered itself south of Garcelles and at the edge of the forest south-east of the village. Seeing these concentrations of tanks almost took our breath away. We could not comprehend the behaviour of the Canadians. Why did those overwhelming tank forces not push on their attack?
>
> Waldmüller and I agreed that we could not let the tank units start out against us. The enemy tanks must not be allowed to drive another attack. An enemy tank division sat attack-ready on either side of the road. That attack could not be allowed to get started – we must attempt to grasp the initiative.

The Germans had been granted the time they needed to bring the *Hitlerjugend* into action!

The Other Side of the Hill

Meanwhile, the Allied Front from Point 122 to Caillouet had been secured by 4 Cdn Bde and the last German troops in that area had fallen back towards Cintheaux where they had been corralled by Kurt Meyer.

Hitlerjugend's key commanders: *Sturmbannführer* Olboeter (III/26 SS Pz Gr Regt), *Standartenführer* Kurt Meyer and *Obersturmbannführer* Mohnke (26 SS Pz Gr Regt).

In the 6 August change to the Phase Two plan, exactly which formation was responsible for the hamlet of Gaumesnil that lay beyond the Phase Two bombing safety line had not been properly coordinated between the Canadian divisions. When this came up as an issue on the morning of 8 August, with the protection of armour, A Squadron of the Sherbrooke Fusiliers was sent forward on their own at about 1030 hours. Exactly what happened is mainly recorded by Major Radley-Walters as, according to the regimental war diary, 'The Int office, which was at Main HQ 2 Cdn Armd Bde, at CORMELLES and which was mounted in an M14 (half-track), was destroyed when American HE bombs fell short of their target ... All regt records on hand were destroyed.'

Major Radley-Walters, however, recalls that he was in position with his eight remaining tanks at 1115 hours, with the squadron's tanks inside the wall around the modest château building. In the event, A Squadron would not be joined in Gaumesnil by a company of infantry from the Royal Regiment of Canada until after the German counter-attack had begun and the bombing had ended.

An entry in the Royals' war diary referring to events later in the day, however, has a slightly different version of events:

When the Coys moved up, the Tank Commander on the spot gave the information that tanks had been all round GAUMESNIL, but no one as yet had attempted to enter the village. The two Coys, therefore, advanced and entered GAUMESNIL at approx 1530 hrs, encountering no opposition although a few stray prisoners were collected.

It may be that the 'Tank Commander' was from B Squadron, which was further up the ridge, and that the infantry occupied the rest of the village not knowing that Major Radley-Walters' tanks were in the area.

Meanwhile, east of the Caen-Falaise road, the Shermans of 1 N Yeo had pushed forward to the southern edge of the orchard beyond St Aignan and Captain Boardman commented that it was 'all rather quiet', but he noted that there was a distinct gully in front of them. 2 Troop of C Squadron had pushed forward across the feature, which is known to the inhabitants of the area as le Petit Ravine. This feature, though shown on going maps[9] did not show up as the 30ft-deep ravine it was on either the 1:50,000 or 1:25,000 scale maps so its presence was unexpected. By crossing the ravine, No. 2 Troop was standing directly in the path of *Kampfgruppe* Waldmüller's counter-attack.

Around 1030 hours the tempo of events started to increase on the Allied left, presumably as the 89th Division had restored command and control in front of this part of the Allied penetration. The war diary of 1 N Yeo recalls 'Heavy mortaring and some shells started to come down, C Sqn on left attempted to exploit into village; shot up strong point ROBERT-MESNIL and got as far as wood North of that village.'

During this shelling the commanding officer was wounded by a mortar bomb while visiting B Squadron. A little later, at 1115 hours, an enemy armoured vehicle, supporting remnants of 1055 Grenadiers, was seen advancing from Mesnil-Robert Farm. Reported as an assault gun, it engaged a C Squadron Sherman that was manoeuvring on the edge of the orchard and with its first shot it knocked it out at a range of 400 yards. The flash was spotted in a hedge near the farm – the squadron replied in kind.

The German Counter-Attack

Before midday *Standartenführer* Meyer had taken his commanders forward to the edge of Cintheaux to look out over the open ground across which they were going to attack towards the nearby hamlet of Gaumesnil, the orchards south of St Aignan, the village of Cramesnil and the high ground of Point 122. They retired to the small market square to coordinate and, as Meyer wrote:

> During the last briefings with Waldmüller and Wittmann[10] we watched a single bomber approaching. It flew across the terrain several times and then set a visual marker. The bomber appeared to us to be some sort of airborne command post. I immediately ordered the attack so that the troops would be out of the bombing sector. Once more I shook Michel [sic] Wittmann's hand and mentioned the extremely critical situation. Our good Michel laughed his boyish laughter and climbed into his Tiger.

The arrival overhead of the American master bomber's aircraft had galvanized the *Kampfgruppe* into action as the main force of 8th USAAF bombers would only be twenty minutes or so behind.

The aim of the attack was to get to grips with the Allies assembling for the next phase of TOTALIZE and in a close-quarter battle seize the initiative and inflict disruption and delay. The main part of *Kampfgruppe* Waldmüller, with 200 Panzergrenadiers, 20 Mk IV tanks and 10 assault guns, was to attack on the right through St Aignan, while *Hauptsturmführer* Wittmann with the 8 to 10 Tigers of 101 *Schwere Panzerabteilung*, reinforced by the 4 *Brummbärs*, was to attack west of the Caen–Falaise road, astride the hamlet of Gaumesnil.

Lieutenant Colonel Hopwood noticed that 'At approximately 1200 the shelling and mortaring increased in intensity' and the 1 N Yeo war diary records '1220 Tigers (VI) reported moving towards A Sqn'. The counter-attack had begun. Kurt Meyer decided not to go with Waldmüller but to remain in Cintheaux near the Caen-Falaise road.

First into action were the Tigers. As already recorded, they were in the cover of the hedgerows south-east of Cintheaux and therefore further forward than the rest of *Kampfgruppe* Waldmüller, which was assembling around further back in the dead ground of Le Petit Val between Cauvi-

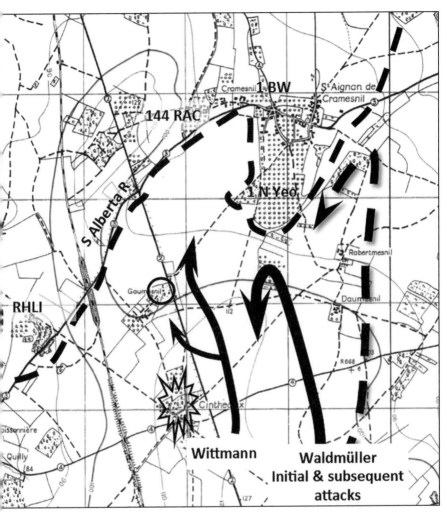

The counter-attack of *Kampfgruppe* Waldmüller.

court and the Cintheaux–St Sylvain road. From his observation post Kurt Meyer witnessed the attack:

> They [the Tigers] cross open terrain at high speed and make use of small dips in the land for their firefights ... I am standing at the northern edge of Cintheaux while enemy artillery aims destructive fire at the attacking panzers. The Tiger of Michael Wittmann races into the enemy fire. I know his tactics during such situations, it is called: Straight ahead! Never stop! Get through and gain an open field of fire!

Wittmann had taken five of the Tigers on an axis 150 yards east of the Caen–Falaise road heading towards Cramesnil followed by a weak

A German *Sturmpanzer* IV (*Brummbär*) armoured infantry support gun.

Sturmbannführer Waldmüller giving orders during the Normandy campaign.

A Tiger belonging to 101 *Schwere Panzerabteilung* ready to go into action.

company of Panzergrenadiers. The tanks were deployed one behind the other so as to minimize the target presented to anti-tank gunners from head-on. The further he advanced, however, the less useful this tactic became as to the left in Gaumesnil were the predominantly 75mm-armed Shermans of A Squadron Sherbrooke Fusiliers and to his right, 1 N Yeo in the orchard and Triangular Wood south of St Aignan. Wittmann was in effect leading his men into a classic fire-pocket or 'killing area'.

This poses a question: had he and Kurt Meyer not spotted either of these threats during the recce from the edge of Cintheaux? It is probable that over a distance of nearly 1 mile that 1 N Yeo in the cover of the orchard could not have been seen, but at only 700 yards it is unlikely that they, their *Panzerjäger* crews and the 89th Division's infantry would not have seen Major Radley-Walters' tanks arriving in Gaumesnil. The breaking-down of the high wall to the south of the château to Sherman gun-barrel height must have been obvious. It is therefore likely that the pair of Tigers and *Brummbärs* advancing to the west of the road were to deal with the Gaumesnil threat head-on.

The primary arc of fire of Major Radley-Walters' Shermans of the Sherbrooke Fusiliers was south across some 700 yards of open country to the northern outskirts of Cintheaux. From around the village and out of the dead ground came the panzers that presented the greatest threat to them. *Hauptscharführer* Hans Höflinger was heading for Gaumesnil and described the early course of the attack from his perspective:

Then we drove off, Michel right of the road and I left, four others with Michel and the brother of Heinz von Westernhagen with me.

The Gaumesnil Château wall where A Squadron gathered has since been rebuilt back to its original height.

Approximately 800 metres to Michel's right there was a small wood which struck us as suspicious and which was to prove fateful to us.

As the Tigers approached his position, Major Radley-Walters was keeping his squadron firmly in hand over the radio:

I just kept yelling, 'Hold off! Hold off!' until they got reasonably close. We opened fire at 500 yards. The lead tank, the one nearest the road, was knocked out. Behind it were a couple of SPs. I personally got one of the SPs right on the Caen–Falaise road.

Höflinger was commanding the Tiger that was knocked out immediately to the south of Gaumesnil. He recalled:

Hauptscharführer **Hans Höflinger.**

We began taking heavy fire from anti-tank guns once again. Then my tank received a frightful blow and I had to order my crew to get out as it had already begun to burn fiercely. My crew and I dashed toward the rear and got through.

Several B Squadron Fireflies joined the battle, having come down onto the forward slope of Point 122 around La Jalousie when the attack began, but at this stage of the action they were at more than 1,000 yards range against the frontal armour of their targets.

158

Wittmann v Ekins

Hauptsturmführer Wittmann, a renowned SS panzer ace who after service in the *Reichswehr* and a period back on the family farm in the Rhineland, joined the *Leibstandarte* and rose through its ranks as it expanded to become a division. First in armoured cars in the early campaigns of the war and then in assault guns and Panzer IIIs on the Eastern Front, Wittmann gained an impressive list of 'kills'. In 1943 he became a Tiger platoon commander and was awarded the Knight's Cross of the Iron Cross in January 1944, to which, with his mounting tally of 117 enemy AFVs, was added the Oak Leaves, presented personally by Hitler at the Wolf's Lair (his Eastern Front military HQ). At the beginning of the Normandy campaign he was awarded the Swords to his Knight's Cross for blunting the 7th Armoured Division's advance through Villers-Bocage when his Tigers ran amok among the tanks of the 1st County of London Yeomanry and the Queen's Regiment's infantry vehicles. This action became a propaganda coup for the SS and the enhanced story that was promulgated by the *Kriegsberichter* still contributes to Wittmann's enduring renown as a premier panzer ace.

The diminutive Trooper Joe Ekins, a shoemaker from Rushden in Northamptonshire, decided to volunteer for the army and get the regiment of his choice rather than wait for conscription and a random allocation. During 7/8 August he was in the unaccustomed gunner's seat of Velikiye Luki,[11] a Sherman Firefly belonging to Lieutenant James' 3 Troop, A Squadron 1 N Yeo. He was normally radio-operator but had fired a

(*Left*) *Hauptsturmführer* **Michael Wittmann, acting commander of 101** *Schwere Panzerabteilung*. (*Right*) **Trooper Joe Ekins, A Squadron 1 N Yeo.**

159

couple of 17-pounder rounds during pre-D-Day cross-training. Joe Ekins recalled 'Someone came up on the air and said that there were Tigers approaching. I saw them through the gun sight, but they were 1,200 yards away advancing north towards us.' Captain Boardman ordered three Sherman 75s and the Firefly into action.

The German attack began. Watching from the high ground around Point 122, Major Welch, whose battery of 4 Fd Regt RCA was supporting the Royals, saw the panzers head north across the fields. He was 'astonished at the cool arrogance of the German tank commanders, standing up exposed in their turrets, looking for targets through their binoculars, their guns traversing all the time.'

Hauptscharführer Hans Höflinger describes the course of the attack when his earlier concerns about the wood on the right came back to haunt him: 'Unfortunately, we couldn't keep the wood under observation on account of our mission. We drove about one to one-and-a half kilometres, and then I received another radio message from Michel which only confirmed my suspicions about the wood.'

Joe Ekins gave his account of the same events:[12]

We saw them coming and I was the only one who could do anything about it; the 75mms would have to be within 300 yards to do anything to a Tiger. Sergeant Gordon, our tank commander said to us 'Wait until they are about 800 yards'. So, we waited and then he pulled us forward out of the orchard. You need to get out of the trees to traverse the gun. 'Target the last Tiger.' There were four coming across in line ahead. It was something we had learnt, fire at the last tank. Gordon said, 'Fire when ready', which I did and immediately the loader loads another one and I fired again. I think I hit with both. I fired twice at the same target and he started to smoke. Sergeant Gordon immediately said 'Reverse back into cover' and I could see the gun of the second Tiger starting to traverse around towards us. He had obviously seen us and fired at us as we reversed back into cover. Either the shell hit the turret lid or he was hit by a branch of a tree because Sergeant Gordon was knocked out.

Three shots were fired back as Velikiye Luki jockeyed into cover. According to Joe, after getting Sergeant Gordon out of the Firefly:

A few minutes later the troop officer, Lieutenant James, got into the tank and ordered 'Driver advance.' So we pulled out of the orchard again and I fired at the second tank. His gun was still pointing at us. We fired one round and he blew up; we must have hit his ammunition. We pulled back into the orchard.

According to Höflinger, 'Michel called [on the radio], "Pak right ..." but didn't complete the message. When I looked out to the left I saw that Michel's tank wasn't moving. I called him by radio but received no answer.'

Wittmann's Tiger 007 with its turret displaced by the internal explosion and by being moved to remove the tracks.

Radio-operator in Tiger 312 or 009, *Sturmmann* Balho was a witness to the shot that knocked out Wittmann's Tiger: 'We had already been hit and forced out of the burning Tiger into the crops. I saw the wake of a shell going through the barley and it hit *Hauptsturmführer* Wittmann's tank. It came from the right.'

It is commonly reported in accounts of the fighting in Normandy that the passage of high-velocity tank or anti-tank rounds could be seen like the wake of a torpedo in the tall wheat or barley, with tank crews even saying that they had been able to take evasive action.

Joe engaged the targets from his left to right and this Tiger, call sign 007, was his second target engaged at 800 yards and was the only enemy tank to suffer an internal ammunition explosion in this action, which displaced the turret.[13] Joe's testimony as to the internal explosion combined with Hans Höflinger's and Balho's testimony is important in identifying who knocked out 007 (as positively as one can in the circumstances).

Lieutenant James jockeyed Velikiye Luki forward into action again and by this time the surviving two Tigers had swung north-east away from the Caen-Falaise road and deeper into the killing area: '... when we came out again the third Tiger was milling around; he probably knew the other two had gone and he was looking for some cover.'

This Tiger could have been damaged by the fire from the other 1 N Yeo Shermans whose Sherman 75s were 'peppering it with high explosive' or a Sherbrookes' A Squadron tank that was covering the squadron's flank, i.e. facing east, or it could have been B Squadron between Gaumesnil and Point 122. It was probably having difficulty steering, hence 'milling about'. So much fire was falling around the leading Tigers that Joe Ekins found it difficult to engage his third target. He eventually fired twice, knocking out his third Tiger in twelve minutes. The 1 N Yeo war diary records that the

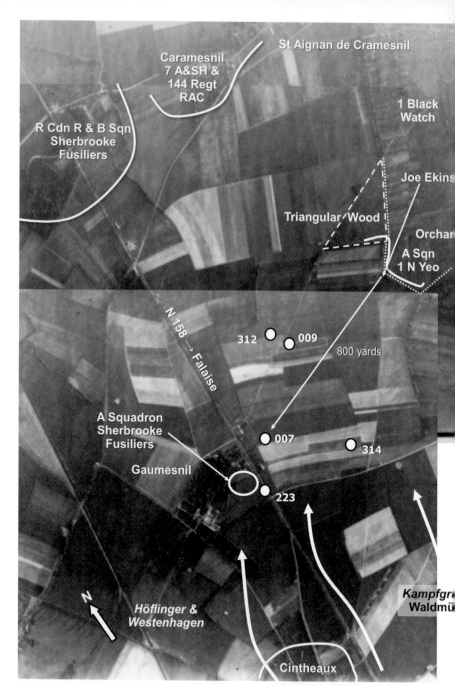

A montage of air photographs showing the action against Wittmann's Tigers.

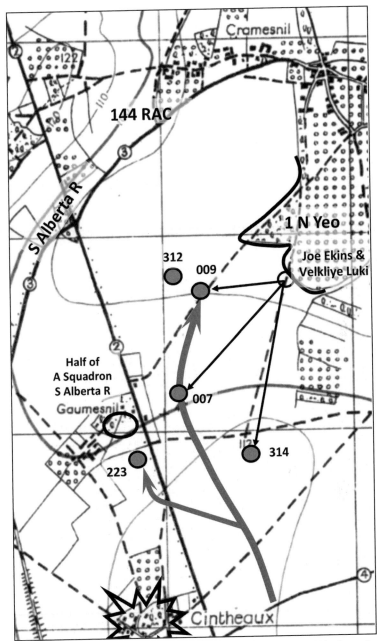

Joe Ekins targeted and hit the three Tigers 314, 007 and either 312 or 009 in that order over the course of twelve minutes.

three Tigers were 'brewed at 1240, 1247 and 1252 all without loss'. The final Tiger was knocked out by a Firefly of 144 Regt RAC or B Squadron of the Sherbrookes.

Having had a grandstand seat alongside the Sherman Fireflies of 144 RAC during the action of the afternoon, Major McKinnon of 7 A&SH concluded 'We had ample evidence that our 17-pounders will make mincemeat of the Tiger if hit on the side plates.'

Hans Höflinger, with his tank knocked out near Gaumesnil, was now on his feet 'de-horsed':

> I stopped to look around and to my dismay discovered that five of our tanks had been knocked out. The turret of Michel's tank was displaced to the right and tilted down somewhat. None of his crew had got out. I climbed into von Westernhagen's tank and, together with Heurich, whose Tiger was undamaged, tried to get to Michel's tank. We could not get through. Dr. Rabe also tried it, but in vain.

Even though five Tigers were knocked out, a total of eight were claimed by the Sherbrooke Fusiliers, 144 Regt RAC and 1 N Yeo but Colonel Jolly of 144 later withdrew his regiment's claim for one Tiger. In the uncertainty of war, one can never be sure who knocked out which tank and only echo the sentiment that in the great scheme of things it doesn't really matter. One arm of the German attack had been decisively defeated by British and Canadian armour.

Kampfgruppe Waldmüller

Meanwhile, Waldmüller had closed up and was in action. Across the open plain Kurt Meyer was watching:

> The panzers are hurled into the steely inferno. They have to prevent the enemy attack, they have to destroy their schedule. Waldmüller and his grenadiers are right behind. The brave infantrymen follow their officers. An endless chain of bombers is approaching from the northwest, town after town is being wiped out. There is only one answer: get out into the open fields.

A Firefly of C Squadron 1 N Yeo was among the first to see the attack developing and with the fire of M10 Tank Destroyers, the infantry's 6-pounder anti-tank guns with the new Armour-Piercing Discarding Sabot (APDS) round, plus artillery defensive fire tasks, the moving panzers facing the 'steel inferno' were outgunned.

Getting the attack under way as quickly as possible had sacrificed some coordination, but it did avoid the USAAF bomber strike. Kurt Meyer continued:

> We can observe that the Canadians, too, are being dropped on by the American bomber fleet. The last waves of the 678 four-engined

An SS NCO shouts his orders.

bombers which had started out fly over the determinedly attacking *Kampfgruppe* Waldmüller without dropping a single bomb on the panzers.

Well forward to the regiment's left, a Firefly commanded by Corporal Giles spotted four Mk IVs followed by infantry approaching from the south-east and in quick time knocked out three of the panzers. At the same time Lieutenant James' troop was in action again, along with Joe Ekins, with their attention now firmly south. Velikiye Luki had another four panzers followed by infantry heading for them, but this time they were Mk IVs and Lieutenant James gave the order to engage. With a single shot at 1,200 yards range Ekins knocked out his fourth panzer of the day. However, there was little time to congratulate themselves as there was 'a loud bang. We had been hit and we all bailed out. Lieutenant James was wounded by mortar fragment and was evacuated.' Captain Boardman witnessed what happened to Velikiye Luki:

I saw one of my troop commander's tanks being hit and brewing. He [Lieutenant James] was wounded and came and lay down behind my tank. I got out of my tank when I could. His arm was hanging off, held on by a thread. I thought of cutting it off but thought better of amateur attempts and I got the Black Watch to evacuate him. He survived but his arm was never much use.

Trooper Joe Ekins joined the de-horsed crewmen who were now a reserve to replace those who were wounded. Despite his success with the 17-pounder, he never sat in a gunner's seat again.

By 1255 hours the Germans had worked their way forward into a position south of the orchards and as far north as the Gaumesnil Farm complex. However, with the Tigers on their left flank knocked out, 1 N Yeo's fire from the orchard was already driving both panzers and Panzergrenadiers to more covered approaches in the hedgerows between Gaumesnil and Mesnil-Robert.

Here they were able to make their way through reasonable cover around to the flank. Captain Boardman recalled:

> Hundreds of infantry were pouring up this belt of trees – a good line of attack for them to take – not easy to deal with them. If they got to the defile [the Petit Ravine] with their *Panzerfäusts* we would be in trouble. I had all my machine guns going at them and left a lot of them lying about.

Attack of *Kampfgruppe* Waldmüller on Saint-Aignan-de-Cramesnil and the Orchard.

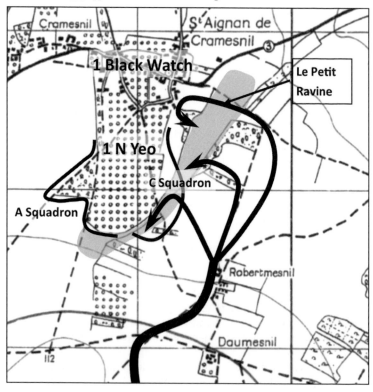

Meanwhile, as Sergeant Finney recalled with his tank being 'rocked with the blast of exploding shells, and shrapnel rattling like hailstones on the turret', calls for supporting fire were increasingly desperate. Such was the situation at St Aignan that fire missions were allocated to the heavier guns of the AGRAs and, as Captain Boardman went on to explain, during this battle such fire didn't always go to plan:

> Our own artillery, the mediums, gave us a hell of a stonking during the day which destroyed my bed roll amongst other things on the outside of the tank. It took quite a long time, it seemed like a long time, to persuade the Gunner forward observation officer to put his shells elsewhere!

The German move around the eastern flank had taken the Panzergrenadiers into some confused fighting with C Squadron's 2 Troop forward of the ravine who were able to knock out several Mk IVs before themselves being picked off by a well-positioned enemy tank leaving a gap in the line, which 3 Troop filled in a deadly game of cat-and-mouse that lasted from 1300 to 1345 hours. It is believed that the squadron commander eventually knocked out the Mk IVs but during this time the remnants of C Squadron were driven back onto the Black Watch, with some of the *Hitlerjugend* claiming that they had 'recaptured' St Aignan before being ejected. *Sturmmann* Helmut Wiese, the driver of a Panzer IV of 5 Company of 12 SS Panzer Regiment, encountered one of the Black Watch's 6-pounder anti-tank guns:

> There, at the edge of the woods, enemy soldiers are bringing an anti-tank gun into position. I report to the turret, it is a new target for the front MG. Our gun opens up as we are at full speed. 'Stop! Stop! Back! Back! Faster!' Otto, the commander, yells this order. I know that the engine is running at the highest speed; it cannot go any faster. I look at the instruments, the tachometer is showing in the red ... As I look through the vision port I am blinded by an exploding brightness. There is a bang as if a full pop bottle is bursting after falling onto a tiled floor. Direct hit to the front, I thought ... Then the Panzer is shaken as if by the first of a giant; brightness, screaming, braking, splintering sounds, nothing remotely human. Then, smell of sulphur and absolute calm. The panzer is on fire. 'Bail out!' Otto orders. I unlock the hatch and push it upward; it only opens a few centimetres and flames immediately come through. The turret is blocking the hatch. I watch as our radio man, Egon, pulls his legs through his hatch. That is the way out. I crawl across the gearbox and the radio towards the hatch, there is no more air; it is getting so hot, I want to get out, I have had it!
>
> Then, I see a face far away, see arms stretched out towards me and hear shouts: 'Helmut, come out!' I push and pull, find fresh air.

A *Hitlerjugend* Panzer IV and its young crew.

Finally, I am outside, jump off and drop to the ground. Egon had come back and got me out, thanks, comrade! Egon helps me to get up and I am on my feet again. Bullets are whistling by and hit the hull. We run around to the side away from the enemy, Otto is there. But where are Arno and Karl? Otto points to the turret, the side hatches are still closed, and he yells: 'Both were killed immediately, I was still inside!' They were left in the turret, a terrible realization.

Meanwhile, panzers had, however, got into the ravine that led around in front of A Squadron's position. Captain Boardman was on the southern extremity of the orchard and recalled that

> Not very far in front of us was a dangerous defile which the Germans used as a covered way for tanks. I remember German tanks sticking their heads up and taking on our tanks. I had been around the squadron in my tank and suddenly I saw one coming up hull down 100 yards away and coming round on to me. I called to Routledge my gunner 'traverse left, on and fire', fortunately we got him. That was the longest ten seconds of my life, whoever got off the first shot was going to win.

While Captain Boardman was lucky, several other 1 NY's tanks became casualties the same way.

Rottenführer Eckstein, gunner in *Oberschar-führer* Rudolf Roy's *Panzerjäger* IV earned 'the Iron Cross First Class for his outstanding bravery in the attacks on an enemy armoured formation at St Aignan de Cramesnil. There he alone knocked out eight enemy tanks.'

The Germans mounted a final attack on the orchard with infantry supported by tanks firing from cover. 3 Troop had by now all been knocked out and A Squadron's surviving tanks redeployed sometime before 1400 hours to cover the gap and engage the Germans advancing through the tall barley. Engaged by machine guns and artillery fire, the attack was brought to a halt.

Rottenführer **Eckstein.**

One story, as this final attack culminated, is of a *Hitlerjugend* Panzergrenadier standing up and shaking his fist at the British positions in the orchard before turning and walking away. Captain Boardman recalled that 'About 30 minutes later a lot of stretcher bearers came up and we stopped to let them take away their dead and wounded.'

The German counter-attacks had spent themselves, but they had not caused the expected disruption and delay to the advance of the two armoured divisions. They had, however, inflicted significant losses on 1 N Yeo. Captain Boardman commented 'Very few tanks got back to the harbour that evening. Some more came back during the night.' The regiment lost a total of eighteen tanks, a squadron's worth, beyond repair during Phase One and the counter-attacks. Waldmüller admitted a total of about fifteen panzers knocked out. The tank return for 9 August, however, shows the loss of four Panthers and twenty-seven Mk IVs, while no AFV figures are available for the *Panzerjäger* Battalion but crew casualties in the reporting period ending 8 August is forty-six killed, wounded and missing, which is indicative of significant losses.

The Canadian post-operational analysis of Kurt Meyer's counter-attack stated that

> it would have been more favourable, considering tactical aspects, if SS *Kampfgruppe* Waldmüller, reinforced with Tigers, had awaited the Allied tank assault in the south-eastern area of Cintheaux, then, exploiting the temporary bafflement and organisational disturbance caused by initial losses, had launched a counterstroke. In this case at least the exact enemy positions would have been known by all tank commanders taking part.

NOTES

1. German mortars were responsible for more Allied casualties in Normandy than any other weapon system.
2. *Obersturmbannführer* Wilhelm Mohnke, Commander of 26 SS Panzergrenadier Regiment. Later he commanded the *Leibstandarte* in the Ardennes and was the last commander of the Berlin Garrison in April 1945.
3. The Ordnance ML 3in mortar had a range of 2,800 yards and the Ordnance ML 4.2in Mortar 4,100 yards versus the 25-pounder's 12,253 yards.
4. Gazetted 21 December 1944.
5. General Simonds 'felt that at the time there was a school of thought which considered that it was quite wrong to use heavy bombers for tactical operations, that they were being diverted from their primary strategical tasks and that to employ them in that role was misusing their characteristics.'
6. *Obersturmbannführer* Hubert Meyer, Chief of Staff, 12th *Hitlerjugend* Panzer Division was adamant that no Tigers were in the forward area at this stage of the battle. Interview with the author 2009. Other sources, however, indicate that the handful of surviving Tigers of *Panzerabteilung (Fkl)* 301, probably just three, may have been forward in support of the 89th Division. 'Fkl' stands for *Funklenk*, i.e. the radio control for the Borgward B IV remote-control explosive vehicles.
7. Main divisional headquarters was in the cover of woods and buildings around Tombeau de Marie Joly. German practice was that the commander gave an outline of the plan, leaving the chief of staff to produce its detail and orders. This enabled the commander to be forward with his tactical headquarters. The British commander spent far more time in his headquarters overseeing the detailed planning and production of orders.
8. *Begleit-Kompanie* or escort companies were infantry with the range of heavy support weapons that gave them significant punch. Most were not used as 'escorts' but as the divisional commander's 'firemen', i.e. a mobile reserve for plugging gaps.
9. 'Going maps' were specially prepared and printed by Intelligence and Royal Engineer Geo Sections to show the nature of the terrain in a particular area, road types, obstacles and country across which the 'going' was slow.
10. *Sturmbannführer* Westernhagen, the commander of 101 *Schwere Panzerabteilung* had been taken ill and *Hauptsturmführer* Michael Wittmann had taken his place in command and took over the command Tiger call sign 007 as his own Tiger was already in workshops. Wittmann did not like the command variant, as it carried thirty fewer rounds.
11. A Squadron's tanks were all named after Russian towns.
12. BHTV/author's interview, May 2009. Available on DVD, Wittmann v Ekins.
13. All five Tigers were subsequently 'pulled' by Canadians or Poles in order to remove their tracks so that the individual links could be used to up-armour Shermans against the hollow-charge *Panzerfäust* and *Panzershrek* rounds. During this process the original location and orientation was changed and 007's turret would have been left behind when pulled as shown in the photographs.

Chapter Eight

The Armoured Advance

If the bomber strike that began at 1330 hours had virtually no impact on Waldmüller's counter-attack or the battle fought around St Aignan, the same cannot be said of the armoured division moving up through the rear of the two Phase One infantry formations. They were all disrupted to a greater or lesser extent.

By midday the Polish Armoured Division was beginning to appear behind St Aignan and forming up ready to go through the forward positions once the bombing was complete. The distance they had covered in their overnight march from the divisional concentration areas north-east of Bayeux to the south of Caen was on nearly 20 miles of crowded roads in the still-compact beachhead. British and Polish military police had their work cut out to prioritize the conflicting requirements of an operational move and routine logistic transport attempting to cross each other. The Polish 10th Armoured Cavalry Brigade (10 Armd Cav Bde) was, however, complete in its assembly area at Bras by 0800 hours on 8 August. After a breakfast, A1 and A2 logistic echelons were left in the village, while the rest of the brigade started to regroup in the open, where they were joined by the flail tanks of the 22nd Dragoons returning from their Phase One tasks.

Major General Kitching, whose 4th Canadian Armoured Division was forming up astride the Caen-Falaise road, commenting on the lateness of the start of the operation, wrote that 'it was assumed that it would take several hours of daylight to organize the full-scale assault by two divisions on the German defences in that area.'[1] Although Generals Kitching and Maczek (Polish Armoured Division) were unhappy about the pause between Phases One and Two, Kitching was not wrong about the time needed to deploy and negotiate the traffic!

As the morning progressed the two armoured divisions started to move forward from their assembly area hides in the southern outskirts of Caen, villages and factories to their Forming-up Places (FUP) on the original start line. Their first problem was to carry out a passage of lines through the two infantry divisions and armoured brigades in front of them. War diaries abound with descriptions of a 'nightmare move', 'congestion' and 'chaos', with the Governor General's Foot Guards describing progress as 'distressingly slow'.

Initially the main obstacle for both armoured divisions in their march to their FUPs was that both had to thread their way through the gun batteries and their associated columns of ammunition wagons. Not only that, the guns of the infantry divisions and AGRAs were at the same time moving up, generally by sections of two guns, onto the Verrières Ridge and new battery locations from where they could best support their battalions.

Polish tank crews prepare for battle during TOTALIZE.

The Polish Armoured Division waiting to move forward on the morning of 8 August 1944.

It wasn't just a problem for the tanks, as Lieutenant George Blackburn recalled. He was one of the gun position officers (GPOs) and had been sent forward to lay out the new battery position and having just put in all the marker posts for his individual guns, the first packet of tanks from the 4th Canadian Armoured Division drove straight through the area following a conveniently southerly-orientated set of tank tracks. He flagged down the leading tank of the next packet for advice:

> The solution, he tells you, is quite simple. Erect any kind of barrier, regardless of how flimsy around your position and the tanks will respect it. Once the new diversion is marked by a few tank tracks, the barricade will no longer be necessary. Tanks meticulously follow a well-established track because of their fear of mines. Show him where you want to go and he will start a new track.

As the armoured columns made their way further forward they encountered another problem and that was traffic jams and diversions caused by the ongoing operations to secure the remaining Phase One objectives and generally making the captured area secure. The Lake Superior Regiment's war diary records that they were 'Stalled near Rocquancourt all the morning ... No advance was made until 1200 hours when it became possible to make slow progress.' General Kitching summed it up when he said, 'putting some 50,000 soldiers into an area 2 miles by 4 miles ... particularly when there is a battle going on in the middle of it is not a good idea.'

A formal studio photograph of Major General Kitching.

The plan for Phase Two which the two armoured divisions were to execute had been changed on 6 August with the arrival of the news that the *Leibstandarte* had left the front south of Caen for Operation LÜTTICH. In the revised plan, rather than the divisions attacking sequentially, now against far less opposition on the high ground (Bretteville-St-Sylvain) north of the River Laison, both the Canadians and the Poles would attack concurrently, with the infantry of the 3rd Canadian Division following the Shermans of their fellow countrymen. In short, General Simonds now wanted to go for both Phase Two and Three objectives at the same time.

The objective was to break through the second German position on the high ground mentioned above as rapidly as

173

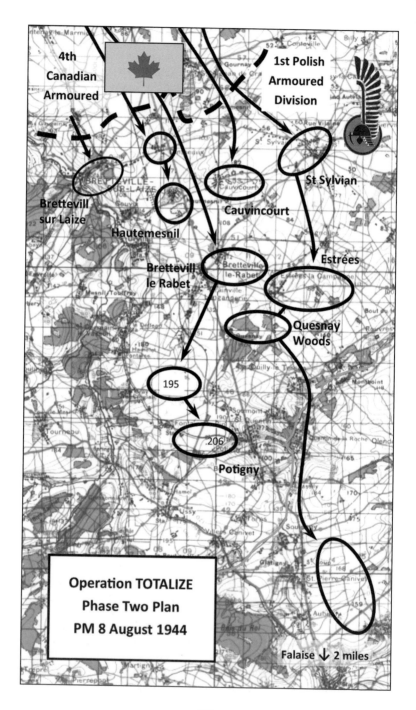

4th Canadian Armoured

1st Polish Armoured Division

Brettevill-sur-Laize

Hautemesnil

Cauvincourt

St Sylvian

Bretteville le Rabet

Estrées

Quesnay Woods

195

206

Potigny

Operation TOTALIZE
Phase Two Plan
PM 8 August 1944

Falaise ↓ 2 miles

possible and with developing momentum exploit south towards Falaise. Major General Kitching's 4th Canadian Armoured Division was to attack west of the Caen–Falaise road and capture the high ground of Points 195 and 206 to the west of Potigny. The 1st Polish Armoured Division, commanded by Major General Maczek, was going to swing around and through the Black Watch and 1 NY at St Aignan, heading via Cauvicourt across the Laison to Point 170. These were ambitious aims, requiring the Poles to make an advance of 10 miles, or nearly 14 miles from the original start line. The 3rd Canadian Division, with little of the transport that had been available to the infantry in Phase One, was to advance in the centre to positions around Bretteville-le-Rabet, extending as far south as Point 140. From these positions they would also be covering what would be, with the passage of the Poles across the Laison, an open left flank.

In the prevailing optimism and sense of expectation in Headquarters II Canadian Corps, the reality of what was being asked of the armour had not been properly considered. In addition to their myriad of other difficulties, there was friendly fire to make matters worse.

The Bombing

'When the use of heavy bombers in the battlefield, very close to our own troops, was first put forward I expressed doubts; it seemed to me that the army had no idea of the risk that the troops would be running.'

Air Marshal Sir Arthur Harris

General Simonds explained the need for the second bomber strike, saying it '... was essential because in an attempt to break through and penetrate to a depth of some four to five thousand yards, an attack is liable to fade out when it runs out of full artillery support.' To that end the bombing that was to precede Phase Two was designed to facilitate the advance and soften up the second German defensive line that was to be breached by the armoured divisions, with targets extending from Bretteville-sur-Laize, via Haut-Mesnil to St Sylvain. The Canadian Historical Section describes the targets and methodology in more detail:

The support requested for the daylight attack on 8 Aug was more comprehensive. Again, the flanks of the advance were to be struck, the bombers being requested to attack Bretteville-sur-Laize and Gouvix on the right and St Sylvain on the left, as from 1300 hours, simultaneously with the advance of 4 Cdn Armd Div down the highway. The tanks would be preceded by a moving curtain of bombs falling on targets at Cintheaux and the woods south-east of Robertmesnil, thence southward to cover Cauvicourt and Haut-Mesnil and the farther woods and copses. This carpet bombing was to be concentrated into 30 minutes, when the air attack would be shifted south for 45 minutes' further bombing to neutralise the enemy guns at the time when the armoured advance should be gaining momentum. The targets at this stage were

Bretteville-le-Rabet and Grainville-Langannerie on the Falaise road, the Laize valley to the west and south from Urville and Estrées-la-Campagne and the Quesnay Woods to the east.

It was originally intended that RAF Bomber Command would carry out the second strike, but weather and re-arming meant that a second run in twelve hours was unlikely to be delivered as aircraft would probably not land at their home station. Consequently, it was only on 7 August that the second strike was taken on by the 8th USAAF bombers. The problem was

The bomber targets for Phase Two and the misbombing.

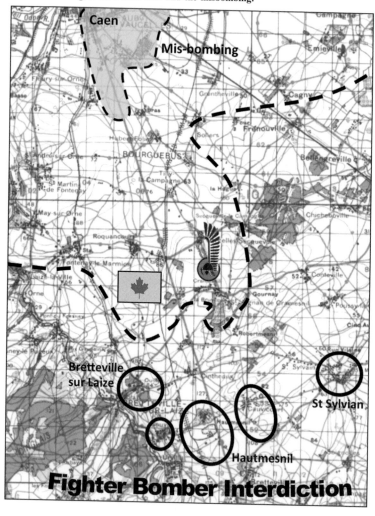

that the American aircraft that normally bombed large industrial targets by daylight did not have the same precision bombing aids as their RAF counterparts and, therefore, in this case had to rely on visual identification of targets in a rural setting. As the UK weather was set to deteriorate, the arrival of the master bomber was advanced to 1230 hours.

During the morning, at the behest of the USAAF, Headquarters II Canadian Corps passed orders to the Commander Royal Artillery of the 4th Canadian Armoured Division for a battery to be ready by 1200 hours to fire red smoke as target indicators for the American bombers:

A special convoy was rushed up to 23 Cdn Fd Regt, and the shells reached the gun area at 1100 hours. By 1200 hours the regiment was ready, and after much anxiety the smoke was fired at 1225 hours. Five minutes later the gunners heard the deep vibration of the silver Flying Fortresses flying over to continue the bombardment which was to crush the German resistance.

Starting at 1226 hours 497 B-17s of the 8th USAAF began dropping 1,487 tons of bombs. Due to flak and sundry other problems, including obscuration of the target, 184 aircraft aborted their mission. Nonetheless, for the German officers assembled in Cintheaux to receive orders for the counter-attack, the sight of the sky full of bombers was alarming. Kurt Meyer, however, recalled that 'A young soldier from Berlin cried out "What an honour from Mr Churchill, a bomber for each one of us." Actually he was quite right. More bombers were approaching than we had soldiers lying on the ground.'

With the bombs falling and so much dust being thrown up from the chalk plain, despite the efforts of master bombers, aircraft mistook the targets and bombed Cormelles and the surrounding areas, hitting in varying degrees all those who were preparing to take part in Phase Two. Some of their bombs were dropped on the rear part of the 4th Armoured Division, hitting 10 Cdn Bde's column, including the Algonquin Regiment (Alq R), which was waiting to move up from Ifs. Also hit was the tail of the Polish Armoured Division and according to General Maczek's report '... our AA Arty lost 44 men (killed and wounded).' The situation was extremely difficult as the area was packed with various munition dumps which exploded for forty minutes after the bombing as a result of fires caused.

Also put out of action were a group of Polish-speaking British officers whose task was liaison and translation between divisional and the various headquarters of the Polish division. This was to have an obvious impact on coordination during the afternoon.

The 3rd Canadian Infantry Division, following the armoured divisions out of Caen, was bombed as it was beginning to concentrate in Faubourg-de-Vaucelles. Significantly Major General Keller's tactical headquarters was hit and he was wounded at the worst possible moment for such an

B-17 Flying Fortresses completing a bombing run.

occurrence, just as his division was going into battle. He is recorded as shouting as his stretcher was loaded onto an ambulance 'Roberts, bring me my pistol! I'm going to shoot the first American I see!' Brigadier Black-adder took command in his place and was himself lucky as 'Just as the head of the 8 Cdn Inf Bde convoy was nearing the old barracks there [Faubourg-de-Vaucelles], the suburb received a heavy weight of these badly misplaced bombs.'

In this brigade, the North Shore Regiment alone suffered nearly 100 casualties, with 'one company being totally ineffective for the operations of the next two days.' Private Les Wagner of the Queen's Own Camerons of Canada was a witness:

We watched and cheered as they went over when suddenly one wedge veered off its southern course and turned west, towards Caen.

A ripple of consternation went along the slope and I saw the yellow smoke of friendly identification flares start up. We watched in horror as the whole 'wedge', as if one plane, released its bombs and watched them fall like elongated sheets of rain, and the centre of Caen boiled up in a low erupting line of dust and debris. Then another 'wedge' veered off its southern course and then another, three in all I think. Since the main body of our division was running the Caen bottleneck at the time, we had casualties, mainly in Divisional Headquarters, our General for one, and one Company of the Seventh Brigade. We cursed the Americans for this mindless follow-my-leader, for that was what it appeared to be. We cursed the lack of adequate ground-to-air communication, and most of all we just cursed, from sheer frustration.

As a finale, the headquarters of 9 AGRA was hit and put out of action, which reduced the fire support available for most of the afternoon to 4 Cdn Armd Bde and according to the Alq R war diary 'Wild rumour began to circulate to the effect that the bombers had really been captured by the enemy, who was flying them against us!'

Explanations for the misbombing vary, but the United States Air Force provides the following explanation of this tragic incident:

> Short bombing within friendly lines resulted from gross errors on the part of two twelve-plane groups. In one case, faulty identification of target by the lead bombardier led him to drop near Caen, although fortunately some other bombardiers of the formation cautiously refrained from dropping with him. In the second instance, a badly-hit lead bomber salvoed short and the rest of the formation followed in regular routine.[2] Canadian troops were thereby in some measure disorganized, and suffered casualties amounting to 25 killed and 131 wounded.[3]

Canadian troops watch the bombing and shelter from some near-misses.

The bombing probably had a deeper impact on friendly forces moving in the open than on the well dug-in Germans. It certainly downgraded Allied performance and with the gun positions in particular suffering; the envisaged level of artillery support was not forthcoming at crucial moments.

The 1st Polish Armoured Division

Organized as a standard British and Commonwealth armoured division, General Maczek's principal manoeuvre unit was his armoured brigade (10 Cav Bde), which consisted of the usual three armoured regiments and a motor battalion (10 Rifle Regt or 10 Dragoons) mounted in half-tracks. His second formation was a lorried infantry brigade (Rifle Brigade or 3 Pol Inf Bde). They were given the following 'Tasks to be executed in two phases':

> First Phase: The Armd Bde to seize first objective (area S of Estrées-la-Campagne and the Hill 140 (1347)). Rifle Bde was to form a pivot in the area of Cauvicourt.
>
> Second Phase: Rifle Bde was to change over with the Armd Bde, which was to attack the second objective (area of Hills 170 & 159 N of Falaise).
>
> Total operation to be covered by reinforced 10 Mounted Rifle [Dragoons] Regt from the E in order to maintain closest contact with 4 Cdn Armd Div in the W.

At 1235 hours, while the bombs were still falling ahead of them, the Poles on the left flank were already moving forward. Two companies of infantry in half-tracks from 10 Dragoons, reinforced with M10 Tank Destroyers, were to advance through the La Hougue/Secqueville-la-Campagne area which was expected to have been secured by 153 Highland Brigade during the morning, but with the delays in securing Tilly the sequencing of the operation had broken down. Secqueville had not yet even been attacked by the Gordon Highlanders. Consequently, the Poles became irrevocably entangled in that battle, leaving the left flank of the main attack exposed for two hours.

Meanwhile, 10 Cav Bde's leading tank regiments, 24 Lancers and 2 Tk Regt, both reinforced by a company of 10 Dragoons, a squadron of flails and a platoon of engineers, started their advance, passing through the British lines. Captain Boardman of 1 N Yeo was towards the right of the area where the Poles would be conducting their passage of lines and recalls their enthusiasm to get into battle with the hated enemy:

> When the Poles eventually came through they were as if they were going on a hunt. We knew that there was a mass of German tanks beyond the ridge and we just couldn't stop them; they were so impetuous. We tried to warn them over the radio about the German

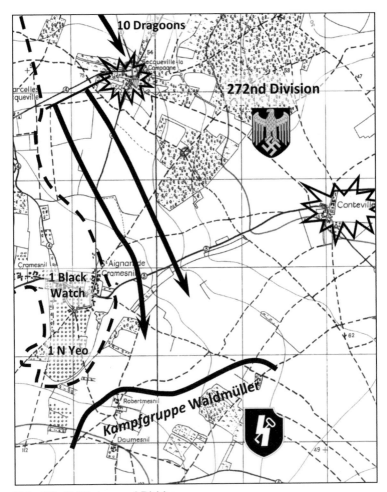

Fate of the Polish Armoured Division.

tanks but we couldn't get through and when I dismounted and tried to talk to them they ignored me.

The Poles ran straight into the panzers of *Kampfgruppe* Waldmüller, which were still in the cover of the hedgerows, woods and orchards in an arc centred on Mesnil-Robert. General Maczek reported that at

1425 hours, 2 Tk Regt was stopped in [its] attack by twenty German tks, probably of German Tiger type and Mk IV, operating from area 108556 [Mesnil-Robert]. 24 Lancers were under enemy arty fire. The Comd 10 Armd Cava Bde required arty on the discovered targets.

Cromwell tanks of the Poles' Recce Regiment, the 10th Dragoons, lined up and ready.

The sight of the far-too-closely deployed Polish Shermans concerned the Yeomanry onlookers as they passed by, but quickly they had become appalled as one after another tank was brewed up. One witness counted sixteen palls of smoke rising from blackened hulls in his area alone.[4]

The Polish field artillery had not been as badly affected by the mis-bombing as the Canadian batteries or those of the AGRAs but even so, it took quite some time for them to get into action as they were moving forward at this time. It had been planned that during this phase the Poles would, while moving their guns as far forward as possible, rely on the Highland Division's artillery. The loss of the British Liaison Section to call for fire was keenly felt from the start. General Maczek continued:

> At 1450 hours, two Arty Regts opened fire with good results. At 1520 hours contact with 4 Cdn Armd Div was established at the co-ordinate 082558 [near Gaumesnil]. In that time, 2 Tk Regt fell into a very difficult situation, its flank being menaced by German tks. The CO Bde, [eventually] arrived with help, covering the flank with 2 Coys, 10 Mounted Rifle Regt and with one A Tk Bty.

After a protracted bombardment the Poles attacked again at 1550 hours and this time they advanced far more cautiously. On their right towards the open terrain that German tanks and anti-tank guns now dominated so effectively they made little progress and on their left a different danger lurked among the hedges around Mesnil-Robert, where SS Panzergrena-diers waited with *Panzerfäusts*. By nightfall the Poles had only made gains

A 5.5in gun of one of the AGRAs firing in support of Phase Two.

General Montgomery and Major General Maczek.

of just over 1 mile but in the process had lost more than forty tanks knocked out or requiring repair.

General Maczek reported that:

The ground was difficult for an attack by the armour, having several small woods and high hedges. In spite of fairly distant horizons, the ground was very favourable for the enemy's A Tk defence.

The enemy was not sufficiently neutralized by our own Air Force and arty, so that the Bde could attack without heavy losses ... Our [Polish] arty very efficiently and quickly supported 2 Tk Regt.

There was a constant threat to the left flank, which will be henceforth a menace to the div ops and my permanent worry.

After all day fighting, the armd regts set out for the night bivouac. 3 Rifle Bde took over the sector and protected it for the night.

One of General Simonds' comments applies here:

A well trained division comes into the field in top form but is very inclined to start by saying 'This is war now, all the things we have been learning about can be thrown over the fence – away we go.' They tend, when they first go into action, to discard a lot of the minor lessons of training and they get one or two sharp lessons.

Secqueville-la-Campagne

Also on the left flank, now behind the fighting echelons of the Poles but tangling with their logistic transport, the village of Secqueville was to be attacked by the 51st Highland Division. In General Rennie's orders, 153 Brigade was, following the capture of Tilly and Lorguichon, tasked as follows:

Occupy and clear SECQUEVILLE LA CAMPAGNE and wooded areas in 0959 and 1058.

CODEWORD – BRIG

This op will NOT commence until the area stated in para 8 (a) [33 Armd and 154 Bde objective] is firmly held. 'B' Sqn 141 RAC Regt [Crocodiles] will be available to sp this op.

B Squadron 141 RAC had fought alongside the 51st Highland earlier in the campaign where their effectiveness in clearing woods and villages with flame had been amply demonstrated to the Jocks. In this battle they would be in support of Lieutenant Colonel The Honourable Cumming-Bruce and his 1st Battalion the Gordon Highlanders (1 Gordons) who were to take Secqueville-la-Campagne area on the afternoon of 8 August 1944.

By late morning, once the Phase One objectives had been secured, the Highlanders of 153 Bde had been relieved in Soliers by 146 Bde of the 49th Infantry Division but it took time for 1 Gordons to receive and mount their Kangaroos. Once mounted, the battalion drove through the traffic to a concentration area east of Rocquancourt in preparation for their dismounted attack on Secqueville. Colonel Cumming-Bruce recounted:

> Time was very limited and no detailed reconnaissance was possible except by myself [the Commanding Officer]. 1 GORDONS moved on foot to an assembly area at LORGUICHON Wood and eventually joined up with the tanks and Crocodiles on the start line at GARCELLES SECQUEVILLE as the attack started.

In addition to the Crocodiles, as indicated above, they were belatedly joined here by the Shermans of 148 Regt RAC and a platoon of 4.2in mortars from the divisional machine-gun battalion 1/7 Middlesex. Of the Germans' 272nd Infantry Division, a fair amount was known:

> The enemy was known to be holding the village and was also dug in between the latter and GARCELLES SECQUEVILLE. Reports during the morning had shown considerable enemy movement in the vicinity of SECQUEVILLE [LA-CAMPAGNE] and woods to the East ... stiff opposition was expected. Luckily the heavy enemy shelling of GARCELLES slackened as the battalion formed up, and only sporadic fire and one particularly accurate defensive fire concentration were met during the advance.

The plan was for two companies of Gordons, with a squadron of tanks in close support, to advance astride the road and go straight into the village, leaving D Company and the Crocodiles to mop up patches of wood in

The 1 Gordons' attack on Secqueville-la-Campagne.

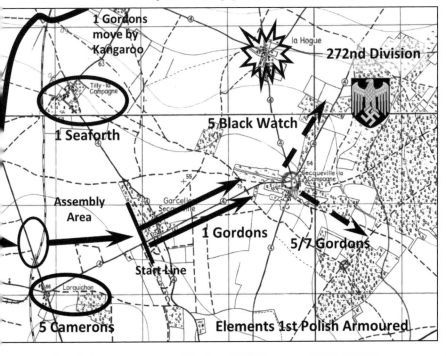

front of the village. The other two squadrons of 148 Regt RAC were to provide flank protection and direct fire support as necessary.

During planning, a 'through artillery programme was laid on to deal with the surrounding area, La Hougue in particular', but at the time the attack was launched only a single field regiment was actually available. This was due to the dislocation of the artillery and its ammunition supply caused by the bombing and the demands for fire from the armoured divisions who were in action further forward.

In B Squadron, 141 Regt's war diary there is an example of poor battle procedure that led to difficulties during the attack:

> Major Ryle went to tie up with the Inf Comd at 1400 hrs but owing to a protracted O Group he was not himself able to hold one until 1610 and with a 1630 H hr the Tps were not able to mate up properly with their opposite numbers. This may account for some of the subsequent confusion.[5]

Another factor in the 'confusion' was that the rear echelons of the Polish Armoured Division, whose exact location was not known by the Gordons, were reported in the area between Garcelles-Secqueville and the objective. Consequently, timed fire missions were only fired from H-Hour onwards on the village itself. The B Squadron war diary describes the resulting 'general melee':

> The Poles chaffing at the leash had been released over their start line . . . and off they went gleefully rubbing their hands in anticipation, so the whole attack was a gleeful pandemonium of Polish tanks, 148 RAC and Crocodiles milling around with the infantry 'hither and thithering' with the greatest calm and gaiety!

Major Martin Lindsay, the Gordons' second-in-command,[6] was leading the battalion forward to join the CO and the company commanders in the woods at Garcelles-Secqueville. He wrote:

> As soon as I could I turned off [the road] and across a field, five hundred fighting men well dispersed following behind me. Then I heard the awful groaning of Moaning Minnies and looked around to hear the crack and see the burst as some twenty smackers landed just about where we had left the main road. But as luck would have it they came down between two companies.

The attack got under way but in the confusion the leading Crocodile troops found themselves up with the leading companies and their 6 Troop had to be called forward from reserve to support D Company in the clearance of the woods. Meanwhile Major Lindsay, waiting in Garcelles to bring up the battalion's anti-tank guns and mortars, was trying to read the battle:

> There seemed to be a good deal of shelling coming both ways and I couldn't tell what was happening. So I nipped back and got a carrier

Canadian Jeep ambulance used to evacuate casualties from Regimental Aid Posts.

and ran up to see Harry [Cumming-Bruce]. I found him with his Tac HQ at a hedge junction just short of Secqueville-la-Campagne. The earth all around was burnt out by our flame-throwers. He told me that all the companies except one were on their objectives and that I should bring up the anti-tank guns, but that the most important thing was to see to the evacuation of our wounded who were now going back in Jeeps, some sitting up, others lying on stretchers.

Colonel Cumming-Bruce recorded that:

The support from the artillery concentrations, mortar fire and Crocodiles was very effective, and although the enemy in the village fought hard, all objectives had been captured by 1800 hours, an hour after the attack started. Sixty-five prisoners from 1055 GR were captured and many more had been killed during the action. Patrols pushed out along the tracks through the woods to the East, but few enemy were seen.

In the meantime, the other two battalions of the brigade had moved up in the available Kangaroos and as one was committed, the next took its place.

5 BW passed through 1 Gordons and cleared the small wood to the north-east of Secqueville-la-Campagne and occupied La Hougue, followed by 5/7 Gordons who advanced into the wood from the south-east of the village and by 2100 hours had cleared a substantial part of it.

The 4th Canadian Armoured Division

It could be said that the Poles had advanced 'impetuously' but the reverse was true of Major General Kitching's tanks. Based on briefings by fellow armoured commanders on their experiences, particularly during Operation SPRING, caution was their watchword. Another difference was that while the Poles had run into ad hoc positions in difficult terrain around Mesnil-Robert, the Canadians faced the Germans' layered defence in more open country. This stretched back from Cintheaux to the high ground around Haut-Mesnil and on to the area encompassing Quesnay Woods, Point 195 and the River Laison. Here time had been granted to *Kampfgruppe* Krause to deploy and dig in.

The plan that General Kitching developed was based on the necessity for a speedy capture of the self-same high ground that the Germans were busily occupying and en route, the villages of Cintheaux, Haut-Mesnil, along with its large quarry, and Bretteville-le-Rabet. With Bretteville-sur-Laize, beyond the right flank being the objective of 5 Cdn Bde (2nd Canadian Division's Phase One reserve), there was only a frontage of at the most 3,000 yards and as little as 500 yards at some points for the division to deploy on, and Kitching's options were further limited by the German defences in the villages. Experience had shown from Operation GOOD-WOOD onwards that tanks attempting to bypass villages in broad daylight would lose heavily in the process. The solution was a compromise. Both

Tanks of the 4th Canadian Armoured Division at the beginning of Phase Two.

Buildings of the Haut-Mesnil Quarry on fire.

Kitching's brigades would advance together; the infantry capturing the villages and also taking over ground seized by 4 Cdn Armd Bde, with the area up to and including Haut-Mesnil subsequently being handed over to the following 3rd Canadian Division. This would release 10 Cdn Bde to move on to the objectives on the high ground. To assist 4 Cdn Armd Bde maintain momentum, following the example of the previous night, Kitching mounted the Alq R (detached from 10 Cdn Bde) in a variety of half-tracks and armoured cars, which it was intended would speedily deliver the infantry to Bretteville-le-Rabet, some 4.5 miles beyond the start line. Once relieved, 10 Cdn Bde, now following in the wake of 2 Cdn Armd Bde, was to take over Bretteville-le-Rabet and resume command of the Alq R.

The plan was, however, poorly disseminated and coordinated, as the rush to get the operation going on the night of 7/8 August had in many cases precluded proper battle procedure at brigade level and below. Most of the twenty-four hours had been spent in those painfully slow moves to concentration areas, with 4 Cdn Armd Bde regrouping from I Corps. It is quite clear from the war diaries that there were different understandings of, for instance, Brigadier Booth's 4 Cdn Armd Bde plan. The key part of that plan rested with Halpenny Force based on the three tank squadrons of Lieutenant Colonel Halpenny's Grenadier Guards of Canada (Grenadiers) and the four rifle companies of the Lake Superior Regiment (LSR), which was the brigade's motor battalion. They formed three company/squadron groups, with the fourth infantry company in reserve and were supported by a self-propelled anti-tank battery and flail tanks. This single battle group believed it was to secure in sequence Bretteville-le-Rabet, Point 195 and finally Point 206, some 12,000 yards from their start line; a very tall order for the combat power of a single battle group. This raises questions as to whether this was what Brigadier Booth really intended unless, of course, he was expecting negligible opposition following the bombing.

The attack got off to a slow start with the leading elements of Brigadier Jefferson's 10 Cdn Bde becoming entangled with the Royals of the 2nd Canadian Division who were heading down from Point 122 to join A Squadron, Sherbrooke Fusiliers in Gaumesnil once the bombing had finished. This and the other factors already discussed, coupled with the

The 4th Canadian Division's Phase Two.

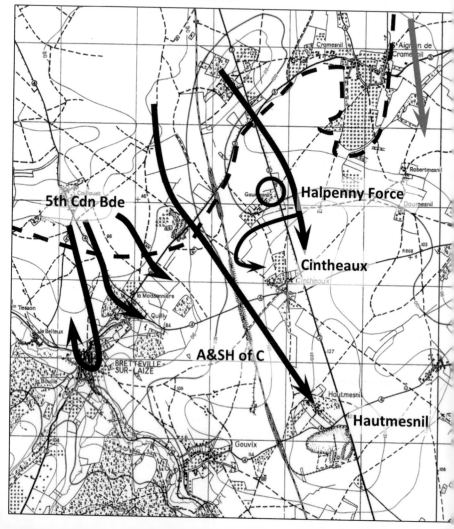

expected weight of artillery support being conspicuously absent, meant that the attack began tentatively. In the case of the 4th Canadian Armoured Division, the effects of the bombing were compounded by poor radio communications. With all these sundry difficulties General Kitching's division was in fact having to 'thread the eye of a needle' through the 2nd Canadian Division's units, without adequate indirect fire support. The general explained: 'At the time, my division was accused of being slow in getting to our start line ... because of our very restricted frontage, had only about 500 yards in which to manoeuvre. This was the normal frontage for a squadron to operate in.'

Another reason for the cautious advance was that in moving up, virtually every unit had lost tanks along with other vehicles to mines. It is often said that there were none but in the case of the Canadian Grenadier Guards alone they lost three tanks. Their war diary records: 'On the way down two of No. 1 Sqn's tanks (Sgt Walker and Cpl Brookes) went up on mines near Rocquancourt, later it was found that one of No. 2 Sqn's was similarly lost.'

While this was a small cost in comparison to what was to come, losses before actually getting into the fighting have a disproportionate effect on levels of caution. The Grenadiers make another point in their war diary: 'On reaching Rocquancourt No.1 Sqn deployed and experienced difficulty proceeding due to traffic especially at Rocquancourt where it was running nose to tail across the main rd.'

Eventually they were through and advancing south from Point 122. Colonel Halpenny's leading squadron of the Grenadiers came under fire from Cintheaux as they passed to the east of Gaumesnil, where Wittmann's Tigers had been knocked out. This village was the objective of the Argyll and Sutherland Highlanders of Canada (A&SH of C) the South Alberta Regiment (SAR)[7] but they were still on their start line. Consequently, the Grenadiers' No. 1 Squadron commanded by Major Amy was brought to a halt with the familiar black smoke pouring from Shermans:

> On arrival at 077556 Major Amy reported four Panther tks burning in the fd to the east of the main rd. These had been shot up, it is believed, by our Typhoons.[8] Maj Amy attempted a left flanking move skirting the town [Cintheaux] but was held up by 88 fire from the wood [around Gaumesnil Farm] Lt Smith reported seeing a Panther pulling out to the east. He opened fire, but was hit himself, wounded and his tk set in flames. At this point it was considered that No. 1 Sqn had been weakened too much to make cracking of the CINTHEAUX defences practicable.

The remains of the squadron and Major Radley-Walters' in Gaumesnil were to give covering fire, while No. 3 Squadron was brought up and looped around across the open ground to the east but in doing so they

A typical SS soldier wearing a camouflage smock and helmet cover.

came under anti-tank fire. The war diary recorded that 'It was appreciated that progress to the east of the town was impossible since it was open ground covered by 88 fire from both sides.' In the absence of the crushing weight of the 720 guns assembled for the operation, the twenty-odd Shermans firing 75mm HE was a poor substitute, especially as they were fighting their own battle of survival.

By late afternoon the lack of progress infuriated senior commanders and the airwaves reverberated with demands for movement and action, but such was the state of communications within the 4th Division that General

Kitching had to get in his Jeep and find the tactical headquarters of Brigadier Booth, commanding 4 Cdn Armd Bde:

> I had the greatest difficulty in locating him and he would not answer calls on the radio. When I finally found him, he was nearly two miles away from the battle and fast asleep in his tank. I personally had to climb up on the tank to wake him and tell him to go and see what was happening. I was so angry that I ordered him out of the tank and gave him a tongue-lashing for five minutes. He was almost in tears when he went forward.

The resulting exhortations for his leading battle groups to get moving were largely fruitless, as these messages recorded in 4 Cdn Armd Bde's signals log record:

> 1617 You are reporting no opposition so push on. If there is opposition then I should know about it.
> 1702 Fetch Sunray [radio nickname for a commanding officer], what is hold up? Push on ... no opposition in front – yet the going is very slow. I am not waiting any longer ...
> 1736 Put Sunray on set. Put Sunray on set. Get Sunray immediately!

Meanwhile, Major Smith of the Grenadiers' No. 3 Squadron was pinned down and dispatched a troop back and around to the west of Gaumesnil. Using the shape of the ground, Lieutenant Phelan's Shermans were able to work their way into a position from where they could engage the German anti-tank gunners whose attention was firmly fixed on the open ground to the east. The Grenadiers' war diary gives an account of this remarkable action:

> ... having observed flashes from the corner of the orchard, at 079543, Lt Phelan fired HE and advanced, finding he had shot up an 88mm gun. Moving around the north of the orchard, he winged a 2cm gun in the corner, and moving across to the bldgs at 078540 he got two more 2cms. With his tp covering his advance, he dashed across to 075535 which appeared to be a prepared posn of some kind. Across the open stretch he was fired on by 88s from the hedge running SW from CINTHEAUX. This hedge was plastered with HE and co-ax by his tp sgt and it was found to contain three 88mm and one 2cm all of which were knocked out. On going over the mound at 075536 he saw 3 SP guns, two immediately to his front and one withdrawing at 075531. All three were fired on and halted; one of these at 075536 going up on impact with a tremendous flash. Joined by the rest of his tp he proceeded to round up prisoners, and whilst dismounted so doing another SP gun exploded killing one man and wounding five others. Not daunted they nevertheless rounded up 28 POW. About 15 dead men were counted around the gun posns. Two of his tks had become cas. A Coy of the

See map on p. 194

A & SH (Maj Farmer) arrived on the scene, and they took over the job of mopping up the town.

Running amok, Lieutenant Phelan's troop claimed to have knocked out eleven guns and *Sturmgeschütz* but the Halpenny Force had lost seventeen tanks. For this action Phelan was awarded the Military Cross and Sergeant Hurwitz received a Military Medal.

An armoured attack on a village rarely equates to capturing it but in this case 'After a short mortar preparation' the Argylls' A and D companies, supported by C Squadron of the SAR, only took 'a few minutes' to clear and secure Cintheaux between 1800 and 1816 hours. The war diary records that 'The Germans left in the town were too dazed by the artillery and aerial bombardments to put up much opposition. About 42 prisoners were taken, most of them from A/Tk units.'

At some stage the war diary of the 2nd Battalion, SS Panzer Regiment 12 records that the three Tigers that survived the earlier counter-attack were withdrawn from the Cintheaux area before they were enveloped and cut off.

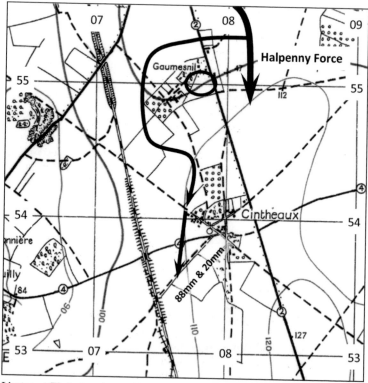

Lieutenant Phelan's action at Cintheaux.

One of the Cintheaux StuGs knocked out by the main road being passed later in the battle by the armoured cars of the 3rd Canadian Division.

During the action to capture Cintheaux with a very narrow front and with overlapping and interlocking enemy anti-tank fire dominating the open ground to the east of the village, the two battle groups, Halpenny and the Argylls, became tangled on the even narrower front to the west. This took some time to sort out and may have contributed to Colonel Halpenny's subsequent decisions.

As late as 1900 hours Brigadier Booth ordered his two leading battle groups on to the next objectives. Two companies of Argylls, supported by the tanks of the SAR, were to advance on foot and together take Haut-Mesnil, described as 'a scattering of buildings about a huge quarry', while the tanks of Halpenny's Grenadiers and the infantry of the LSR were to motor on to seize Bretteville-le-Rabet.

By the time it would have been possible to get moving, Colonel Halpenny decided it would be dark and therefore he ordered the tanks of the Grenadiers Guards of Canada to leaguer-up near Cintheaux for the night. The three hours of daylight that remained may have been enough to advance the 4 miles to Point 195 but probably not to complete its capture and consolidation. Colonel Halpenny chose not to risk the operation and instead start at dawn on 9 August. The Argylls, however, advanced the mile on foot to Haut-Mesnil but here they were brought to a halt by stiff enemy resistance. The village was the location of the headquarters of the 1st Battalion, 25th SS Panzergrenadiers.

Untersturmführer Willi Klein, Waldmüller's adjutant, having established the battalion headquarters just south of the Cauvicourt-Gouvix road prior to the attack, had set about preparing an ad hoc defence of Haut-Mesnil

The Haut-Mesnil Quarry today.

An SS machine-gun crew with their MG-34 mounted on a Lafette tripod.

Untersturmführer **Willi Klein.**

with soldiers of the battalion's command company. These were supplemented by rounding up, reputedly by force, men of the 89th Division who were making their way south towards Falaise. In addition, batteries of 88mm guns had been brought up and sited either side of the Caen-Falaise road.

The war diary of II Battalion, SS Panzer Regiment 12 records that tanks were present as well: 'We collected the retreating infantry of the *Wehrmacht*, and the established positions south of Haut-Mesnil; 2 Panzer IVs and 5 Panther Vs also arrived here.'

The Argylls had attacked with two companies and had secured a foothold in the northern outskirts of the village but when the SAR's Shermans attempted to envelope the Haut-Mesnil village and quarry they came under anti-tank fire and were busy fighting for their lives rather than supporting the Argylls. The commanding officer of the 23rd Field Regiment, in direct support, commented that '... during these actions we never received one request for fire support and we began to think we were just along for the ride'. The fire of twenty-four 25-pounders could have made all the difference, blasting the infantry and tanks onto their objectives. Inexperience was repeatedly showing at every level, and questions the effectiveness of pre-invasion all-arms training in the 4th Canadian Armoured Division.

The attack after a two-hour fight ground to a halt and 'The company commander decided that the quarry was too large to risk a one-company attack on it during the night. Accordingly, 'B' Company was ordered to contain it during the dark and enter and capture it at first light.'

The Argylls had an uncomfortable night with the enemy at close quarters while the tanks pulled back to a safe leaguer.

Bretteville-sur-Laize

Meanwhile, during the afternoon it was the 2nd Canadian Division who took on responsibility for the capture of Bretteville-sur-Laize in Simonds' revised Phase Two plan. The attack by 5 Cdn Bde was delayed until mid-afternoon as the artillery was still firing in support of 6 Cdn Bde's attacks on May and Fontenay. The Calgary Highlanders (right) and *Le Régiment de Maisonneuve* (left) attacked from Caillouet, the battalions being supported by tanks of A and B squadrons of the 1st Hussars respectively. The advance was across more than a mile of open terrain, with the tanks supporting them from cover on the high ground forward of Caillouet. The advance through smouldering wheat, much to the surprise of the battalions, was not contested by enemy infantry or the artillery but the war diary records concern over 'evil-looking woods' to the flanks.

The Maisies cleared the houses to the north of Bretteville as far as the hamlet of Ouilly and Point 84 from where they and the supporting tanks were able to cover the descent of two of the Calgary Highlanders' companies through the wood into the ruins of the village. The enemy infantry of the 89th Division were few, but put up a fight that required them to be cleared out and supporting tanks helped destroy a number of machine-gun positions in and beyond the village. With a handful of prisoners, the rifle companies began to dig in by around 1630 hours.

If the capture of Bretteville had been easy, the Germans woke up to the fact and as Canadian support and logistic vehicles came forward they were engaged from the wooded hillside west of the river and suffered more casualties than during the capture of the village. Lieutenant Colonel Mac-Laughlan's carrier was engaged and destroyed, but a tank was brought up to silence the enemy position.

After going around Bretteville coordinating its defence, Colonel Mac-Laughlan requested permission to withdraw from the village onto 'dominating high ground to the north'. The reason has never been adequately explained, but following his experience during Operation SPRING the commanding officer probably felt exposed and isolated and managed to persuade Brigadier Megill that this was the case. Consequently, with brigade permission, the Calgary Highlanders' four rifle companies left the village but German artillery forward observation officers spotted them. Lieutenant Ed Ford recalled:

We had been taught never to be caught on a forward slope in daylight and at Bretteville we were ordered to come back up over that slope. We were fired upon and we got a lot of casualties and ... had to help evacuate the wounded ... I could never understand how anybody could order a battalion up over the brow of a hill in broad daylight.

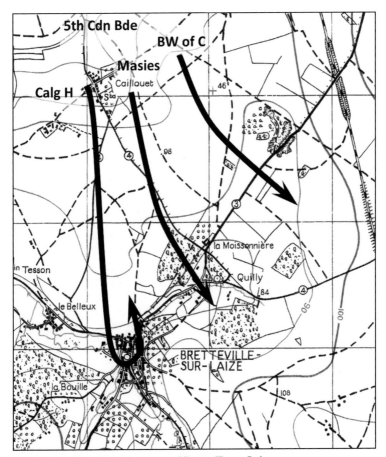

The 5th Canadian Brigade's capture of Bretteville-sur-Laize.

Caught in the open, the battalion suffered 3 officers and 31 other ranks wounded and 8 ORs killed in this withdrawal.

Meanwhile, the Black Watch had come up on the left of the Maisies and dug in around a small Quarry and eastwards towards the railway line.

Conclusion

For the Canadians the day of 8 August 1944 was not to be a re-run of 'the Black Day of the German Army' in 1918, but before looking at it from their perspective it is worth looking at the German. General Eberbach reported the situation to *Feldmarschall* von Kluge at 2100 hours:

> I SS Panzer Corps has established a defensive line of Pak [anti-tank guns] and Flak, which it has held until now. It is questionable if this

199

line can be held tomorrow when the enemy attacks in earnest. The new division [the 89th] has practically been reduced to 50 per cent, the same holds true for the HJ. I would be happy if I could assemble twenty panzers tonight.

Von Kluge replied, 'We have to accept the fact that the decisive time will be tomorrow or the day after.'

Even though *Standartenführer* Kurt Meyer makes much of how few troops and how little resources he had, it is quite clear that the Germans

Feldmarschall **von Kluge and General Eberbach.**

had at the crucial times and places sufficient men and equipment to present serious resistance. The Canadian official history records that 'The 2nd Division reported that during the day it had encountered strong resistance from an 88-mm. Gun screen manned by G.A.F. ground troops. III Flak Corps had arrived and was making itself felt.' In confirmation the Fifth Panzer Army's evening situation report at 2125 hours recorded that 'General Pickert states that south of Langannerie [south of Bretteville-sur-Laize] an 8.8cm. tank trap has been constructed. In addition, he has also ordered forward a flak *Kampfgruppe* from the Orne.'

In addition, the *Hitlerjugend*'s divisional history, written by its chief of staff *Obersturmbannführer* Hubert Meyer states that forward of the *Luftwaffe* guns, those of *Flakabteilung* 12, were in position astride Bretteville-le-Rabet. There was by the evening of 8 August a powerful blocking position in place based on the most capable anti-tank gun of the day.

For General Simonds his expectations following the singular success of the night advance had been dashed and he summed up the afternoon's operations on the ground in 1947:

> Phase II did not go off with the bang we had hoped and there were, I think, three or four contributory factors. I had stressed very strongly to the two armoured divisional commanders that, when the time came for them to pass through, they were to take up the battle regardless of the position reached by the infantry divisions. In other words, there was to be no quibbling about whether they should wait until one of the infantry divisions had taken some part of their final objective. At that stage we had two AGRAs each of five medium regiments, one in support of each armoured division. All likely targets on the flanks and front had been carefully registered and given code names. In order to keep the tempo going, I again stressed to the armoured divisional

An 88mm dual-purpose anti-aircraft/tank gun of the type issued to III Flak Corps.

commanders that they must not get involved in probing out the position before they called down fire or the fighter bombers. Neither did so and this was one of the reasons why the pass through was rather sticky. In the case of the Polish Armd Div, this was largely a question of language difficulty and we hadn't the understanding that we built up later on.

The final factor was what General Simonds described as 'roadboundness':

This was an inevitable failure of training in England, where it is very difficult to get away from the roads. There were cases where there was all the room in the world to deploy across country but nevertheless the armour kept to the road and, in due course met the anti-tank gun sited to cover it. It must be borne in mind that both these divisions were in action for the first time and my remarks have not been made in any sense of reflection. They both did extremely well, but had they been in the form they reached two weeks later they would have gone straight through.

NOTES

1. There were in effect two H-Hours: 1100 hours when the armour started to move forward from the start line south of the villages and outskirts of Caen to conduct their passage of lines, and the beginning of the attack proper at 1335, after the bombers had engaged targets progressively further south between 1300 and 1345 hours and the bombs were falling well beyond the bomb line.
2. Enemy flak hit the lead aircraft of a squadron of the 351st Bomber Group which caused the release mechanism to activate and the rest followed their leader.
3. Craven, *The Army Air Forces in World War II*, vol. III (Chicago, 1951). The casualties were, of course, far greater than quoted.
4. The Sherman was referred to as the 'Tommy Cooker' by the Germans and the 'Ronson' by the Allies because it lit 'first time and every time'. The reason is often said to be petrol ignition but diesel versions suffered equally badly from 'brewing'. The problem was not solved until wet ammunition stowage was introduced in the autumn of 1944.
5. An enduring rule of battle procedure is that a commander takes one-third of the time available for his planning and orders, leaving two-thirds for his subordinates down the chain of command for their own planning and preparations.
6. Major Lindsay had been commanding officer of 8 Para but prior to D-Day he had left Bigot Top Secret papers unattended while he went to the lavatory. He was reported by his second-in-command Terence Otway, sacked and replaced by Otway. Major Lindsay served with distinction throughout the campaign with his regiment, the Gordon Highlanders.
7. The South Albertas was the divisional recce regiment, but in this case it was being used as a conventional armoured unit. At this early stage of the battle it is hard to see what it could have done on such a narrow front and with the Germans in their layered defence. Their recce task would have begun once the breakthrough had been completed.
8. There were no reported fighter bomber sorties over the immediate battle area because of air space deconfliction measures.

Chapter Nine

The Second Day of TOTALIZE

For the headquarter staff of both armies there was little sleep during the night of 8/9 August 1944; the Canadians and Poles in the armoured divisions planned and organized a resumption of the offensive, while the Germans struggled to establish a coherent defensive line with which to contain the coming attack. Meanwhile, for the soldiers who were to be pitched into the renewed battle there was only a few hours of fitful dozing at best.

At 2100 hours on 8 August, contrary to armoured doctrine that had seen Colonel Halpenny, for instance, bringing operations to a halt three full hours before dusk, General Simonds ordered the attack to continue overnight. General Maczek in his operational report, however, wrote that the armoured regiments had pulled back at dusk and that '3 Rifle Bde took over the sector and protected it for the night (the Bde was to have executed a night attack, which "was not realized").' The reason for the attack on *Kampfgruppe* Waldmüller being 'not realized' was that the Germans had been seen pulling back from the Mesnil-Robert area at last light as a part of the general rebalancing of their defences across the front.

The Defenders

During the evening *Feldmarschall* von Kluge had authorized the release of elements of other panzer divisions to I SS Panzer Corps, but commanders argued that they were either so weakened in strength or locked in battle that they were not available. Consequently, II SS Panzer Corps was ordered to dispatch the thirteen operational Tigers of 102 *Schwere* Panzer Battalion across the River Orne to join the *Hitlerjugend*'s defence on the road to Falaise. Additional guns from III Flak Corps were also being moved from other parts of Normandy to bolster the defence.

The remarkably concise orders issued by the *Hitlerjugend*'s (chief of staff), *Oberführer* Hubert Meyer, were a mixture of confirmation and adjustment of those issued the previous morning:

Kampfgruppe Waldmüller (reinforced I/25) will defend itself on the hills north of Maizières, north of Rouvres to Hill 140 inclusive, northwest of Assy. For this, *1. Kompanie SS-Panzerjägerabteilung* 12 will be attached to it;

Kampfgruppe Krause (reinforced I/26) will defend itself in the sector of the hills north of Ouilly–Hill 183 at the Route Nationale;

III/26 [*Sturmbannführer* Olboeter] will defend itself on the high terrain around Hill 195 (3km north-west of Potigny) and will absorb all arriving stragglers of 89 Inf-Div;

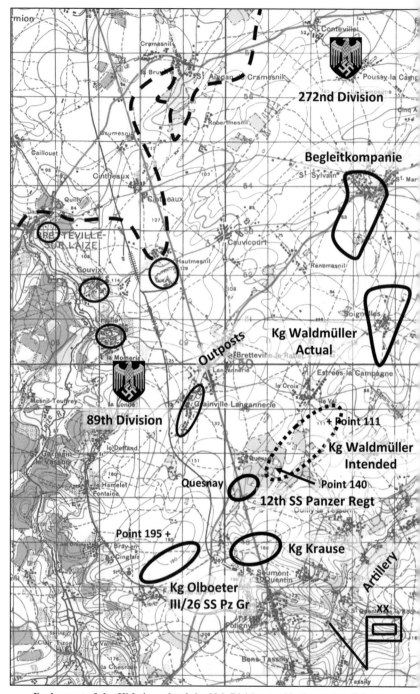

Deployment of the *Hitlerjugend* and the 89th Division astride the road to Falaise.

Panzerregiment 12 [*Obersturmbannführer* Max Wünsche] with attached heavy SS-*Panzerabteilung* 102 will assemble in the Quesnay forest (2km north-west of Ouilly). From there, it will carry out limited attacks to enable the setting-up of the defences and prevent a breakthrough by enemy tank forces along the Route Nationale.

The war diary of Panzer Regiment 12 records that overnight 'the assigned Panzer VI (Tiger) tanks were withdrawn from their positions south of Haut-Mesnil in order to establish new positions eastwards at Soignolles.' These are believed to be the three surviving Tigers of 101 *Schwere* Panzer Battalion plus another three from repair:

> *Artillerieregiment* 12 with attached *Werferabteilung* 12 will take up position south of the Laison in such a manner that it can go into action anywhere in the sector of the Division;
>
> *Flakabteilung* 12 will take up positions along the Route Nationale north of Potigny with the two 8.8cm batteries so that it can destroy enemy tanks which have broken through. The 4 *Batterie* (3.7cm) and the attached 14/26 (2cm) are available for air defence.

Note: During the night, *Flakabteilung* 12 and elements of III Flak Corps in action at Bretteville-le-Rabet on the western flank exchanged positions:

> *Aufklarungsgruppe* [Reconnaissance] Wienecke will establish and maintain contact with 272. Inf-Div;
>
> The *Divisionsbegleitkompanie* [Escort Company] will leave *Kampfgruppe* Waldmüller and assemble in Montboit (1.5km east of Ouilly) as Divisional reserve;
>
> The Divisional command post will remain at La Brèche-au-Diable [buildings in some broken country near Tombeau de Marie Joly].

Well before dawn available elements of the *Hitlerjugend* were assembled, having overnight occupied blocking positions with the aim of 'holding the line St Sylvain–Bretteville'.

Surviving elements of the 89th Division that had not been co-opted by the *Hitlerjugend* were, according to Hubert Meyer, concentrated west of the Caen-Falaise road.

II Canadian Corps' Plans

General Simonds' requirement was for his armoured divisions to press on and take their objectives and not to give the Germans an opportunity to regroup, but these formations lacked the training and experience to do this quickly or effectively at night. In the case of the 4th Canadian Armoured Division, General Kitching ordered Brigadier Booth to secure Bretteville and Point 195. Halpenny's battle group was to advance past the toehold in Haut-Mesnil held by the Argylls of Canada and secure Bretteville-le-

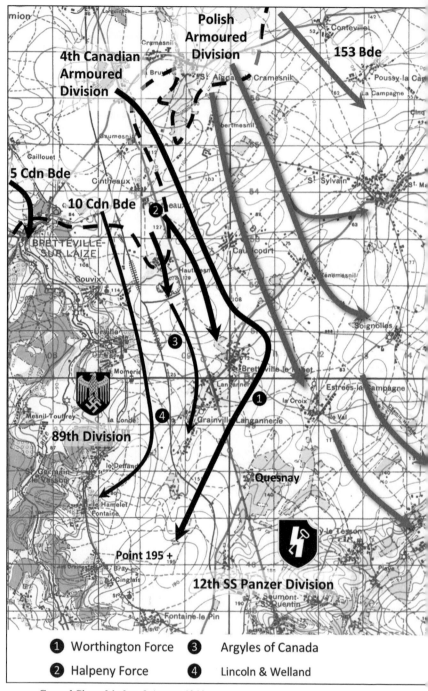

General Simonds' plan, 9 August 1944.

Rabet, leaving the Argylls to secure the Quarry area. This would enable another battle group, the Worthington Force, to go on past the village and seize Point 195 some 7,300 yards deep in the German position. This was to be completed by dawn at the latest and would create the conditions for the seizure of the ridge of high ground north of the River Laison. The remainder of the two armoured divisions were to be prepared to follow, seize that ridge and exploit towards Falaise. It was soon clear that the Poles would not be able to advance until after first light.

The Worthington Force

Lieutenant Colonel Worthington, the commanding officer of the British Columbia Regiment (BCR) was the overall commander of the force that consisted of his three squadrons of Shermans and two infantry companies of the Algonquin Regiment, B and C, plus the usual attachments. He was summoned to a brigade O Group (orders group) at midnight where Brigadier Booth gave his revised plan to the two battle groups. Worthington returned to his headquarters and formulated his own plan and gave his orders to squadron and company commanders at 0130 hours.

These orders were apparently given in a confident manner with the expectation of light opposition around Point 195, mainly from second-rate troops, but the regimental intelligence officer, Lieutenant Jenkinson, recalled that this concealed his colonel's concerns about the operation:

> Col. Worthington commented quietly and off the record about the changes in the original plan. He recounted the Principles of War and how so many of them had been violated and that we would need luck if we were to 'bring it off'.

The essence of Colonel Worthington's orders was recalled by one of the company commanders, Major Monk:

> We will likely be beyond our artillery support but may have some air co-operation. The Algonquin Regiment is under command. The Brigadier's intention is to seize the high ground feature, spot height 195 ... My intention is to seize and hold this feature until the rest of our troops can reach us.

> Method – we will move out of this harbour [near Point 122], cross the highway ... about 300 yards south of where we are now, pass through the Lake Superiors [Halpenny Force's infantry around Cintheaux] who are dug in at this point, advance south on the east side of the highway, taking advantage of ground until opposite the objective, then re-cross the highway and assault the hill from the south-east.

Assembled in a column adjacent to the Caen-Falaise road, the Worthington Force started moving at 0230 hours led by C Squadron. The first opposition encountered was machine-gun fire from a wooded hedge just east of

Cintheaux. These were probably elements of the 89th Division that had not been properly cleared by the SAR and the Argylls. After a delay of about twenty minutes while the hedgerow was cleared, the column moved on but in less than a mile was again engaged, this time from Cauvi-court Church at a range of some 700 yards. Opposition became stiffer as they passed into the gap between Haut-Mesnil to the west and Cauvicourt to the east. It will be recalled that A and D companies of the Algonquins held the northern part of Haut-Mesnil and the southern part was held by elements of 1st Battalion, 25th SS Panzergrenadier Regiment, under the command of *Untersturmführer* Willi Klein. How-ever, with an armoured battle group bypas-sing him Klein withdrew from Haut-Mesnil before dawn on 9 August and joined the rest of Waldmüller's command near Soignolles.

See map on p. 210

The main problem for Worthington, how-ever, came just beyond Cauvicourt when they were brought under fire from a company of 88mm guns and other flak guns that now covered the flanks of the next village, Brette-ville-le-Rabet. This village was the objective of Halpenny Force, but the lead squadron of Grenadier tanks was only just arriving to the north-west of the village. The sequencing of the operation had broken down when Halpenny's command had been slow getting away from their leaguer north-west of Cintheaux. In the dark, elements of the two battle groups became confused.

Lieutenant Colonel Donald Worthington, the British Columbia Regiment's CO.

As recorded by the adjutant in the war diary, there was a pause while it was decided 'whether we should wait for them to clear the town or not. Then the CO gave the order "Move on anyway, while we still have surprise".' Having disen-tangled themselves, the Worthington Force started to bypass Bretteville and its 88mm guns to the east:

It was so dark I could only see the red back lights of the tank in front. Sometimes we crawled along. Finally, we just stopped and waited for first light. There were breakdowns. My troop pulled out around a broken-down Sherman and promptly got lost – there were too many tank tracks. The Regiment was being led by Lt 'Wing Ding' Wilson –

208

(*Left*) The British Columbia Regiment's cap badge. (*Right*) The Algonquin Regiment's cap badge.

he made a right turn but everyone else turned left – didn't believe 'Wing Ding' could navigate ... that's how we got lost.

Then having swung around the village they came across a broad straight road, which in the dark they mistook for the Caen-Falaise road, the only broad straight road to be seen on the map! This was in fact the old Chemin Haussé built by William the Conqueror and as far as the tank commanders were concerned it seemed to be heading in the right direction and they turned right on it, as if they were heading to Falaise.

For a formation that habitually didn't operate at night, with only a new moon and early morning mist rising and unboxed compasses that didn't work well near the steel bulk of a tank,[1] this was an easy mistake to make. At 0530 hours, with the silhouette of high ground in front of them seeming to confirm their direction, they pressed on down Chemin Haussé. This was to be the culmination of several errors that set up another of the tragic incidents in Operation TOTALIZE.

The Worthington Force continued south-east for about 3 miles and as recorded by the adjutant of the BCR: 'As we approached ... we sighted enemy soft skin vehicles, armoured cars, and half-tracks. These were duly shot up as we proceeded and many of the enemy were killed.'

In the dark the column had achieved surprise and driven straight through scattered elements of *Kampfgruppe* Waldmüller. Other small groups of enemy troops were engaged before, as expected, the road started to climb uphill onto a ridge in the first light of dawn. First up were C Squadron and Worthington's regimental headquarters. They motored to a position south of Point 111, below the crest and a mile to the east of the wooded Point 140. They took up position in a hedged paddock, and at 0655 hours

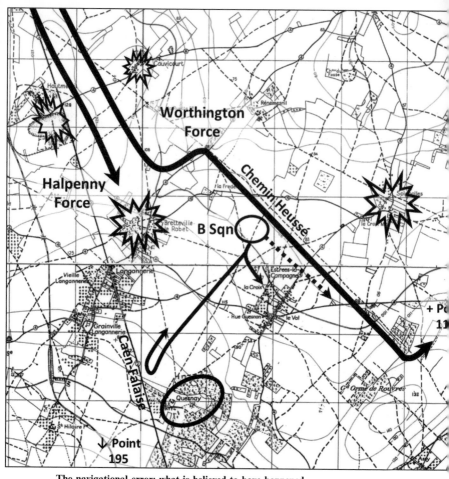

The navigational error: what is believed to have happened.

signalled Brigadier Booth that they had reached Point 195 and that there was 'No evidence of enemy occupation – but recent signs. Few lorries destroyed, slit trenches and tools about. We are holding until our friends come fwd [forward] to consolidate.'

Meanwhile, further back down the column which had inevitably become split up, the officer commanding B Squadron, Major Carson, realized that he was in the wrong place and was to the north of Estrées-la-Campagne. While poring over his maps, one of the Algonquin companies caught up and a platoon was dispatched to check out Estrées, which they reported clear of enemy. Major Carson had already sent a troop off to Point 195 and was just about to lead the rest of B Squadron off when Colonel Worthington came on the radio and ordered him to 'advance to high ground in front'. There was nothing for it but to follow the distinctive Sherman tank tracks up onto the ridge.

The Sherman troop dispatched to Point 195 was well on its way but paused at Point 151, a mile short of the objective. After being on their own for some time, with no sign of the rest of the battle group following, they headed back towards Estrées.

Meanwhile, on his arrival with the rest of the battle group, Major Monk (C Company) realized that 10 Platoon, which had been bringing up the rear, had not followed them. Instead, on being engaged by the enemy they had swung their vehicles at them and charged, debussing on the enemy position, which was centred on a pair of 88mm guns. The twenty-odd *Luftwaffe* gunners were no match for Canadian infantry in full cry and with bayonets fixed. Only five Germans survived being killed or wounded in the brief fight.

The leading squadron and companies had again been lucky to slip through the German blocking position under cover of dawn and a little ground mist, but now in daylight A Squadron of the BCR was caught out in the open by Waldmüller's *Kampfgruppe* in Soignolles and panzers that had come forward to the outskirts of Estrées. Lieutenant John Stock of B Squadron was an onlooker:

> We suddenly saw that A Squadron, which was slightly off to our left, were having a tough time of it. These were the first [of our] Shermans that we had actually seen destroyed in battle. We had seen many films of the 8th Army in action in Africa, with smoke slowly curling out of the turrets of knocked-out tanks, but not so with Shermans.

Canadian Sherman tanks on the move.

When a Sherman was hit by anti-tank fire, particularly from the 88, there seems to be an immediate explosion and flames roared 20 or 30 feet out of the top of the turret. This was followed by two or three explosions of high-octane gas and the high-explosive shells and the ammunition racks exploding. As I watched through binoculars, the first tank that I saw hit ... the whole tank became a roaring torch of flame. Most of the rest of the squadron followed suit.

Only two of A Squadron's tanks survived the devastation to reach Worthington. What had happened?

With the renewed sound of battle, *Obersturmbannführer* Max Wünsche, commander of SS Panzer Regiment 12, had immediately dispatched panzers, probably Mk IVs, north-east from their hides in Quesnay Woods towards Estrées, *Standartenführer* Kurt Meyer had been up before dawn and was at an observation post on the high ground above his divisional headquarters. From there he claims to have seen British armour up on the Hill 140 feature. Getting on to the radio he found that Max Wünsche was aware and had already dispatched a reconnaissance. *Obersturmführer* Meitzel went up onto Point 140 and reported 'There are no German forces

Obersturmbannführer **Max Wünsche.**

212

Pz IV of II Battalion 12th SS Panzer Regiment.

on the hill. There are enemy tanks on the high ground.' Kurt Meyer continued his account:

> Meitzel moved back in his armoured car to gain a more accurate picture of the enemy. As soon as he crossed over the ridge, his car received a hit. He was thrown out of the open turret. He was quickly surrounded by enemy infantry and captured.
>
> Reconnaissance soon clarified the situation. An enemy *Kampfgruppe* had occupied the high ground and dominated the Laison valley with its weapons. That menace had to be eliminated at once if we were to hold the sector for the rapidly approaching 85th *Infanterie* Division ... The situation called for rapid action. The high ground had to belong to us once again.

The high ground east of Point 140, it will be recalled from the *Hitlerjugend*'s orders the previous evening, was to have been held by *Kampfgruppe* Waldmüller. However, with elements of his command scattered across the battlefield from Haut-Mesnil via Cauvicourt to Mesnil-Robert and beyond, he was unable to do more than withdraw them to Soignolles. Allied artillery now restored to its normal efficiency overnight, which made the prospect of withdrawing across open country to the high ground uninviting. The advance of the Worthington Force to Point 111 had, as far as Waldmüller was concerned, cut him off; a situation that would only become worse once the Poles advanced.

While the Germans prepared their counter-attack, up on Point 111, the BCR's B and C squadrons along with the Algonquins' B and C companies prepared their positions in the uneasy quiet, believing that they were near Point 195. This was in fact some 4.5 miles to the south-east. It wasn't just the Worthington Force that believed that they were on Point 195. Based on reports, optimistic reports climbed the chain of command from Brigadier Booth upwards that the Worthington Force had slipped past Bretteville, where the fighting was still going on, to secure their objective.

At this stage Worthington had thirty-one Shermans that were distributed around the rectangular field making use of the limited cover of the bank and hedge. Interspersed were the infantry, who were struggling to dig in in the rocky soil of the ridge, supported by their M5A1 half-tracks, most of which mounted Browning machine guns. The only indirect fire available was from the Algonquins' 3in mortar platoon.

The calm on the ridge did not last long. Kurt Meyer explained the plan and what happened:

Wünsche shouted a few words to his veteran tank crews and pointed to Hill 140. It was our intent to attack with some Tiger tanks from the west and with 15 Panthers from the east. While the [five] Tigers slowly left the woods and approached the ridge, the Panthers rattled down the valley road towards Krause's sector so that they could wheel inward there. During the movement of the two tank groups, the hill came under artillery and mortar fire. Our only 88mm battery waited for targets in vain. The enemy tanks wouldn't venture beyond the ridge. Two Tigers took up firing positions ... They had snuck through the undergrowth unnoticed by the enemy and were on his flank. The first 88mm rounds slammed out of the barrels. Two Shermans exploded noisily. The enemy hammered at the Tigers they had spotted ... The Tigers had chosen to fix the enemy with fire; they exploited their greater firepower. More and more enemy tanks were burning, sending tell-tale smoke into the sky.

With the Worthington Force fixed, the Panthers were making their way around the south of Point 140 and the ridge. Kurt Meyer was with the Tigers when he

... suddenly saw the first Panthers. The enemy tanks were cornered at that point. Death and destruction hit them from the east. Pinning them through superior firepower would guarantee us success! Each thicket and perilous spot was peppered with gunfire. The entire ridge-line was systematically covered. Smoke cloud after smoke cloud merged together. We could hardly believe that each cloud represented a tank's grave. The lack of foot soldiers prevented us from penetrating into the tree-encrusted northern slope of the ridge. Two bicycle companies of the 85.Infanterie Division were expected at any moment.

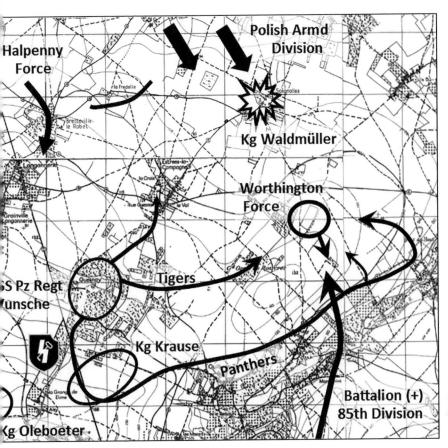

The German counter-attack.

Worthington was not willing to simply await the arrival of the rest of the division but took the battle to the enemy. He ordered a troop of tanks to manoeuvre and bring the enemy under fire from their flank, but in heading down off the high ground the troop was engaged and destroyed. A second and more direct attempt was made at around 0900 hours by two much-reduced troops of B Squadron to clear a wood approximately 400 yards to the south and towards the crest of the ridge, which appeared to be being used by the enemy.

Despite heavy fire, particularly from the Tigers to the right, two Shermans of No. 4 Troop made it to the wood, covered by the fire of No. 3 Troop.[2] Here the pair started to fire main armament HE rounds and machine guns at a series of enemy trenches occupied by leading elements of the 85th Division. Once stationary in the wood, the Tigers were able to engage effectively. One shot skimmed over Lieutenant Stock's tank and smashed into a tree but seconds later another 88mm shot hit the tank, going through its front right side and brewing the tank. The two crewmen

215

in the front of the hull were killed, while the resulting explosion blew the other three out of the turret as they struggled to save themselves. The second tank was hit along with two from squadron headquarters that had come up to join them.

The 1st Battalion12th SS Panzer Regiment records this part of the battle:

> Three panzers took position on the right flank. *Untersturmführer* Fila attacked the enemy from an advantageous firing position and destroyed the four Sherman tanks threatening the left flank, but after this an anti-tank gun on the right flank knocked his tank out.

The de-horsed Canadian crewmen managed to overwhelm some of the German infantry and shelter in their trenches but they were almost surrounded, and most were wounded in some way. Colonel Worthington sent his intelligence officer forward in a half-track to rescue them. Amazingly he made it to the wood and back, while other crewmen crawled back through the standing crops.

At about 1000 hours, with the arrival of the increasing numbers of *Wehrmacht* infantry, the Canadians now faced counter-attack:

> The tanks pushed onto the track in the woods with the bicycle companies of the 85 *Infanterie* Division, which had just arrived, and increasingly pressured the Canadian positions. At that critical juncture and taking advantage of the air attack, SS-*Obersturmführer* Meitzel suggested to his captors that they surrender.

With the infantry now dug in around the hedgerow and enemy mortar fire lifting, they were able to join the surviving tanks in halting the German attack. The enemy withdrew, leaving the ground north of the ridge covered with field-grey heaps. The cost to the Canadians was also high, with half the thirty-one tanks that had reached Point 111 knocked out. In addition, Colonel Hay of the Algonquins was wounded.

The 'air attacks' mentioned by *Standartenführer* Meyer were in fact Allied Typhoons who believed that they were taking on enemy tanks in front of the Poles, who were at that moment still some 3 miles north. Kurt Meyer saw the fighter-bombers overhead and worried that they would go for his tanks, but they must have been attracted by the smoke of burning Shermans near Point 111, as Meyer later wrote:

> The aircraft described a curve and then dived on the Canadian *Kampfgruppe*. They were above us like lightning, making a banking turn and attacked the Canadian battle group. Not a single aircraft attacked a Tiger or a Panther. The hill was covered in the smoke of exploding tanks in a few moments.

The friendly air attack was brief, as yellow smoke grenades were thrown and air marker panels displayed by the BCR. The Typhoons returned to

Typhoons of 198 Sqn RAF on their airfield at Plumetot north of Caen.

the area regularly throughout the day but the German tanks remained in cover for most of the time, so the attacks by the aircraft were speculative and Meyer stated they caused little damage to the panzers.

As casualties mounted it was decided to evacuate the casualties back north in up to six M5A1 half-tracks. According to Meyer, he

> saw two half-tracks break out of the woods and race towards the north at around 1100 hours [1200 Allied time]. One Tiger in my vicinity opened fire, but the vehicles were able to get away. Fire could not be opened against the vehicles until they were far away due to the thick vegetation. According to prisoner statements, one of the half-tracks carried the wounded Lieutenant Colonel A.J. Hay of the Algonquin Regiment.

Meanwhile, the 4th Canadian Division's attempts to locate Worthington Force by radio, for example using artillery fire on known locations around the area where Worthington reported he was, failed. Finally General Kitching, Commander Royal Artillery, took to the air in a spotter aircraft to find the missing battle group, but he and all others who could see and hear the battle on the ridge to their front left assumed it was the Poles in action. Kitching thought that Worthington had overshot and little did anyone think that the missing battle group, who were in contact by radio throughout the day but becoming steadily increasingly difficult to reach, were miles to the east of where they reported they were.

During the course of the afternoon Colonel Worthington decided to send back his last remaining eight mobile tanks. Seven of them made it back to the advancing Poles, leaving those that were 'mobility kills' to continue to support the Algonquin infantry. At about that time the first Canadians surrendered at *Obersturmführer* Meitzel's suggestion. The prisoner, now captor, led about twenty-three men away from what they were convinced was the scene of impending annihilation.

Throughout the afternoon the Germans had continued to launch counter-attacks and close in on the Algonquins. It was during one of these attacks sometime after 1700 hours that Lieutenant Colonel Worthington was killed by a mortar bomb.

A British artillery officer wrote:

> At 1830 hours a strong enemy counter-attack came in. It was met by infantry and tank crews with small-arms fire and grenades. Serious losses were inflicted on the enemy who withdrew. At this stage in the battle I saw one soldier shot through the thigh and with a broken leg still throwing grenades. Every man who was still conscious was firing some type of weapon.

With the commanding officer dead, no sign of relief and no let-up in the counter-attacks, it was decided that once it was dark the survivors would break out north. They were, however, too late as when the last light faded the Germans attacked again. Lieutenant Gartley was one of the few who escaped to report:

> At last light the Germans started to line up an attack to wipe out the remainder of the attacking force that had moved in so boldly that morning. The first information of this was in C Coy area when we heard machine-gun and rifle fire; hence the roars of a tank and the shouting of infantry. Almost simultaneously we heard shouting to our rear as another force was moving in from east to west along the dead ground.

Sturmbannführer **Jürgensen.**

The cost was high. The BCR lost forty-seven tanks, nearly all Shermans in this their first action. Of their crews, forty were killed in action, thirty-eight wounded and thirty-four were taken prisoner. The level of casualties among the Algonquins' infantry was unusually similar, with forty-five killed, thirty-eight wounded and forty-five taken prisoner. Only a handful of survivors exfiltrated down from the ridge and through the German lines to the Poles at Renémesnil.

For the battle against the Worthington Force, *Sturmbannführer* Jürgensen commanding the fifteen *Hitlerjugend* Panthers in action on 9 August on

218

One of the Worthington Force's tanks being examined after the battle.

Point 140 was awarded the Knight's Cross of the Iron Cross. His citation, written by *Standartenführer* Meyer, reads:

> The enemy had broken through the positions of the 89. *Infanterie* Division on the previous day ... *Sturmbannführer* Jürgensen immediately attacked with his tanks. Regained the commanding Hill 140 and brought the enemy to a halt. That made it possible to recapture, as ordered, the positions on most favourable terrain. That in turn made it impossible for the enemy to break through to Falaise.

While a breakthrough to Falaise was not made on 9 August, the Worthington Force did draw in the majority of the available panzers.

Bretteville-sur-Laize

While the 4th Canadian Division was mounting operations down the line of the Caen-Falaise road, the 2nd Canadian Division continued operations on the corps' right or western flank. The Calgary Highlanders had entered the village of Bretteville-sur-Laize on the evening of 8 August but had pulled back to the high ground, losing heavily to enemy artillery in the process. The Canadian TOTALIZE report records:

> The two battalions of 5 Cdn Inf Bde had spent a comparatively quiet night on the high ground on the outskirts of Bretteville-sur-Laize, joined during the hours of darkness by the Black Watch, who occupied a large quarry to the east.
>
> In the morning the Calg Hldrs were ordered to reoccupy the ruins from which they had withdrawn the previous evening. But the retracing of steps was not easy because during the night the enemy [the

89th Division] had anticipated us and had posted his men in commanding positions among shattered houses and broken walls. Deadly fighting ensued, snipers stalking sniper, riflemen exterminating machine-gunner. The tanks were busy too firing at the enemy on the high ground south of the village. But by early afternoon the village was securely in the hands of the Calg Hldrs once more.

The Calgary Highlanders' war diary for 9 August concludes that 'Together with two German officers and 19 other ranks, the battalion could settle down to enjoy a hot meal.'

A well-camouflaged Panther.

The Main Axis South

At the same time the Worthington Force was beginning its odyssey to the south-east before dawn, Lieutenant Colonel Halpenny's leading squadron (No. 2) of the Canadian Grenadier Guards was heading for its objective of Bretteville-le-Rabet on the Caen–Falaise road. About halfway between Cintheaux and Point 195, more or less the same point where the Worthington Force had also come under fire: '... the vanguard of the force became heavily involved. Snipers were everywhere, inflicting severe casualties. The supporting armour went into action and soon succeeded in penetrating the defences.'

Other than the *Luftwaffe* anti-tank guns flanking the village, the defenders of Bretteville were primarily from the 89th Division, probably around 300 strong.

No. 2 Squadron of Grenadiers shot up the village from the flanks, with the regimental war diary recording that 'Considerable speculative shooting was engaged in and tracer bullets were about as thick as snow in a snow-storm.' The Grenadiers' war diary continued:

> Gradually everyone stopped firing, and it was then possible to observe flashes coming from an anti-tk gun at 010501 which was silenced with HE by Lt Grieve. No.1 Sqn then regrouped for the attack on Bretteville, No. 2 Sqn and RHQ returning to their previous harbour at Gaumesnil. The clearing of Bretteville was to be carried out by No. 1 Sqn and a coy of the LSR [Lake Superior Regiment], another coy of the LSR being in reserve.

The infantry of the Lake Superior Regiment, along with the help of the tanks of No. 1 Squadron in close support, broke into the village but

An SS anti-tank gun crew wearing 'peas pattern' camouflage uniforms.

once in, amid the rubble and burning buildings, the fight to secure it had become protracted:

> The initial clearing was done by No.1 Tp under Lt McKinnon who entered covered by the fire of the rest of the sqn from the north of the town. Surprised by 88 fire, Lt McKinnon's tk was brewed up and he was wounded.

The battle against determined opposition forced Lieutenant Colonel Murrel to commit C Company and had to be given D Company of the Algonquins and a company of Argylls as a reinforcement. No. 1 Squadron provided considerable assistance: 'high-explosive rounds against single infantrymen were quite in order and speculative shooting on hedges and houses flushed the enemy infantry who were co-axed by the score.' [Coaxial machine gun mounted alongside a tank's main armament] The whole battalion was required to clear the sizeable village in detail before it was reported clear at 1500 hours.

The Lake Superior Regiment's war diary reports: 'The enemy's losses here were heavy: 200 men of 89 Inf Div were taken prisoner, and scores more were killed.'

The attack on Haut-Mesnil and Bretteville-le-Rabet.

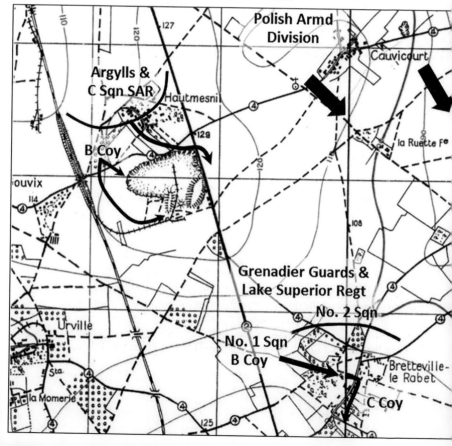

German prisoners of war being marched to the rear.

A mile north of Bretteville, at first light on 9 August, the Argylls who had remained deployed around Haut-Mesnil overnight, fully occupied the village, which had now been evacuated by *Untersturmführer* Willi Klein. Another company of Argylls put in an attack on the quarry south of Haut-Mesnil, supported by the tanks of C Squadron of the South Alberta Regiment (SAR). The area had already been bypassed before dawn by the two armoured battle groups, but to enable 10 Cdn Bde to move on foot (unprotected) through the area and on to the villages beyond Bretteville-le-Rabet, Grainville-Langannerie, etc., another quarry to the west needed to be cleared.

In the Haut-Mesnil quarry were numerous tunnels that had been enlarged by the Germans for the planned storage of V-1, A-9 and A-10 ballistic missiles. During the battle so far, they had been used for shelter, storage and command but the quarry was now the front line. The fighting was over quickly and the quarry cleared during the morning, yielding some twenty-five prisoners as well as many vehicles.

With the quarry secured, with the Lake Superiors gaining the upper hand in Bretteville and at 1200 hours 9 Cdn Bde (3rd Canadian Division)

The Haut-Mesnil Quarry.

taking over Cintheaux and Haut-Mesnil, during the early afternoon General Kitching was able to give orders to Brigadier Jefferson's 10 Cdn Bde. They were instructed to clear the adjoining villages of Langannerie and Grainville-Langannerie, which dominated the route onwards towards Point 195. On receipt of these orders the Shermans of the SAR were re-grouped to support the infantry of the Lincoln & Welland Regiment (L&WR) and the Argylls who would clear the villages.

The L&WR battle group advanced west of the road at 1415 hours, with two companies forward supported by A Squadron of the SAR and passing through the positions of one of the Argylls' companies, which was now to the south of the Haut-Mesnil Quarry. They were followed at 1430 hours by the remainder of the Argylls, with C Squadron of the SAR tanks. Together they attacked the straggling village of Langannerie with the L&WR on the right and the Argylls left, and with the fire of the tanks they broke through the orchards and into the houses.

On the left the attack by the Argylls went well, but on the right the L&WR faced greater obstacles. Their war diary recorded:

A Coy advanced against comparatively light opposition but B Coy met very stiff resistance. C and D Coys advanced through A and B Coys to seize the portion of the town beyond the Church and occupied positions to cover the exits to the town. C Coy had particular difficulty in house to house fighting.

In the process A Squadron, fighting in close support, lost two tanks to mines but even though the pair were no longer mobile they were able to help the infantry with HE and machine-gun fire. The fierce house-to-house fighting with the grenadiers of the 89th Division was helped to a successful conclusion with the aid of rocket-armed RAF Typhoons operating unusually close to their own troops and 'By 1800 hours the village was consolidated.'[3]

Meanwhile, 4 Cdn Armd Bde was to continue its efforts to reach the division's objectives on the high ground. Brigadier Booth's plan was to use the tanks of the Governor General's Foot Guards (GGFG) west of the Caen-Falaise road with the remaining company of Algonquins, namely A Company along with a slice of Support Company, who were to head up on to Point 195.

The 4th Canadian Armoured Division's advance south, the afternoon of 9 August 1944.

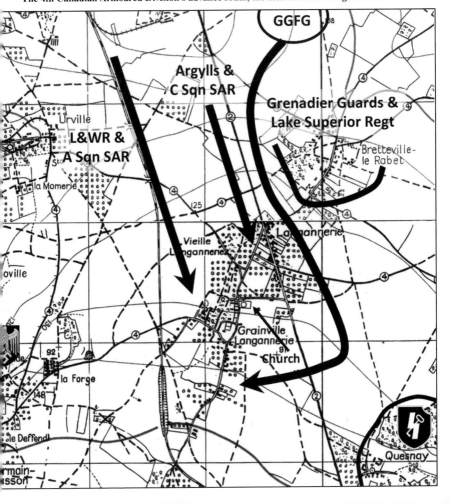

The GGFG battle group orders were issued by Lieutenant Colonel Scott at 1200 hours, reflecting Brigadier Booth's insistence that 'opposition be bypassed and make for Point 195 with all speed'. At this stage it is clear that the GGFG still believed that the Worthington Force was at Point 195 and that they were marching to the relief of the BCR. The situation immediately ahead of them, however, was far from clear. Not only was there the issue of the exact location of the Worthington Force, but also how far south the Canadian infantry had reached and the enemy; where were they and how many? The central issue was who or what was in the Quesnay Woods that lay adjacent to the Caen-Falaise road. To assist the Foot Guards, the armoured cars of A Squadron Manitoba Dragoons would push forward to Point 195 and report.

Originally the battle group was given an H-Hour of 1330 hours but in the event, regrouping of the supporting arms was delayed. However, such was the pressure from above to get moving, the GGFG were forced to set out on their first attack of the campaign at 1430 hours before the well-rehearsed battle procedure and regrouping had been completed. Battle procedure can of course be abbreviated, but it requires experience and attempting it during a unit's first battle is rarely a recipe for success.[4] In this instance, however, the Foot Guards regained some balance as they motored forward. The Grenadiers operating on the open left flank lost four tanks to long-range fire in their approach march from the Gaumesnil area and paused in the open ground between Bretteville and Estrées before advancing again through the woods and villages at the foot of the ridge and on up to the high ground.

Their war diary commented: 'Little resistance was encountered until we reached the gap between BRETTEVILLE-LE-RABET and LANGAN-NERIE. There we encountered enemy A/Tk guns and at least one Tiger tank, which was knocked out by Sgt. McLean's crew with a 17-pdr gun.'

According to the SAR, who were behind the GGFG in the outskirts of Grainville-Langannerie from where they saw the increasing number of palls of smoke billowing from knocked-out Shermans,

> ... unwisely, they [the GGFG] positioned themselves on a forward slope while their commanding officer held an O Group. They were hit from three directions by anti-tank fire and enemy tanks that sniped at them from the edge of Quesnay Wood to their rear and were even attacked by miniature robot tanks.

No. 1 Squadron of the GGFG, in heading through the defile between the two villages where fighting was still going on, had in effect blundered into 10 Cdn Bde's battle. Either that or it was another case of sequencing breaking down, based on expectation that the villages would have been secured:

> Things became fairly hot and confused. No.1 Sqn tried to by-pass to the right but we were met by heavy 88mm fire from the area of

QUESNAY ... Major Laidlaw's tank was hit and he and his wireless operator were killed.

Fourteen of the Foot Guards' Shermans were left as smouldering hulls when they withdrew to cover around the edges of Grainville-Langannerie, from where they engaged enemy infantry positions until a final withdrawal into the village at last light. Most of the damage was done by flak and anti-tank guns, plus a single Panther of the 1st Panzer Battalion; the only one left in the wood 'to secure our position' after the deployment to take on the Worthington Force and, probably a mix of *Hitlerjugend* and *Luftwaffe*, in daylight in open country proved decisive.

By 1300, when they withdrew to a better position in some dead ground, the Grenadiers had after their first day in action only fifteen tanks left, just 25 per cent of their starting strength.

By the end of the afternoon the 4th Canadian Armoured Division had gained a little over 1 mile of ground south down the Caen-Falaise road. The high ground of Point 195 and 206 beyond still eluded them and the *Hitlerjugend* still sat firmly astride the road. Matters were, however, little better in the Polish sector.

The Polish Armoured Division

The Poles' introduction to battle on the afternoon of 8 August had been a brutal one. At dusk the 10 Armd Cav Bde had withdrawn to reorganize and handed over their modest gains to the infantry, but the overnight

A captured Borgward B IV. Originally conceived as an ammunition carrier, it was later used as a demolition vehicle.

A Bren-gunner in the ruins of a village.

attack on Mesnil-Robert that they had been ordered to carry out was not necessary. General Maczek explained in his report:

> 9 August 1944 – During the night of 8/9 August, 3 Rifle Bde prepared itself for the attack, but did not carry it out, as the enemy withdrew, and [at first light] after only short fighting, reached the SE boundaries of woods Robertmesnil, taking forty-eight prisoners. Our losses were insignificant.

This required the Poles' plans to be recast and 'Between 0900–1000 hours, a conference of COs [commanding officers] was held and the orders for a further move were given.' The objective of the Polish Armoured Division was the high ground of Point 140 and the crossings of the River Laison a short distance beyond. 153 Highland Brigade was to advance and cover the Poles' left flank.

General Maczek, however, appreciated the problem that faced him on a direct southerly approach via Soignolles. This was where the main strength See map on p. 231 of *Kampfgruppe* Waldmüller had reached before daylight. Consequently, he decided on an additional south-easterly advance to St Sylvain and then south on to the high ground. H-Hour for the advance would be 1100 hours.

228

Polish officers planning during TOTALIZE.

St Sylvain village and the surrounding area was, however, held by I SS Panzer Corps' and the *Hitlerjugend*'s *Begleitkompanies* still under command of *Kampfgruppe* Waldmüller. The *HJ*'s divisional history provides some detail:

> The Division's *Begleitkompanie* had moved into a defensive position between St Sylvain and the Château du Fosse, located approximately one kilometre south-west of the town. The Muance stream, running on its right wing in a north-easterly direction, offered sufficient protection from tanks. The *Korps' Begleitkompanie* was in position to the left of the *Division's Begleitkompanie*.

Elements of the motor battalion of 10 Armd Cav Bde, 10 Mounted Rifle Regt advanced on the area under the command of 3 Polish Brigade. General Maczek commented that '10 Mounted Rifle Regt very successfully and courageously reconnoitred St Sylvain',

> ... but when it was discovered that St Sylvain was occupied by a strong enemy force with the support of hy mortars and arty, the task of capturing it was given to 10 Mounted Rifle Bn, which reinforced 8 Rifle Bn.

Attacking immediately to the west was 2 Tank Regt, advancing between Château du Fosse and Renémesnil supported by the remainder of the

10th Motor Rifle Regt. Their attack fell on the *HJ*'s *Begleitkompanie*. *Unterscharführer* Freund was among them:

> The position was located in the middle of open terrain. In front of us was a wide and easily observed field of fire, to our back a huge harvested grain field, the sheaves standing upright. A wooded area was behind the grain field ... We could see the tanks rolling toward us a long distance away. However, the first push was directed at our neighbour on the left, the *Korps' Begleitkompanie*. But then, all hell broke loose in our corner also. Suddenly, enemy tanks were sitting among our fox holes. One of the tanks was even right next to the *Kompanie* command post, located in a fair-sized camouflaged depression in the ground, covered with tree trunks. The two 7.5cm Pak [anti-tank] guns, attached to the *Kompanie*, fired without pause at the enemy tanks now coming at us from dead ahead. After several of them had been knocked out, the others stopped, suddenly and as if frightened ... They opened fire on the two Pak guns. In the meantime, two of the tanks driving around among our positions had been destroyed, including the one next to the *Kompanie* command post. The other two or three immediately withdrew in the direction of the chateau. Our two Pak guns had been silenced by the concentrated enemy fire. But suddenly, the forward observer of our I.G. Zug [infantry gun platoon],[5] *Unterscharführer* Kurt Breitmoser, appeared next to me and yelled: 'Let's go, come over to the Pak!'
>
> The two guns were sitting not far from us. One of them was destroyed, but the other still seemed in working order. However, all the crews were casualties. We loaded for the first time and Kurt Breitmoser pointed the gun deliberately at the tank closest to us. Direct hit! We were able to fire two more shells, then there was a sudden bang and we were hurled backward a few metres, landing in the sand. I was unharmed, but Breitmoser had been wounded in the head. His face was covered with blood and he hurried back to find a medic. However, it did not take long before Breitmoser showed up again, his head bandaged up to the eyes. In answer to our surprised looks and questions he only said: 'There's no way I can leave you alone here, even if there isn't a helmet to fit me.'

The Divisional *Begleitkompanie* was eventually overrun and that of the corps effectively destroyed. *Unterscharführer* Freund was among those who escaped:

> During the evening we withdrew eastward across the grain field to the wooded area. The enemy infantry first tried to pursue us. However, after our MGs had set the sheaves of grain on fire with tracer bullets, the enemy attack, carried out with great superiority, was fought off.

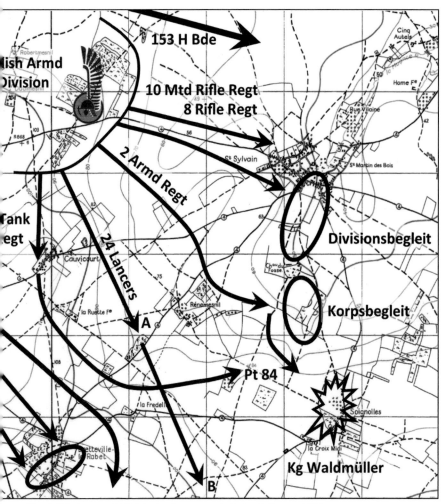

The Polish Armoured Division's advance south during 9 August 1944.

St Sylvain remained in enemy hands throughout the day, but in the Polish Armoured Division's centre 2 Tank Regt was halted before the village of Soignolles and surrounding copses at around 1600 hours. They had advanced just under 3 miles. It is probably this battle group that engaged the Worthington Force on the high ground until the yellow identification smoke caused them to desist. The identity was confirmed in mid-afternoon when the tanks that escaped from the ridge reached Polish lines. The loss of the translator section during the bombing the previous day continued to inhibit the passage of information as to the whereabouts of the Worthington Force.

Meanwhile, further to the west, 1 Tank Regt battle group attacked with 24 Lancers echeloned behind them. They were to face the main body of

Kampfgruppe Waldmüller, supported by towed anti-tank guns and *Panzer-jäger* IV. The advance started well and General Maczek recorded:

> Between 1220 and 1255 hours, 1 Tk Regt reached the W outskirts of Cauvicourt and 24 Lancers the wood 110520 [see map Point A]. In the foreground appeared several times tks of Tiger type, numbering 10 to 15 against which the regts were fighting and suffering losses. About 1600 hours 1 Tk Regt captured Hill 84, distinguishing itself in this fighting. 24 Lancers seized the NW boundary of la Croix, 1149 [see map Point B].[6]

1 Tank Regt was the only force that had stood a chance of breaking through to the Worthington Force, but they were halted with losses on the open ground short of the ridge.

As far as the Germans were concerned, with the Worthington Force on the ridge behind him, the Polish attacks had fixed and isolated Wald-müller's *Kampfgruppe*. Consequently he was ordered to hold his positions, which with the exception of the losses described above to the *Begleitkom-panies*, he did remarkably well, containing the Poles' advance. However, losses of men and anti-tank guns mounted, neither of which could be replaced. Hubert Meyer wrote in the divisional history that 'At 2120 hours 5 *Panzerarmee* reported to the *Heeresgruppe* [army group] that the total Panzer inventory of I *SS-Panzerkorps* was only 15 Panzer IVs, 5 Panthers and 15 Tigers (after *Tigerabteilung* 102 was assigned).'

Ground had been made by both armoured divisions during the day, but stout resistance by the *Hitlerjugend* had blunted their attacks and a break-through across the high ground of Point 195 and the River Laison still eluded General Simonds and II Canadian Corps.

NOTES

1. The Caen-Falaise road runs at approximately 165 degrees in a south-south-easterly direction, while Chemin Haussé runs in a south-easterly direction on a bearing of 133 degrees.
2. The Tiger's power traverse was slow and therefore had difficulty in hitting rapidly-crossing targets. The speed and agility of the Sherman was one of its advantages in Normandy.
3. A standard load for these aircraft was eight 60lb RP-3 rockets, the equivalent of a destroyer's broadside. Eighteen Typhoon squadrons, including Canadian, were a part of the 2nd Tactical Air Force in the North-West European Theatre.
4. Montgomery habitually tried to give new divisions a gentle introduction to battle. One member of the 43rd Wessex Division, after following the main advance in Operation EPSOM, described their christening as being like the 'noisy battle inoculation we had taken part in before D-Day'. There was no such luxury for the Canadian or Polish armoured divisions.
5. Infantry gun platoons were a part of the German infantry regiment's 13th Com-pany. Bt the time of Totalize the 25th Pz Gr Regt was equipped with eleven 75mm infantry guns.
6. These Tigers were from *Sturmbannführer* Weiss's 102 *Schwere Panzerabteilung*.

Chapter Ten

The End of TOTALIZE

*'Stopping a breakthrough towards Falaise by the superior enemy was
no longer possible.'*
Obersturmbannführer Hubert Meyer

On the night of 9/10 August 1944, Lieutenant General Simonds still did not
have his breakthrough. Nor did he have even a toehold on the high ground
en route to Falaise, but he was not prepared to let matters rest and once
again ordered the battle to be continued overnight by his two armoured
divisions. Events of the night would, however, create an opportunity to
crown TOTALIZE with success.

For the Germans it was a case of extracting what they could of *Kampfgruppe* Waldmüller and sorting out the units of the 85th Division that had
straggled across the River Laison and been thrown into battle as they
arrived. With the balance of the division unable to march during daylight
because of air interdiction patrols, it would be some time before they could
take over in what was a fluid situation. The 89th Division, which it seemed
had been overwhelmed, gradually grew in strength as men returned from
positions that had been bypassed or had otherwise exfiltrated through what
was now Allied territory.

On Hitler's insistence, Operation LÜTTICH had absolute priority. Consequently, despite the threat that the Canadians were posing to Falaise, the
Panther battalion of the 9th Panzer Division was ordered to head west
rather than be attached to I SS Panzer Corps as originally planned.

General Maczek wrote of Polish operations on the evening of 9 August:

> For the night, 9 Rifle Bn took over Cauvicourt from 10 Armd Cavalry
> Bde. At 1930 hours, the Motor Rifle Bn started to attack St Sylvain.
> The action was preceded by heavy bombardment by arty and Air
> Force. By 2200 hours St Sylvain was occupied up to the area incl the
> church, and by 2400 hours St. Martin de Bois was also taken.

St Sylvain had been the focus of effort on the Poles'
left flank for most of the day but the final capture
of the village was aided by the withdrawal of the
Hitlerjugend's *Begleitkompanie* who were by this
stage reduced to a handful of stragglers.

Kampfgruppe Waldmüller managed to gather
many of its disparate elements as dusk settled but
they were attacked by the Poles' 1st Tank Battalion
as they started to pull back from Soignolles during
the evening. Fortunately for Waldmüller, caught in

Obersturmführer **Hurdelbrink.**

233

a potentially very difficult situation, two *Jagdpanzer* IVs commanded by *Obersturmführer* Hurdelbrink and *Oberscharführer* Roy were still in position, with 75mm gunner *Rottenführer* Eckstein knocking out tank after tank of the leading Polish squadron. By 2200 hours the attack was beaten off and the Panzergrenadiers continued their march south unopposed as the attack was not renewed.

Point 195

The leading elements of the 4th Canadian Armoured Division had been battering away at the German positions all day in their attempts to reach the point where the Caen-Falaise road crosses the high ground. During the afternoon the tanks of the GGFG came to within 500 yards of Quesnay Wood before being thrown back to cover in the outskirts of Grainville-Langannerie. The high ground and the gateway to Falaise remained in enemy hands.

Generals Simonds and Kitching were not happy and they ordered the attack to resume under cover of night. 18 Cdn Armd Car Regt (12th Manitoba Dragoons), the corps recce regiment, had been active on the flanks of the division during the afternoon. D Squadron, mounted in Staghound armoured cars, had noted elements of the enemy withdrawing south down the Laize River valley and that the route to Point 180 was clear, while A Squadron confirmed that Quesnay Woods were still strongly held. It was not, of course, a realistic proposition to attack and clear a wood during the night and a successful advance south via Points 180 and 195 would outflank the woods and hopefully lead to a German withdrawal. General Kitching's plan was that 10 Cdn Bde would secure Point 195 by first light and then 4 Cdn Armd Bde would advance to Point 206.

In more detail, a squadron of the Grenadiers was to secure the southern extremity of Grainville-Langannerie (objective CHRISTMAS) and then D Company of the Algonquins was to take the key point of St Hilaire Farm where it was possible for vehicles to cross the railway line. From here tanks of the Grenadiers would advance to Point 180 (objective NEW YEAR), while the Lincoln and Welland Regiment (L&WR) was to advance on foot by a separate route to NEW YEAR and mask from the high ground the straggling hamlets that together went under the name of Saint-Germain-le-Vasson. Even though it appeared that the enemy had withdrawn, clearing a village, a large one at that, at night was an unattractive proposition. However, this time the key element of the plan was to be an infantry operation with the Argylls of Canada being tasked to capture Point 195. The final phase would be an advance by the Grenadiers to Point 195 where they would join the Argylls on what was to be a springboard for the advance of the rest of 4 Cdn Armd Bde (Sherbrooke Fusiliers and South Albertas) to Point 206 the following morning.

At 2200 hours the Argylls were resting after capturing the village of Langannerie, some 2 miles north of Point 195, when the commanding

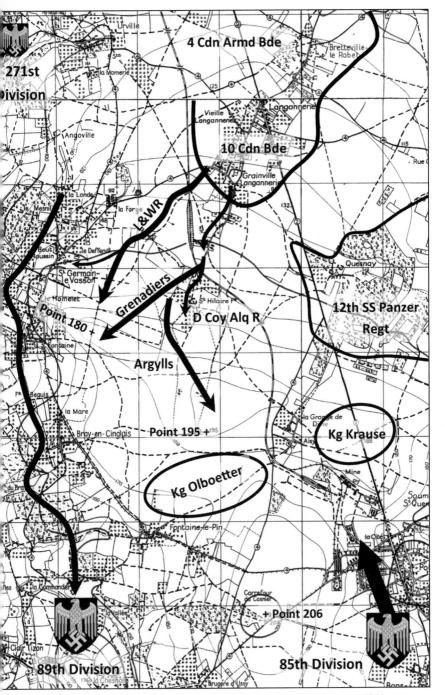

The 10th Canadian Infantry Brigade's operations on the night of 9/10 August 1944.

officer, Lieutenant Colonel Stewart, received orders in signal form from a liaison officer from divisional headquarters to take the elusive feature.

Meanwhile, *Kampfgruppe* Olboeter, based on the 3rd Battalion 26 Panzer-grenadiers,[1] was by the night of 9/10 August well dug in, being sited on the reverse or southern slopes of Point 195. From these positions they had open fields of fire onto the broad and open crest of the feature, but would avoid the worst of the crushing weight of the Allied artillery as it would be map-predicted, i.e. unobserved fire and less than fully accurate.

No. 2 Squadron of the Grenadiers reported that CHRISTMAS was clear at 0030 hours and led by the recce troop, No. 3 Squadron, with regimental headquarters, followed on towards NEW YEAR but lost the CO's tank when it threw a track. Two squadrons were, however, on Point 180 by 0300 hours and were placed on ten minutes' notice to move to attack Point 206. At the same time the L&WR was on the move. They too had been settling down into defensive positions in Grainville-Langannerie when orders came for them to take part in the attack. Their march across open country to NEW YEAR demonstrates the difficulty of night operations, when

> D Coy's guide took a wrong turn, with the result that the coy marched into ST GERMAIN LE VASSON, was cut off, and compelled to remain there throughout the night. C and A Coys were led onto the northern slope of the Bn objective, where they picked up part of B Coy and, together with the Mortars and the A tk Pl they firmed up as well as could be done in the dark.

Unlike the Grenadiers and the L&WR who hoped they would not run into the enemy, the Argylls were sure to encounter German defenders on Point 195. Colonel Stewart elected to eschew the traditional barrage and

Dug-in SS infantry await the coming attack.

advance to contact. Instead he elected to set off in single file following a route piqueted by the Scout Platoon. Thus it was intended that the Argylls would infiltrate, in the dark, onto their objective and take up positions on the hill before the Germans were aware that they were there![2] According to their war diary, 'The Argylls' attack on Hill 195 took the following form':

> A circuitous route, the area to west and north-west of the feature, was chosen, as the area to the east was known to be heavily defended by the enemy. The CO sketched the route to the Scout Platoon and they went out in advance to piquet the advance of the Battalion. The advance began at 0001 hours, at 0430 hours the leading elements were within a few hundred yds of the objective, without as yet having encountered any enemy. There the CO pointed out to the Company Commanders their respective positions – positions that had previously been picked from the map – and then marching troops were dispatched to them forthwith with the instructions to search the area for enemy and 'dig like hell'.

Without a bombardment to herald the attack and a stealthy approach by the Argylls, the exhausted Germans on the reverse slope were unaware that the Canadians were spreading out across Point 195. With bellies pressed to the ground, the Argylls were digging in for all they were worth and as quietly as possible. The war diary continued:

> Meanwhile, the vehicles had reached a bottleneck caused by unmarked hedgerows; the CO and Lieut. Jobless made a rapid recce of the immediate area on foot and, with the aid of wire-clutters, improvised a route that bypassed the obstacle. These two officers then led the vehicles to their areas. At the same time Capt. Whiteside made a recce of the Battalion area and drew up an anti-tank plan, enabling the troop of 17-pdrs and the platoon of 6-pdrs to get into position. Although the unit had reached Hill 195 only about half an hour before first light, nevertheless when morning came, it was well dug in and prepared for counter-attacks.

At 0620 hours on 10 August Brigade HQ reported on the divisional radio net that Point 195 was in Canadian hands. However, up on the hill the trenches, in most cases, especially on the top of the feature where the soil was only about a foot deep, were shallow. Hacking away at the chalk was slow and the Argylls never got down very far. The war diary continued:

> C and B [companies] were forward, supported by A and B Coys. BHQ [Battalion HQ] was slightly in the rear, in an orchard. This difficult move had been made with an almost incredible smoothness. The enemy surrounded us on three sides; yet the only enemy who knew of our arrival were some that B Company had discovered when they reached their company area and whom they used to speed the process

of digging-in. No casualties were suffered by the Battalion during the move and the taking over of the position.[3]

At dawn, the Germans surrounding Point 195 realized that the Canadians were on the feature, or at least a part of the broad plateau.[4] A heavy mortar barrage was followed by the usual hasty German counter-attack focused on a 17-pounder in A Company's position. This, the first attack by *Kampfgruppe* Olboeter, failed with twenty-seven prisoners being taken. *Standartenführer* Kurt Meyer described the scene:

> When I reached the hill Olboeter was in the middle of his soldiers, leading them in a counter-attack. The enemy had broken into the widely dispersed positions and was just about to capture the entire hill. The Panzergrenadiers attacked the enemy spearheads in shock troop fashion.

The ferocity of the German response to the loss of Point 195 was similar to the loss of Verrières and attempts by both sides to cross the ridge during Operation SPRING but worse!

At 0930 hours, as fighting raged to the south, General Kitching held a conference at divisional headquarters back at Verrières. He hoped to plan exploitation from Point 206 but it was apparent, even though information coming back from the brigades was sparse, that earlier optimism was not being realized. The divisional war diary records with a telling comment:

> It has now become apparent that the Div although reaching Point 195, one of its objectives, has not advanced quickly enough and the

SS troops manning an MG42 in the light role.

Germans have been able to organise an A-Tk screen on the gen line South of Point 195 – Quesnay Wood.

Shortly after 0800 hours, the Grenadiers were ordered to advance from Point 180. The plan was that the first bound would be made by No. 2 Squadron up to join on the Argylls on Point 195. 'There they would form up on the feature allowing No. 3 Sqn to pass on to the final objective', i.e. through the Argylls and on up onto Point 206, which was almost 2 miles further south.

The regiment advanced but with German anti-tank guns to either flank, there was precious little dead ground in which the Grenadiers could assemble or take cover. Their war diary records that

at 1155 hrs the regt came under severe 88 fire from the left flank and though no definite clue as to the origin of the fire was given it appeared to come from the left of the crest ... All the comds [commanders] were at this time out of their tanks and coms to Bde were out, so the attack came at a most inappropriate moment. Control was soon exercised by Lt Col Halpenny who issued a regtl fire order to spray the crest and the left front with co-ax and MG.

At this time three of the Borgward B IV radio-controlled tanks operated by *Funklenk Abteilung* 301 were sent over the ridge-line to detonate among the Grenadiers' tanks.[5] 'These were about the size of carriers, carried a white flag on top of their aerials, travelled about 12 to 15 miles per hour and increased our difficulties.'

During the course of the morning it had become obvious to Simonds and his senior staff that without Quesnay and its surrounding woods being cleared of the *Hitlerjugend* and their anti-tank guns, the road down to Falaise could not be opened and his advance would stall. Consequently, the 3rd Canadian Division was ordered to attack and secure the vital woods. This, however, would take hours to plan and organize. In the meantime, the 4th Canadian Armoured Division would continue trying to reach Point 206.

At midday, the tanks of the Governor General's Foot Guards were ordered forward to replace the Grenadiers and advance to Point 206,

but now German fire in the area was so heavy that it was clear that no advance could be made south of 195 until a full-scale assault was made to clear Quesnay Wood. The units in the vicinity had to content themselves with calling down Typhoons and artillery fire on the suspected enemy positions and armoured vehicles.

Despite plentiful artillery and air support from which the Germans suffered cruelly, the blocking position held and there was still no way through to Falaise for II Canadian Corps. Some say that if the Grenadiers had been quicker in following up the Argylls' success things might have been

A Borgward B IV and its smaller cousin, the Goliath.

different, but even though *Kampfgruppe* Olboeter had only recently arrived, the anti-tank screen was already in place, as demonstrated by the way in which they rebuffed the Grenadiers' first attempt on the previous evening.

Throughout the day *Standartenführer* Meyer ordered repeated attacks to regain the position. He wrote: 'The high ground could be held with the assistance of the tanks that were providing cover ... he was exposed to flanking fire from the panzers in the Quesnay woods ... A few could hold out against many there.'

The Germans, however, were not having things entirely their own way. *Obersturmbannführer* Hubert Meyer wrote:

> Without doubt the 8.8cm Flak guns were an important support in anti-tank activities. The high construction of the guns reduced them to only restricted usefulness against tanks. Only at long range were they able to fight tanks effectively without being knocked out quickly by them. Once spotted, they were favourite targets for artillery and fighter bombers.

These *Luftwaffe* 88mm guns were firing at a range of around 2,000 yards from the limited cover available in the area of Point 206.

Obersturmbannführer **Olboeter, commander of III 26th Panzergrenadier Regiment.**

A Sherman tank in the narrow lanes of Normandy.

The final German counter-attack against Point 195 was not beaten off until 1930 hours.

Polish Operations: 10 August 1944

The 1st Polish Armoured Division was ordered to renew its efforts to capture Point 140, cross the River Laison and take Sassy. To achieve this, 3 Rifle Bde was assembled in the area east of Bretteville-le-Rabet. The Polish divisional history, however, indicates that much of the attack was broken up before it got under way by heavy German artillery fire, no doubt directed by observers on the high ground who had a fine view of the open country below.

The 9th Rifle Battalion on the western flank, however, did not receive the cancellation order and began its attack on Point 111 with the tanks leading. *Obersturmbannführer* Hubert Meyer recorded that 'In position on Hill 111 near Rouvres was the bicycle-equipped *Grenadierbataillon* of 85. Inf.-Div' who had arrived overnight.

Despite continuing heavy artillery fire, one Polish infantry company did reach Point 111 and according to reports 'hand-to-hand combat with German troops took place'. The Poles suffered significant losses and fell back, with a second attempt also failing to hold gains. Reinforcements from the rest of the brigade arrived and Point 111 was captured at nightfall. The Poles also claimed to have captured Point 140, but *Obersturmbannführer* Hubert Meyer pointed out that 'the left wing of *Kampfgruppe* Waldmüller was located on Hill 140' and they had not been heavily engaged and remained in place. In capturing Point 111, as a result of their initially unscheduled and subsequently determined attack, the Poles had also established a toehold on the high ground.

Quesnay Woods

With the Poles battling to gain the ridge, the 3rd Canadian Division was brought into play and with Brigadier Blackadder still away commanding the division, the acting brigade commander of 8 Cdn Bde gave his orders at 1500 hours in the tunnels built into the quarry at Haut-Mesnil. His plan

Polish operations, 10 August 1944.

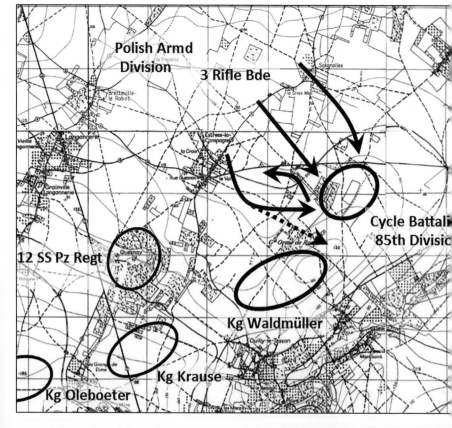

was to attack with two infantry battalions – the North Shore Regiment left and the Queen's Own Rifles of Canada (QORC) right – the latter advancing down the axis of a track running south from Bretteville-le-Rabet to Quesnay. B Company of the QORC was given the task of capturing the flanking hamlet of Le Croix. *Le Régiment de la Chaudière* followed up as 8 Cdn Bde's reserve.

The advance from Bretteville was across more than 1 mile of 'horribly open country' and would be covered by a bombardment, including a creeping barrage by the artillery of the two divisions and the supporting AGRA. The attack on Quesnay Woods was to be launched at 1900, but was subsequently delayed to 2000 hours to allow an air attack on the woods by fighter-bombers.

According to the *Hitlerjugend*'s history, the Canadians 'encountered the "mass" of the *Panzerregiment* which consisted of just twenty-three panzers by then. The only infantry in the Quesnay forest was a part of *Kampfgruppe* Krause.'

The 8th Canadian Brigade's attack on Quesnay Woods.

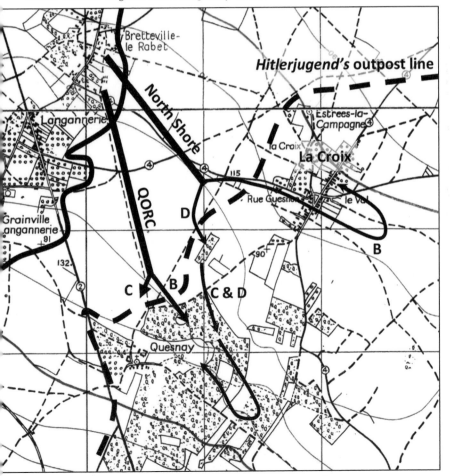

A 5.5in gun of the Canadian AGRA.

The advance just before dusk started well as a result of the combined effort of the bombardment and the *Hitlerjugend*'s fire discipline but at about 500 yards from the wood the enemy opened fire. The Queen's Own Rifles were deployed with B and C companies forward. The war diary records that 'There were tanks firing on them from an unknown source ... Snipers and MGs firing from the woods on the right.' C Company fared little better:

> 14 Pl seemed to get most of it as they were on slightly higher ground. 13 Pl with Coy HQ close behind kept going under small arms fire. Then guns swung over to 13 Pl and MG fire increased, 13 Pl, Coy HQ were pinned to the ground.

C Company was halted at a hedge short of the wood.

By this time both companies had lost their commanders and officer and senior NCO casualties mounted rapidly, but B Company reached the wood despite the enemy's fire which was now concentrated on them:

> 88s and mortars started firing when the coy were 150yds from the woods. There were approx 4 tks in woods ... 12 Pl as told by Cpl Tessier followed the barrage closely and waited at the edge of the wood until the barrage lifted.[6] Two pls got forward but 12 Pl was pinned down in a wheatfield until dark.

The North Shores advanced, with D Company leading, tasked to secure an outlying copse north of the main wood. By 2015 hours they were reporting success, but with the loss of their company commander among other casualties. Their war diary records:

> C and B Coys then moved up. The enemy permitted C Coy to advance well to the right of the woods and into the open before opening fire. The Coy then came under heavy MG fire from dug-in tanks from S. Side of QUESNAY woods, there was also heavy mortaring.

C Company's commander was also killed, but about forty-five men gained the woods, or what was left of them after two days of bombardment and air attack. They were followed by fifty men of D Company.

Small groups from the four companies had successfully reached the extensive woods, but were too few and scattered to make a cohesive attempt to drive the equally few *Hitlerjugend* Panzergrenadiers from the amid the tree stumps and blown-down boughs. It is reported that some Canadians did reach the extremity of the forest, but withdrew when they came under artillery fire. Once the creeping barrage had concluded at the south-eastern edge of the wood, the Canadian gunners that had served the infantry so well during the advance were now unable to provide effective support as their observers were unsure where the infantry were in the remnants of the woods. To make matters worse, the observers who had reached the wood and followed the infantry were now over the crest-line and had the same difficulty with radio communication as everyone else.

Some of the twenty-three panzers in the wood were knocked out and a handful of Germans were taken prisoner, but on an intermittent radio link at 2205 hours the North Shores reported the approach of four Tigers.

Meanwhile, off to the left, in an independent action 'B Coy advanced through the village of LA CROIX but were unable to get very far beyond

A Panther crew relaxing in a wooded hide in Normandy.

SS officers and NCOs planning with an 88mm gun covering the road.

the outskirts due to enemy fire. They suffered a few casualties and withdrew into the village.'

Withdrawal of the QOR began once it was dark, but North Shores with a greater number of men in the wood hung on until just before dawn on 11 August. By then it was obvious to them and their senior commanders that their tenuous hold on the wood could neither be reinforced nor exploited. They withdrew back to Bretteville-le-Rabet. Operation TOTALIZE had culminated, having run out of steam.

The German view of the fighting on 10 August and into the night is that 'it is likely that the deciding factor was the failure of the attack on the Quesnay forest'. If 8 Cdn Bde's attack had been coordinated with that of 4 Cdn Armd Bde they may have overwhelmed the *Hitlerjugend* and opened the way to Falaise.

Conclusion

Despite attempts since the afternoon of 8 August to develop momentum across II Canadian Corps, it was only by plugging away at a highly-competent and motivated enemy that in three days Simonds and his men had advanced 8.5 miles on a south-easterly axis towards Falaise. This was a significant gain, but repeated German resistance had bought time to extemporize a defence and for sufficient reinforcements to arrive. There was to be no breakthrough or success to rival that of their forebears on 8 August 1918, which had been so earnestly hoped for, indeed expected, at the beginning of TOTALIZE.

Canadian historians can be highly critical of the performance of General Simonds and his corps, often overly so, but in this case *Standartenführer*

The great innovation of Operation TOTALIZE: the Priest Kangaroo.

Meyer, who fought implacably against the Canadians throughout the Normandy campaign, sums up the nub of the issue (the underlining here is the author's):

> Every opening phase of a Canadian operation was a complete success and the staff work a mathematical masterpiece ... every Canadian operation bore the mark of intensive planning and was built on sound principles. Canadians never followed up their opening success to reach a complete victory. Every one of the Canadian attacks lost its push and determination after a few miles. <u>Armoured warfare is a matter of using opportunities on the battlefield</u>, therefore the Divisional Commander belongs with the leading combat group.[7]

Fighting continued over the following days, of course, but II Canadian Corps needed rebalancing, replacements and reinforcement. After a pause of three days, on 14 August General Simonds' drive south-east was resumed in Operation TRACTABLE.

Notes

1. The third battalion of the second infantry regiment in an SS panzer division was the division's armoured infantry battalion, mounted in Sdkfz 251 Hanomag half-tracks. The remainder of the infantry in a panzer division was in British terms 'lorried infantry'.

2. The same tactics were used on quite a number of occasions, but successfully by the Hastings and Prince Edward Island Regiment (1st Canadian Division) at Assoro in Sicily and by the Somerset Light Infantry (43rd Wessex Division) at Mont Pinçon only days before.

3. As is often the case, an abrupt change of tactics yields success. The Argylls' British cousins, 2nd Argylls, captured the Tourlauville Bridge in the same manner during Operation EPSOM.

4. *Standartenführer* Meyer states that the Canadians failed to capture Point 195, but *Obersturmbannführer* Hubert Meyer observed in the *Hitlerjugend*'s history that 'The occasional contradictory reports and statements are probably based on the fact that Hill 195 has a rounded top approximately 1.5km wide.'

5. They were established with four companies, one of which was known to be under the command of the 2nd Panzer Division. Presumably another of the companies was with either the *Leibstandarte* or the *Hohenstaufen*. They had thirty-two *Sturmgeschütz* radio vehicles that took control once the driver of the Borgward B IV had abandoned the vehicle within 100 yards of its target. Even though 146 Borgward B IVs were available to the battalion, they made little impression on the battles.

6. If the guns were firing from almost directly behind the axis of an attack, it was possible to get within 75 or even 25 yards of a barrage as most of the shell splinters were carried forward. This of course did not work with high-angle howitzer or mortar fire and the distance depended on the calibre of the gun.

7. Throughout the German defence against II Canadian Corps south of Caen, we find German commanders, Kurt Meyer among them, at the crucial point of the battle. This was well-established German practice, leaving highly-competent, experienced and trained chiefs of staff such as Hubert Meyer to make more routine decisions on the conduct of the battle elsewhere and prepare the detail of orders.

Order of Battle

Lieutenant General G.G. Simonds CB CBE DSO

3 CDN DIV (Major General R.F.L. Keller CBE)

4 CDN ARMD DIV (Major General G. Kitching DSO)

1 POLISH ARMD DIV (Major General S. Maczer CB DSO)

2 CDN DIV (Major General C. Foulkes CBE)

4 Cdn Inf Bde (Brigadier J.E. Ganong)
    R REGT C – The Royal Regiment of Canada
    RHLI – The Royal Hamilton Light Infantry (Wentworth Regiment)
    ESSEX SCOT – The Essex Scottish

5 Cdn Inf Bde (Brigadier W.J. Megill)
    RHC – The Black Watch (Royal Highland Regiment) of Canada
    R de MAIS – *Le Régiment de Maisonneuve*
    CALG HIGHRS – The Calgary Highlanders

6 Cdn Inf Bde (Brigadier H.A. Young)
    FUS MR – *Les Fusiliers Mont-Royal*
    CAMERONS OF C – The Queen's Own Cameron Highlanders of
       Canada
    S SASK R – The South Saskatchewan Regiment

8 Cdn Recce Regt – 14th Canadian Hussars

RCA (Brigadier R.H. Keefler ED)

4 Cdn Fd Regt	2 Cdn A Tk Regt
5 Cdn Fd Regt	3 Cdn LAA Regt
6 Cdn Fd Regt	

RCE

2 Cdn Fd Coy	1 Cdn Fd Pk Coy
7 Cdn Fd Coy	TOR SCOT (MG Bn) –
11 Cdn Fd Coy	The Toronto Scottish Regiment

Under Command 2 Cdn Div:

2 CDN ARMD BDE (Brigadier R.A. Wyman CBE DSO)
    6 Cdn Armd Regt – 1st Hussars
    10 Cdn Armd Regt – The Fort Garry Horse
    27 Cdn Armd Regt – The Sherbrooke Fusiliers Regiment
    1 LOTHIANS (Flails)

56 Bty 6 Cdn A Tk Regt	A Sqn 141 RAC (Crocodiles)
74 Bty 6 Cdn A Tk Regt	79 Aslt Sqn RE (AVRE)

51(H) DIV (Major General T.G. Rennie CB DSO MBE)

152 (H) Bde (Brigadier A.J.H. Cassels CBE DSO)
    2 SEAFORTH   5 CAMERONS
    5 SEAFORTH

153 (II) Bde (Brigadier H. Murray CB DSO)
    5 BW   5/7 GORDONS
    1 GORDONS

154 (H) Bde (Brigadier J.A. Oliver DSO MBE TD)
    1 BW   7 A & SH
    7 BW   2 DERBY YEO

RA (Brigadier W.A. Shiel CBE DSO MC)
    126 Fd Regt   61 A Tk Regt
    127 Fd Regt   40 LAA Regt
    128 Fd Regt

RE
    274 Fd Coy   239 Fd Pk Coy
    275 Fd Coy   1/7 MX (MG)
    276 Fd Coy

Under Command 51(H) Div

33 ARMD BDE (Brigadier H.B. Scott DSO)
    1 N YEO   33 Bty 6 Cdn A Tk Regt
    144 RAC   103 Bty 6 Cdn A Tk Regt
    148 RAC   80 Assault Sqn RE (AVRE)
    22 DGNS (Flails)   B Sqn 141 RAC (Crocodiles)

RCA 2 CDN CORPS (Brigadier A.B. Matthews DSO)
    2 CDN AGRA
        3 Cdn Med Regt   15 Med Regt
        4 Cdn Med Regt   1 Hy Regt
        7 Cdn Med Regt
    RCA 3 CDN DIV
        12 Cdn Fd Regt   13 Cdn Fd Regt
    RCA 4 CDN ARMD DIV
        15 Cdn Fd Regt   23 Cdn Fd Regt
        19 Cdn Fd Regt
    RA 1 POLISH DIV
        1 Fd Regt   2 Fd Regt

In support RCA 2 Cdn Corps RA 49 Div
    143 Fd Regt   185 Fd Regt
    150 Fd Regt
3 AGRA

4 AGRA
    53 Med Regt   68 Med Regt
    65 Med Regt   79 Med Regt
9 AGRA
    9 Med Regt   51 Hy Regt
    11 Med Regt   2 Cdn HAA Regt
    107 Med Regt   109 HAA Regt
    108 HAA Regt

Battlefield Tour of
Operation TOTALIZE

The tour takes the visitor a good 10 miles south from the start lines on the Verrières Ridge to the high ground of Point 195 and the site of the *Hitler-jugend's* headquarters in the hills east of Potigny. Being immediately south of Caen, many of the villages in the early part of the tours were totally destroyed and rebuilt with little of original character remaining and some have become conurbations with numerous new roads, but only a short way into the route the character returns. Much of the country in between the villages is very open and it is easy to visualize the progress of the columns and the advantages that lay with the well-armed defenders using anti-tank guns with a range of up to 2,000 yards.

Map reference: French IGN 1:25,000 Serie Bleue, sheet 1613 SB Saint-Pierre-sur-Dives. This map that covers the entire TOTALIZE area down to and including Potigny is available online from the likes of Stanfords in the UK or from the local hypermarkets in Caen.

Take the N158 south towards Falaise and take the exit signed Bourgué-bus and Soliers. The road to Hubert-Folie was the Scots' start line. From the roundabout take the road south to Tilly-la-Campagne; this at the time of the battle was the railway line from Caen to the various iron-ore mines in the area and at places was a significant obstacle to tanks. Vestiges of the old line can be found in one of the turnings into the Hubert-Folie industrial estate.

Little of the modern village of Tilly-la-Campagne is of interest, but from its outskirts the visitor can see the ground over which the North Novas attacked from Bourguébus in Operation SPRING and the Seaforths from Hubert-Folie in Operation TOTALIZE.

Leave Tilly by the D230a from the centre of the village to Garcelles-Secqueville. To the left is the country transited by the column made up of the Northamptonshire Yeomanry and the Black Watch, and to the right that of 144 RAC and the Argylls followed by 7 Black Watch and 148 RAC who captured Garcelles.

From Garcelles by turning left onto the D41 one can view the route taken by the 1 Gordons battle group on Secqueville. Return to Garcelles and head south to Saint-Aignan-de-Cramesnil on local roads. The wall to the right and the strip wood were the effective boundary between the two columns. Stop by a modern barn short of St Aignan. This is the area from which the Black Watch launched their assault on the village.

Continue into the village and at the road through the centre of St Aignan turn right, pass the Marie and into the short gap between St Aignan and

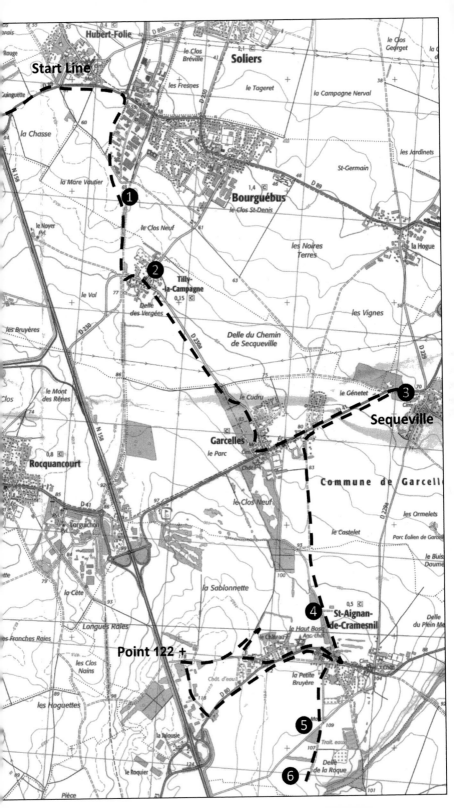

The final leg of 1 Black Watch's assault on St Aignan.

Cramesnil. On reaching the latter village fork right and towards the western end of the village take a minor track to the right, which leads to the area where 7 Argylls debussed and mounted their attack.

Return to the village road and turn right (west) on a narrow lane. This leads up to Point 122. Stop and park short of the N158 and marvel at the view and the approach to it taken by the Royal Canadians.

The view across the N158 and over the area of the Canadian advance.

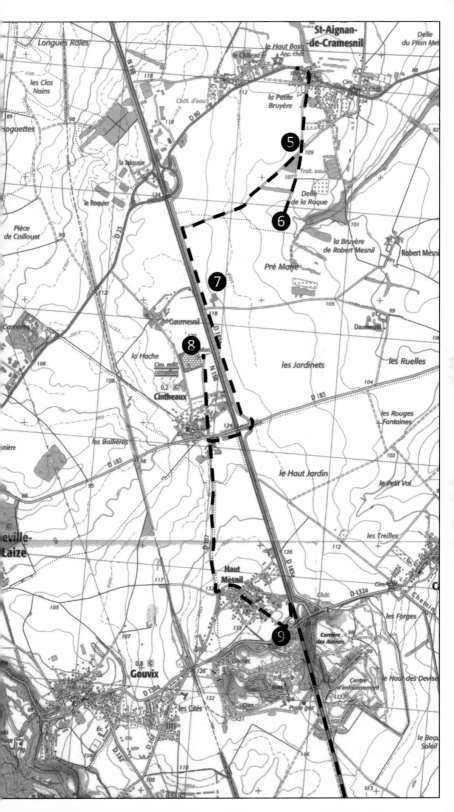

The Northamptonshire Yeomanry's memorial and some of the remnants of battle that still come out of the fields.

Turn left through the industrial estate and left again on the D80 back to St Aignan. In the centre of the village turn right on Rue des Quesnots and follow a minor road south out of the village and stop to examine the Northamptonshire Yeomanry's memorial.

To reach Joe Ekins' forward position take the track south past the Triangular Wood which will be on the right. At the end of the track this is where Velikiye Luki emerged from what was at the time the southern edge of an extensive orchard to engage Wittmann's Tiger. A short walk to the left and the edge of the wood takes one to the end of the Petit Ravine, which was a feature of the C Squadron's battle on their left flank.

Return to the monument and turn left past the Triangular Wood and across the open ground. The slight bend in the road is where two of Wittmann's Tigers were knocked out. Continue and turn left again (south) onto the D183a which runs parallel and adjacent to the N158. In the field between the two industrial buildings on the left is where parts of Wittmann's Tiger and the bodies of the crew were found in the 1980s.

Drive on and up the ramp. Turn right across the bridge over the N158 and drive into Cintheaux. In the centre of the village, where *Oberführer* Meyer gave his orders for the counter-attack, turn right and follow the road to the Canadian CWGC Cemetery. Look north back towards Caen and the walled farm/château of Gaumesnil where Major Radley Walters' A Squadron of the Sherbrooke Fusiliers was ensconced behind its stone

A view of where Wittmann's Tiger was knocked out by Joe Ekins.

Battle damage is still evident on many of the buildings in Cintheaux, a testimony to the savagery of the fighting here.

wall. In good light the repairs to the wall where it was broken down to the height of the Shermans' guns can be seen.

Bretteville-sur-Laize Canadian War Cemetery

Of the 2,874 burials in this cemetery the majority are Canadians killed in the fighting south of Caen during July and August 1944. In common with most burial grounds in Normandy, it is a post-war concentration cemetery with graves brought in from burials as far apart as the southern outskirts of Caen to the north and Chambois to the south.

In Plot 19 to the right of the entrance, a couple of rows in are the graves of Lieutenant Colonel Donald Worthington (British Columbia Regiment) and his brother who were killed just days apart.

In Plot 21, further to the right, there is small patch of eighty British graves mostly dating from Operations TOTALIZE and TRACTABLE. Among them are highlanders and soldiers from the Northamptonshire Yeomanry and the RAC regiments.

Drive back to Cintheaux and from the triangle at the centre of the village head south on the D167 Rue de Pont des Vers towards Haut-Mesnil. On approaching this village turn left onto Rue des Mine and thread your way through the rebuilt village on the Rue des Canadiens.

Near where the Rue des Canadiens joins the ramp between the N158 and the D132a it is possible to get a glimpse of the Haut-Mesnil Quarry (still in use), which was captured by the Argylls of Canada. The view is imperfect due to the increasing amount of vegetation.

The road from Cintheaux to Haut-Mesnil as it was in 1944.

The graves of the Worthington brothers.

The Haut-Mesnil Quarry.

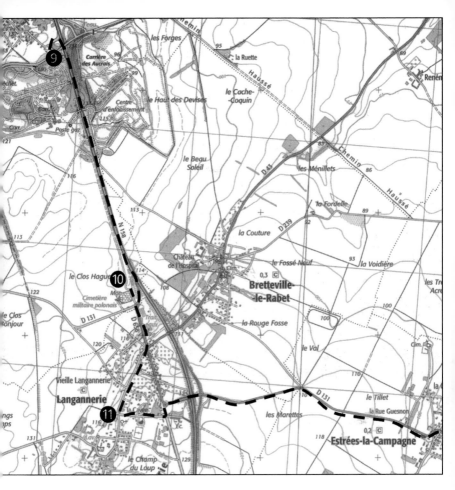

The Polish War Cemetery

10 Take the ramp onto the N158 heading south towards Falaise; after 1 mile take the exit for Langannerie. Follow the signs to the Polish cemetery which is easily visible on the northern outskirts of the village.

This is the only Polish cemetery in Normandy, containing 696 burials of soldiers mainly from General Maczek's 1st Polish Armoured Division, killed in the fighting from 8 August to operations to close the Falaise Pocket at Mont Ormel. After the war, with a Soviet communist government in power in Poland, it was left to the French state to gather the Polish dead from sites across the battlefield. The cemetery was opened in October 1946 and ONAC (the French national office for veterans) maintains the cemetery.

The cap badges of the regiments that made up the division decorate the gates and the centrepiece of the cemetery is a large V-shaped monument with a large aluminium sculpture representing the Polish eagle. The fact

The Polish cemetery.

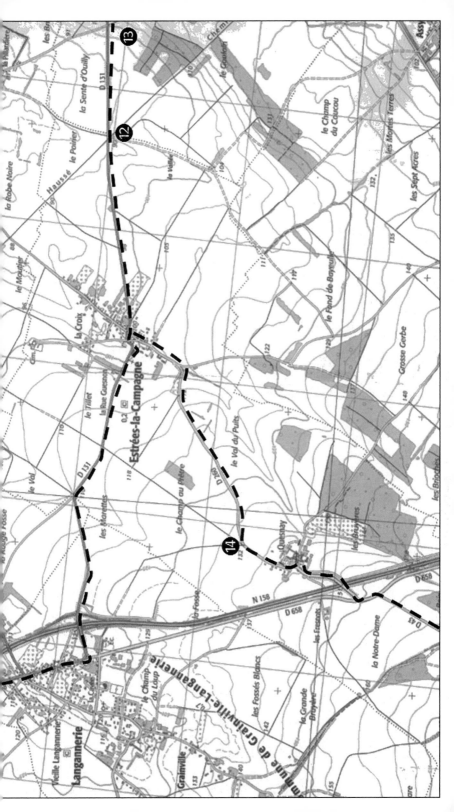

that the French oversaw the building of the cemetery is reflected in the graves; nonetheless it has a distinctly Polish feel.

11 Drive into Langannerie and take the D131 at the roundabout, signed towards Estrées-la-Campagne; a mile beyond the latter village the Chemin Haussé crosses the D131. Today it seems improbable that this track could be mistaken for a major road, but air photographs do show it as being significant and it was dark when the Worthington Force headed along it **12** and up onto the high ground.

Drive on east passing the woods from which the Tigers engaged the tanks of the British Columbia Regiment and the infantry of the Algonquins. Park where safe by the collection of memorials to the men of the **13** Worthington Force who lost their lives in the tragedy that unfolded on this hill side.

Retrace your steps to Estrées-la-Campagne and at the village crossroads turn left onto the D260 towards Quesnay. The shape and extent of the woods that harboured 12 SS Panzer Regiment have changed significantly (see map for comparison). Looking north from the track junctions at **14** Point 132 (now removed some distance from the wood), it is easy to appreciate how significant this position was to events on 9 and 10 August 1944.

Drive on through Quesnay, across the N158 and on to the D43. After just over 1 mile there is an old mineral railway bridge. Immediately after this is a farm track up to Point 196. This is not a public right of way and is **15** rough going. Continue 300 yards south, take the first right turn and follow the minor road onto the reverse slope of the broad Point 195 feature. Park

The layout of the woods has changed significantly since 1944.

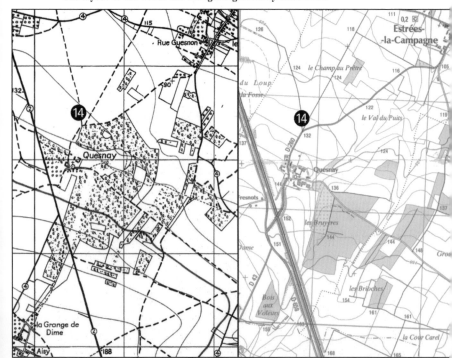

The point where the Chemin Haussé crosses the D131. The memorials to the Worthington Force are on the crest of the hill beyond.

The main memorial to the Worthington Force.

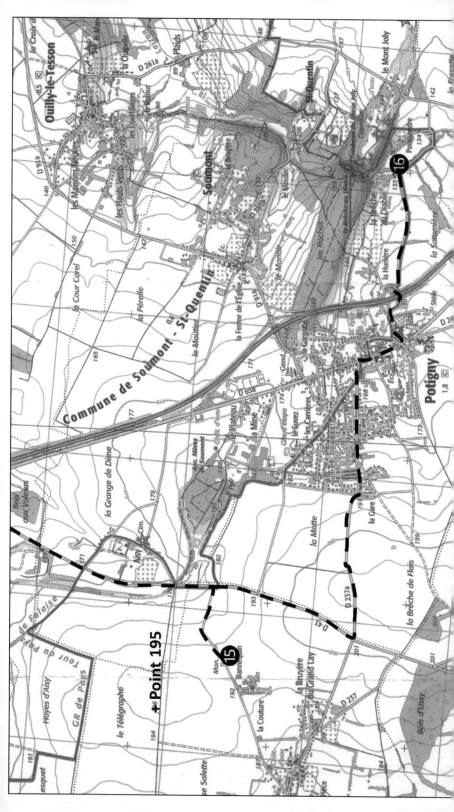

The Argylls of Canada's memorial near Point 196.

The château used by the 12th *Hitlerjugend* SS Panzer Division as their headquarters during Operation TOTALIZE.

16 by the Argylls' memorial. This and the farm further on was the area occupied by Olboeter's III/26th Panzergrenadiers.

Return to the D43, turn right and drive south to the junction with the D237 and turn left to the town of Potigny. Turn right in the town onto the D658 (the old N158). Towards the southern extremity of the town look out for a narrow one-way road on the left, follow it past the church and over the N158, then park at the ninety-degree bend. Nestling at the mouth of La Brèche-au-Diable is the small château used by the *Hitlerjugend* as their excellently-sited headquarters during Operation TOTALIZE.

SS Ranks and their Allied Equivalent

Waffen SS	British Army	US Army
SS-*Brigadeführer*	Brigadier	Brigadier General
SS-*Oberführer*	(not applicable)	Senior Colonel
SS-*Standartenführer*	Colonel	Colonel
SS-*Obersturmbannführer*	Lieutenant Colonel	Lieutenant Colonel
SS-*Sturmbannführer*	Major	Major
SS-*Hauptsturmführer*	Captain	Captain
SS-*Obersturmführer*	Lieutenant	1st Lieutenant
SS-*Untersturmführer*	2nd Lieutenant	2nd Lieutenant
SS-*Sturmscharführer*	Regimental Sergeant Major	Sergeant Major
SS-*Hauptscharführer*	Sergeant Major	Master Sergeant
SS-*Oberscharführer*	(not applicable)	Technical Sergeant
SS-*Scharführer*	Colour Sergeant	Staff Sergeant
SS-*Unterscharführer*	Sergeant	Sergeant
SS-*Rottenführer*	Corporal	Corporal
SS-*Sturmmann*	Lance Corporal	(not applicable)
SS-*Oberschütze*	(not applicable)	Private 1st Class
SS-*Mann*	Private	Private

Index

4.2-inch mortar, 126, 129, 140, 170, 185
17-pound gun, 33, 160, 164, 166, 238
25-pounder, 58, 74, 78, 170, 197
88-mm gun, 30, 55–6, 112, 114, 116, 133, 193, 197, 201, 208, 211, 214–15, 226, 240, 246

Army Group Royal Artillery, 92, 167, 171, 179, 182–3, 201, 243, 244
ATLANTIC, Operation, 16–17, 21, 46
AVREs (Armoured Vehicle Royal Engineers), 70, 98, 100

Beauvoir Farm, 32, 36, 38, 98
BLUECOAT, Operation, 48, 50, 96
Boardman, Captain Tom, 90–1, 93, 153, 160, 165, 166–9, 180
Bofors gun, 68, 78, 79, 92, 105, 108
Bombing, 25–6, 57, 65, 74–5, 91, 100–1, 119, 125–6, 128, 131, 136, 138, 142–4, 153–4, 164–5, 170–1, 175–82, 186, 190–1, 194, 231
Booth, Brigadier, 189–90, 195, 205, 207, 210, 214, 225–6
Borgward B IV, 170, 227, 239–40, 248
Bourguébus, 10, 16, 19, 23, 26, 31, 56, 72, 90, 117, 143, 252
Bradley, General Omar, 9
Bretteville-le-Rabet, 68, 149, 152, 175, 188–90, 195, 201, 205, 207–8, 221, 223, 226, 241, 243, 246

Bretteville-sur-Laize, 25, 45, 55, 68, 74, 102, 138–9, 149, 175, 188, 198–9, 201, 205, 219–20, 258
British Army:
  7 Argyll and Sutherland Highlanders, 60, 77–8, 83, 89, 125, 164
  27th Armoured Brigade, 21, 25
  33rd Armoured Brigade, 69, 77, 184
  7th Armoured Division, 17, 21, 25, 31–2, 36, 55, 159
  79th Armoured Division, 91, 97, 105, 136
  Second Army, 7, 10, 15, 18–19, 21, 45, 46, 50, 103
  21st Army Group, 9, 48, 61, 74, 97
  69 Assault Squadron RE, 98–100
  1 Black Watch, 65, 77, 83–90, 94–5, 137, 165, 167, 175, 252, 254
  5 Black Watch, 158, 188
  7 Black Watch, 64, 77, 89, 124
  146 Brigade, 184
  I British Corps, 14, 16, 19, 73, 189
  XIII British Corps, 70
  4th County of London Yeomanry (4 CLY), 17, 36
  49th Division, 184
  22 Dragoons *see* flail tanks
  1 Gordon Highlanders, 96, 180, 184–6, 188, 202, 250
  5/7 Gordon Highlanders, 188, 250
  Guards Armoured Division, 21, 25

152 Highland Brigade, 68, 72, 84, 117–18, 124, 126, 136
153 Highland Brigade, 68, 72, 82, 117, 160, 184, 228
154 Highland Brigade, 69, 77, 117–18, 137, 184
51st Highland Division, 7, 14–18, 57, 60, 63, 67–9, 71, 73–4, 77, 96–7, 101, 104, 110, 116–17, 184
1st Lothian and Border Horse *see* flail tanks
1st Northamptonshire Yeomanry, 77, 80, 83, 90–6, 153–4, 159, 161, 164, 166, 169, 180, 252, 256–7, 259
5 Queen's Own Cameron Highlanders, 84, 88, 124–5
141 RAC (7 Buffs), 146, 184
144 RAC, 60, 77–84, 89, 91, 96, 106, 125, 146, 252
148 RAC, 89, 124, 186
1 RTR, 32, 36–7
15th Scottish Division, 13
2 Seaforth Highlanders, 117–18, 123–4, 250
5 Seaforth Highlanders, 15, 117–18, 124
59th Staffordshire Division, 52
43rd Wessex Division, 13, 20, 232, 248

Caillouet, 67, 98, 113–14, 144, 152, 198
Canadian Army:
Algonquin Regiment, 177, 179, 189, 214–18, 222, 225, 234
Argyll and Sutherland Highlanders of Canada, 191, 194–5, 205–206, 222–4, 234, 236–9
Black Watch of Canada, 40–5, 70, 199, 219, 249
British Columbia Regiment, 207–19

Calgary Highlanders, 17, 39–43, 45, 101, 198, 219–20, 249
Cameron Highlanders of Canada, 17, 25, 39, 41–2, 117, 124, 128, 131–4, 144–6, 178
1 Canadian Armoured Brigade, 13
2nd Canadian Armoured Brigade, 17, 25, 67, 97, 102, 104, 125, 142, 153, 189
4th Canadian Armoured Brigade, 36, 67, 70, 179, 189, 193, 225, 234, 245
4th Canadian Armoured Division, 61–2, 67, 137, 171, 175, 177, 188, 191, 197, 205, 225, 227, 234, 239
5th Canadian Armoured Division, 13
4th Canadian Brigade, 31–2, 37, 68–9, 97, 113, 116, 137, 142
5th Canadian Brigade, 17, 38, 68, 70, 101, 198, 219
6th Canadian Brigade, 17, 25, 38, 68, 101, 125, 131, 136, 142, 145, 198
8th Canadian Brigade, 178, 242
9th Canadian Brigade, 223
10th Canadian Brigade, 177, 189–90, 223–4, 226, 234–5
11th Canadian Brigade, 62
II Canadian Corps, 8, 10, 13, 16, 19, 23, 25, 48, 56, 59, 65–8, 137, 143–4, 175, 177, 205, 232, 239, 246, 248
1st Canadian Division, 12–13, 62, 248
2nd Canadian Division, 16–17, 31, 59, 63, 68, 97, 142, 144, 190, 198, 219
3rd Canadian Division, 14–16, 26–31, 58, 173, 175, 189, 195, 223, 239, 242
Elgin Regiment, 59

Essex Scottish, 97–8, 104, 106, 110, 112–14, 136, 144–6
First Canadian Army, 7, 10, 19, 50, 61
Fusiliers Mont Royal, 17, 128–31, 146–8
Governor General's Foot Guards, 171, 225–6, 234, 239
Grenadier Guards of Canada, 189, 191, 193, 193, 221, 225–7, 234, 236, 239–40
1st Hussars, 32, 36, 43, 101, 102, 105, 128, 146, 198
14th Hussars (8 Recce Regiment), 68, 97, 105–7, 124, 144
Lake Superior Regiment, 173, 189, 195, 207, 221–3, 230
Le Régiment de Maisonneuve (Maisies), 17, 45, 198–9, 249
Lincoln and Welland Regiment, 224, 234, 236
Manitoba Dragoons, 25, 226, 234
North Nova Scotia Highlanders, 26, 28, 30–1, 252
North Shore Regiment, 243–5
Queen's Own Rifles of Canada, 244, 246
Royal Hamilton Light Infantry, 26, 31–4, 36–7, 46, 98, 104, 107, 109–10, 114, 134, 144
Royal Regiment of Canada, 32, 36, 98, 104, 107–9 114, 134, 140–1, 153, 160, 190
Sherbrooke Fusiliers, 25, 97, 108–9, 112–14, 141, 144, 153, 157, 161, 164, 190, 234, 257
South Alberta Regiment, 14, 191, 194, 195, 197, 202, 208, 223–4, 226, 234
South Saskatchewan Regiment, 17, 128, 134, 136, 145–6, 249
Toronto Scottish (MG), 126, 140

Cassels, Brigadier, 117, 121–4
Chemin Haussé, 20, 210, 232, 264–5
Cintheaux, 25, 138–9, 149, 152, 154–5, 157, 169, 175, 177, 188, 191, 193–5, 207–8, 221, 224, 257–9
COBRA, Operation, 7, 21, 23, 48
Cramesnil, 25, 67, 78, 83–9, 96, 125, 140, 154–5, 254
Crerar, General Harry, 10, 19, 50–1, 57, 61, 68, 73–4, 144
Crocodile, Churchill tank flamethrower, 70, 128, 136, 146–8, 184–6, 249–50
Cumming-Bruce, Lieutenant Colonel, 184–5, 187

Dempsey, General Sir Miles, 12, 45–6
Dietrich, General der SS Sepp, 21, 23, 55–6
Directive M512, 19, 21, 46

Eberbach, General, 56, 139–40, 199–200
Eckstein, *Rottenführer,* 169, 234
Eisenhower, General Dwight D., 9, 10, 19
Ekins, Trooper Joe, 159–66, 257

Factory, the (La Cité de la Mine), 39–41, 46, 146–7
Falaise/Falaise Road, 9–10, 16, 21, 23, 25, 31, 46, 50, 52–3, 56, 67, 77, 81, 98, 104–8, 110, 124, 138, 140, 142, 153–5, 158, 161, 171, 175–6, 180, 197, 203–7, 209, 219, 221, 225, 227, 232–4, 239, 246, 252, 261
Fighter bomber, 17, 45, 48, 216, 240, 243
Fire plan, 28, 39, 42–3, 75, 93–4, 126

Fontenay-le-Marmion, 25, 31,
41–2, 65, 67–8, 101, 125, 128,
131–3, 145
Forster, Lieutenant Colonel, 90–1
Fortress force/area, 61, 70, 100,
107, 110, 112, 142
Foulkes, Major General Charles,
17, 68, 97, 103, 144

Ganong, Brigadier, 97, 133
Gapping force, 70, 98, 110, 112
Garcelles Secqueville, 26, 67, 77,
119, 186, 188
Gaumesnil, 67, 114, 116, 153–4,
157–8, 161, 164, 166, 182,
190–1, 221, 226, 257
German Army:
12 Divisional *Begleitkompanie,*
150, 205 229–30, 232–3
Korps *Begleitkompanie,* 229–30,
232
III Flak Corps, 10, 55, 74, 201,
203
10th *Frundsberg* SS Panzer
Division, 38, 45, 48
1055 Grenadier Regiment, 71,
85, 89, 95, 109, 119, 134, 154,
187
1056 Grenadier Regiment, 113,
128, 146
12th Hitlerjugend SS Panzer
Division, 8, 15–16, 20, 23, 28,
50–6, 60, 74, 93, 110, 116–17,
138, 140, 149, 151–2, 167–70,
200–1, 203, 205, 213, 218,
227, 229, 232–3, 239, 243–6,
248, 252, 267–8
9th *Hohenstaufen* SS Panzer
Division, 20, 37–8, 45, 48, 50,
248
85th Infantry Division, 213, 215,
233, 242
89th Infantry Division, 50–2,
55–6, 76, 110, 112, 117,

137–9, 153, 157, 170, 197–8,
203–5, 208, 220–1, 225, 233
271st Infantry Division, 128, 137
272nd Infantry Division, 23, 25,
38–9, 43, 45, 50, 137, 185, 205
Kampfgruppe Krause (I/26 Pz
Gr Regt), 52, 150, 188, 203,
243
Kampgruppe Meyer, 37–8
Kampfgruppe Olboeter, 203,
235–40
Kampfgruppe Waldmüller, 75,
149–50, 153–5, 164–9 181,
203, 205, 209, 211, 213, 228,
229, 232–3, 242
Kampfgruppe Zollhöfer, 38, 43,
45
1st *Leibstandarte* SS Panzer
Division, 23, 32–8, 48, 50–1,
55, 67, 117, 126, 150, 159,
170, 248
Fifth Panzer Army, 201, 232
I SS Panzer Corps, 8, 21, 23,
37–8, 45–6, 48, 50–1, 75, 110,
143, 150, 199, 229, 233
II SS Panzer Corps, 20, 203
1st SS Panzergrenadier
Regiment, 31
25th SS Panzergrenadier
Regiment, 195
Panzerjäger Battalion, 12, 93,
110, 116, 138, 150, 203
12th SS Panzer Regiment, 150,
194, 197, 205, 212–13, 216,
234, 243
101 *Schwere* Panzer Battalion,
38, 53, 149, 154, 156, 159,
170, 205
102 *Schwere* Panzer Battalion,
203, 205, 232
503 *Schwere* Panzer Battalion,
23
GOODWOOD, Operation, 10,
16–17, 19–21, 25, 109, 143

Grainville-Langannerie, 176, 223–4, 226–7, 234, 236, 261, 264

Griffin, Major Philip, 42–3

H-Hour, 25, 32, 38–9, 123, 125, 156, 202, 226, 228

Halpenny Force, 189, 191, 194, 203, 205, 207–8, 221, 239

Hamerton, Lieutenant Ian, 91, 92

Harris, ACM Sir Arthur, 74, 175

Haut-Mesnil and Quarry, 68, 175, 188, 189, 195–7, 205, 208, 213, 222–4, 242, 259–60

Heinrichs, General, 50–1, 110, 139

Hitler, Adolf, 9, 21, 48, 52, 61, 72, 159, 233

Höflinger, *Hauptscharführer* Hans, 157–61, 164

Hopwood, Lieutenant Colonel, 90, 93–4, 96, 137, 154

HUSKY, Operation 13

Jagdpanzer/Panzerjager IV, 23, 52–3, 92, 110, 116, 234

Jefferson, Brigadier, 190, 224

Jolly, Lieutenant Colonel, 60, 78–84, 164

Jürgensen, *Sturmbannführer*, 218–19

Kangaroo (APC/de-frocked Priest), 57–8, 60–1, 69–70, 73, 85, 93–5, 98, 100, 108, 112, 136–7, 185, 187, 247

Keller, Major General, 177, 187

Kitching, Major General George, 61–2, 171, 173, 175, 188–9, 191, 193, 205, 217, 224, 234, 249

Klein*, Untersturmführer* Willi, 195, 197, 208, 223

Kluge, *Generalfeldmarschall* von, 37, 48, 72, 137, 199–200, 203

Krämer, *Oberführer* Fritz, 37

Krause, *Sturmbannführer,* 52, 75, 150, 188, 203, 214, 243

La Brèche-au-Diable, 205, 268

La Hogue, 25–6, 51, 65, 70, 180, 186, 188

Laison, River, 53, 149–50, 173, 188, 205, 207, 213, 228, 232, 233, 241

le Petit Ravine, 153, 166–8, 257

Lorguichon/Lorguichon Wood, 67–8, 83, 88, 117, 124–5, 184, 186

Luftwaffe, 28, 48, 55, 221, 227, 240

LÜTTICH, Operation, 7, 48, 51, 117

M10 Tank Destroyer, 87–8, 97, 113, 164, 180

Maczek, Major General Stanisław, 63, 171, 175, 177, 180–4, 203, 228–9, 232–3, 261

May-sur-Orne, 25, 37–46, 50, 67–8, 70, 101, 116–17, 125–6, 128–31, 144, 148, 198

McNaughton, General Andrew, 11

Megill, Brigadier, 45, 101, 198

Meiklejohn, Lieutenant Colonel, 78–88

Meyer, *Obersturmbannführer* Hubert, 47, 110, 116, 149–50, 170, 201, 203, 205, 232–3, 240, 242, 248

Meyer, *Standartenführer* Kurt 'Panzer', 74–6, 96, 138–40, 142, 152, 154–5, 157, 164, 169, 177, 200, 212–13, 216–17, 238, 240, 247, 257

Meyer, *Obersturmbannführer* Otto, 37–8, 45, 47

Mk IV tank, 26, 30, 38, 140, 150, 154, 165, 167, 169, 181, 212

Mohnke, 138, 139, 159, 170

Montgomery, General Bernard (Monty), 7, 9–10, 12, 15, 19,

21, 23, 50, 63, 72, 136, 183, 232

Mortain Counter-Attack *see* LÜTTICH, Operation

Movement Light/Monty's moonlight, 46, 92–3, 105

Navigating officers, 78, 81, 84, 89, 98, 105, 194

Nebelwerfer, 10, 22–3, 55, 88

Olboeter, *Sturmbannführer,* 152, 203, 236, 238, 268

Orne, River, 15–16, 19, 21, 25, 46, 51, 60, 69, 103, 143

Panther tank, 36, 38, 52, 140, 149, 169, 191, 197, 214, 216, 218–20, 227, 232–3, 245

Panzerfäust, 81, 83, 166, 182

Panzers numbers US v British, 10

Phelan, Lieutenant, 193–4

PIAT, 29–30, 46, 87, 136, 146

Point 67, 17, 39, 45, 67

Point 111, 209, 213–14, 216, 241–2

Point 122, 25, 31, 67, 89, 97–8, 106–9, 140–2, 144, 153–4, 158–9, 161, 190–1, 207, 253

Point 195, 65, 67, 175, 188, 190, 195, 205, 207, 210–11, 214, 221, 224–7, 232, 234–41

Point 206, 65, 67, 175, 190, 234, 236, 238–40

Polish Army:
    10th Mounted Rifle Regiment (10th Dragoons), 180, 182, 229, 233
    10th Polish Armoured Cavalry Brigade, 180–1, 227, 229, 233
    1st Polish Armoured Division, 62–4, 67, 171–2, 175, 177, 180–4, 186, 227–8, 231, 233, 241, 261
    24th Polish Lancers, 180–1, 231

3rd Polish Rifle Brigade, 180, 184, 203, 228, 241

9th Rifle Battalion, 233, 241

1st Tank Regiment, 231–3

2nd Tank Regiment, 180–2, 184, 229, 231

Potigny, 53, 74, 149–50, 175, 203, 205, 252, 268

Quarry, the, 109–12

Quesnay Woods, 176, 188, 212, 226–7, 234, 239–40, 242–3, 245–6, 264

Radley-Walters, Major, 114, 141, 153, 157–8, 191, 257

Rennie, Major General Thomas, 7, 15–16, 18, 60, 64–5, 184

Robertmesnil/Mesnil-Robert, 68, 153–4, 166, 181–2, 188, 203, 213, 228

Rocquancourt, 25, 31–2, 67, 98, 101, 104, 106–7, 112–14, 128 134–6, 144–6, 173, 185, 191

Runcie, Lieutenant Colonel, 131–2

Saint André, 17, 25, 31, 38–9, 45, 70, 75, 101, 131

Saint-Martin-de-Fontenay, 25, 31, 38–43, 45, 70, 101, 128

Schack, Major General, 43

Scott, Lieutenant Colonel, 226

Secqueville-la-Campagne, 67–8, 96, 117, 180, 184–8, 252

Sherman Firefly, 81, 159–60, 164–5

Sherman flail (Crab), 70, 72, 80, 91–2, 98, 100, 103, 171, 180, 190, 249–50

Sherman tank, 14, 16, 26, 30, 36, 43, 64, 70, 93, 96, 100–1, 112, 124, 128, 141, 144, 153, 154, 157, 160–1, 170, 173, 182, 185, 191, 197, 202, 207–8,

212, 214–16, 218, 224, 226, 227 232–3, 241, 258

Simonds, Lt Gen Guy, 7, 13, 16, 20–1, 23, 25, 36–7, 45–6, 51, 56–7, 59, 61–2, 65, 67–8, 72, 84, 97, 126, 137, 142–4, 170, 173, 175, 184, 198, 201–3, 205, 232–4, 239, 246

SPRING, Operation, 7, 19, 21–48, 50, 55–6, 65, 97, 101, 118, 188, 198, 234, 238, 262

St Aignan de Cramesnil, 67, 85, 91–6, 139, 149, 153–4, 157, 166–7, 169, 171, 175, 252, 254, 257

St Sylvain, 21, 55, 150, 155, 173, 175, 205, 228–9, 231, 233

Stewart, Lieutenant Colonel, 236

Sturmgeschütz/Assault guns, 22–3, 31, 38, 46, 110, 154, 159, 194–5, 248

Sturmpanzer IV (*Brummbär*), 51, 53, 149, 154, 156–7

Tiger tank, 23, 36, 39, 52, 149, 152–70, 191, 194, 203, 205, 214–15, 232, 245, 257, 264

Tilly-la-Campagne, 25–6, 29–30, 32, 36–7, 68, 70, 77–80, 83, 90–4, 117–24, 180, 184, 252

Triangular Wood, 157, 162, 267

Troteval Farm, 25, 31–2, 36, 98, 134

Typhoon, 191, 216–17, 225, 232, 239

Verrières/Verrières Ridge, 16–17, 19, 23, 25, 31–8, 41, 43, 45–6, 56–7, 60, 101, 105, 113, 132, 134, 136, 146, 171, 238, 252

Waldmüller, *Sturmbannführer* Hans, 138, 150, 152, 154, 158, 169, 171, 195, 213, 233

Wisch, SS *Brigadeführer* Teddy, 17, 39, 45, 67

Wittmann, *Hauptsturmführer* Michael, 8, 53–4, 152, 162, 170, 191, 257

Worthington Force, 207–20, 231

Wünsch, *Obersturmbannführer* Max, 205, 212, 214

Wyman, Brigadier, 97, 105, 142

Young, Brigadier, 125, 145–6

Zollhöfer, *Obersturmbannführer,* 38, 43, 45